MICHAEL P. SCHUTT

REDEEMING LAW

Christian Calling and the Legal Profession

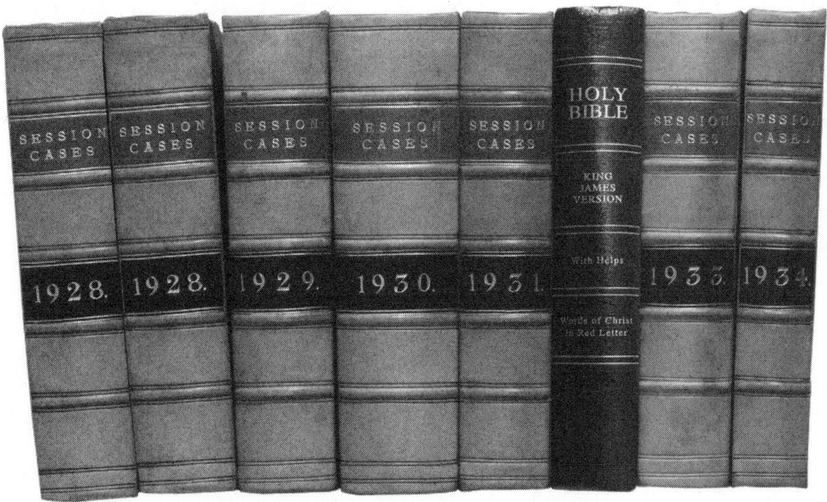

An imprint of InterVarsity Press
Downers Grove, Illinois

InterVarsity Press
P.O. Box 1400, Downers Grove, IL 60515-1426
World Wide Web: www.ivpress.com
E-mail: mail@ivpress.com

InterVarsity Press® is the book-publishing division of InterVarsity Christian Fellowship/USA®, a student movement active on campus at hundreds of universities, colleges and schools of nursing in the United States of America, and a member movement of the International Fellowship of Evangelical Students. For information about local and regional activities, write Public Relations Dept., InterVarsity Christian Fellowship/USA, 6400 Schroeder Rd., P.O. Box 7895, Madison, WI 53707-7895, or visit the IVCF website at <www.intervarsity.org>.

Design: Cindy Kiple
Images: Bible: Rubberball/Getty Images
casebooks: Linda Macpherson/iStockphoto

ISBN 978-0-8308-2599-8

Printed in the United States of America ∞

Library of Congress Cataloging-in-Publication Data
Schutt, Michael P., 1962-
Redeeming law: Christian calling and the legal profession / Michael P. Schutt.
p. cm.
Includes bibliographical references and indexes.
ISBN 978-0-8308-2599-8 (pbk.: alk. paper)
1. Christian lawyers—United States. 2. Practice of law—Religious aspects. 3. Christianity and justice. I. Title.
KF298.S38 2007
340.023'73—dc22

2007011611

P 21 20 19 18 17 16 15 14 13 12 11 10 9 8 7 6 5 4 3 2 1
Y 25 24 23 22 21 20 19 18 17 16 15 14 13 12 11 10 09 08 07

To my parents, Thom and Sharon Schutt,

and my parents in-law, Jack and Norma Jaggers,

who have left a good and godly heritage

through their commitment to divine vocation in

their families, their daily work, their service to country,

and the local congregation

Contents

Acknowledgments

This book would not have been possible without the vision of two men: Jeffrey A. Brauch, dean of the law school at Regent University, and Samuel B. Casey, executive director of the Christian Legal Society. Both of these leaders have dedicated themselves to fulfilling a vision larger than themselves and their own organizations, and it has been my privilege to watch them seek to serve God and his people, never tiring of doing what is good. I am indebted to them for their example of Christian leadership through service and for the opportunity to undertake this project.

Ever since Moses came down from Sinai with the tablets, God's people have been trying to figure out what the law means for daily life, and my efforts are simply applications of the ideas of others that have come before me. Many of these have thought better and more deeply than I have about the topics at hand, and I hope that my repackaging and reapplication of their ideas has done them some justice. Many people have helped me in my attempts to encourage others to think Christianly, in the context of law and lawyering, about serving God and loving one's neighbor. First, I want to thank my colleagues at Regent University School of Law for educating and encouraging me in my own calling. I particularly owe a debt of gratitude to professors Craig Stern, Scott Pryor, Doug Cook, and Natt Gantt for all the time they have spent reading drafts and discussing issues with me, not simply during the writing of this book, but any time I have needed advice and counsel. The Lord has truly blessed me abundantly through my friendships with these beloved colleagues. I also thank Stephen Bretsen at Wheaton College for his careful reading and critique of the manuscript and his excellent insight and suggestions for improving it. His counsel, too, has made this a much better book, and had I been more adept at incorporating his advice, the book would be still better for it.

There have been many pastors, students, lawyers, and teachers who have been willing to talk to me about calling in the church and in the law. Among them I am especially grateful to pastors Dave Anderson, Jeff Julian, Phil Ashey, Glandion Carney, Geoff Bohleen, and Jim Denison. I am also grateful to Robert Rolston, Raymond Dague, Sylvia Chen, Bryan Sanders, Brent Amato, Jamie Lash, Bill Brewbaker, Michael Scaperlanda, Randy Singer, Tom Brandon and the Salado group, and Louis Hensler for their helpful insights. I am also grateful to Ken and Donna Pilgrim for all of their varied and deep support and love (and a secret hideout in the woods from which to write), and to my friends and colleagues on the InterVarsity/CLS working team: John Terrill, Bob Trube, Don Paul Gross, Sylvia Chen, Sue Valentine, and Jeff Gissing—your friendship and fellowship has been invaluable. I also want to thank my assistant, Melinda Lange, my secretary and friend, Mary Bunch, and my research assistant, Emily Smith, for their help and good service. I am additionally thankful for the prayers and encouragement of Judy Capps, Criss Stagg, Marc Kimball, Mitchell Walker, and Clint Rivers, and I deeply appreciate the intellectual and scholarly work of the Law Professors Christian Fellowship, and the insights of Professor Bob Cochran. Thanks also to my Worldview Academy colleagues—Randy Sims, Dell Cook, Bill Jack, Chad Warren, Jeff Baldwin, and Mark Bertrand—for talking through with me so many of the ideas in this book. I am also grateful to my friend Russ Stolle, who has fundamentally shaped my thoughts about life in the law.

I want to thank my family at the Christian Legal Society, especially David Nammo and Dan Kim, for their friendship, love and thankless service to and love for law students. Finally, my family has been my greatest support and encouragement, and I am most grateful to God for my three children and my best friend, a woman who is my finest critic, most diligent editor, and my true love, my wife, Lisa.

Introduction

This book is for those called by God into the legal profession and sent into the world to do good works. This book is about what those good works might be. Our assignment from God is always particular and limited—we are not called to the whole world at once—so vocation must direct us. Our marching orders always come in the particular context of ordinary life and work. So the question is: Can our ordinary work in the law really have redeeming value?

To be sure, law cannot redeem souls. But as co-laborers with Christ, who reconciles all things to himself, "we have a redemptive task wherever our vocation places us in this world."[1] Our God is Redeemer, and he is redeeming law—and politics and dance and architecture and literature and sinners. To the extent that we are used as God's tools in exerting a loving, serving, redeeming influence on the world around us, our law practice can indeed have redeeming value in this world. If we are faithful, we will also have redeeming influence *on* our law practices, our clients, our colleagues, and our professors. Neither we nor our law practice will do any redeeming, of course, but God may be pleased to use us to serve and renew the people and institutions around us.

In working out our calling as agents of God's kingship in a realm as public and political as the law, we navigate difficult waters. On the one hand, we must realize that the "project of bringing heaven down to earth always results in bringing hell up from below."[2] From the Inquisition to Prohibition, from the

---

[1]Albert M. Wolters, *Creation Regained: Biblical Basics for a Reformational Worldview*, 2nd ed. (Grand Rapids: Eerdmans, 2005), p. 73.

[2]Lesslie Newbigin, *Foolishness to the Greeks: The Gospel and Western Culture* (Grand Rapids: Eerdmans, 1986), p. 117.

Thirty Years' War to witch trials, we tend to get it wrong in a thousand different ways. We must remember that the "full revelation of the heavenly city lies beyond the horizon of earthly history."[3] On the other hand, our "vision of the heavenly city" must control our conduct, and "can admit no separation of private from public life."[4]

If God is redeeming the law and the legal institutions in which we operate, we may help bring them, slowly and uncertainly, under his authority as a means to liberate captives, vindicate the rights of victims, exercise stewardship, punish wrongdoers, and do justice—though never fully while in this world. Yet our calling as lawyers is not some quest to control and transform cultural and legal institutions. Our calling is humbly to love and serve our neighbors—clients, pastors, spouses, law partners, and actual neighbors on our block—through the limits and the freedom of the roles to which God has called us. This service will, in fact, transform the world around us, because our neighbors will be better off for being served and loved, but our goal is not world transformation. It is service.

In the following pages, we will explore the potential for law—law practice at the bar and bench, and legal scholarship by law teachers and law students—to be a ministry of good works to those around us, a calling from God to love and serve our neighbors with the skills and opportunities he has given us. We'll seek to recognize our responsibilities to particular communities, across particular roles, and in particular circumstances as lawyers within the body of Christ.

[3]Ibid.
[4]Ibid.

PART ONE

THE LOST LAWYER

1

The Lost Lawyer

It was easy to be a Christian at the University of Texas Law School in the mid-1980s. There weren't many of us, and not one law professor came out of the closet as a believer, yet there was an enthusiastic weekly meeting of the Lawyers' Christian Fellowship and freedom to speak one's mind in the classroom. In addition, a handful of Christian friends in the law school and from church provided plenty of fellowship.

But my Christian colleagues and I were hungry for a deeper walk as Christians in the law. We desired more than just sweet fellowship and civil debate. We wanted to know what it means to serve God in the law, and perhaps even a prerequisite: whether it was a good thing to try to serve him as a lawyer in the first place. We wanted some "right answers" too about the purpose of the criminal law, for example, or the reasoning of Justice Holmes, or the underlying jurisprudence of comparative negligence. We wanted to be more than Christians muddling through the law. We wanted to be Christian lawyers, our faith integrated with our calling. We found little guidance in the classroom, from our texts, or from practicing lawyers and professors. Or from our pastors and priests.

Today, as then, Christian law students hunger for an authentic integrated approach to their studies and ultimately their professional calling. And the law students of yesterday march today through their legal careers still searching for integrity, still looking for answers, still disappointed in their own shallow approach to issues of faith and law practice. Many still ask themselves whether their life's work is pleasing to God.

This struggle is not new. For almost three hundred years American lawyers have wrestled with their moral identity.[1] But in a legal system whose development was influenced by the orthodox Christian worldview of the likes of William Blackstone, James Kent, and John Marshall, the old questions about the possibility of serving God in the law were not as fundamental as they are today. In fact, until relatively recently, law schools assumed that Christian virtue was a prerequisite to true success as a lawyer.[2] Any conflicts over substantive legal theory—contracts, private property, or criminal justice, for example—were fights about the *proper* biblical perspective on the subject.

Today, however, this perspective is more than forgotten—it is turned on its head. Law professor Joseph Allegretti tells the story of leaving law practice to attend Yale Divinity School. He had been at seminary only a week when another student, who had also been a lawyer, told him that she had quit practicing law because "a Christian can't be a lawyer."[3] Most lawyers recount stories of laymen asking how a Christian can be a lawyer, and more than one Christian businessman has confessed to me that he "hates lawyers." When I tell people that I teach at a Christian law school, many quip that "Christian lawyer" is an oxymoron. And I often hear reports from law students that their pastors aren't sure that a Christian can be a lawyer. Of course this shifting foundation within the legal profession is of a piece with other shifts in society over the past century, and its causes are as deep and wide as the reasons for decay and change elsewhere.

This book is not an attempt to return the legal profession to mythical "good old days" when "we were all Christian." But to claim that nothing can be done about the state of the profession would be faithless and false. As followers of Christ we must address our failure to live as his followers in the legal profession and to think theologically about our work.

---

[1]See Charles Warren, *A History of the American Bar* (1911; reprint, Buffalo, N.Y.: William S. Hein, 1980), pp. 4-5; Stephanie B. Goldberg, "Identity Crisis," *American Bar Association Journal* (December 1994): 74; Jerome J. Shestack, "President's Message: Respecting Our Profession," *American Bar Association Journal* (December 1997): 8 (quoting Timothy Dwight, telling graduates in a 1776 Yale commencement speech, to "shun legal practice like 'death and infamy' ").

[2]See, for example, David Hoffman, *A Course of Legal Study* (1846; reprint, Buffalo, N.Y.: William S. Hein, 1968), pp. 26-27. "A science so . . . dignified and important should be cultivated by those alone, who are actuated by the principles of the purest and most refined honour. . . . To be great in the law, therefore, it is essential that we should be great in every virtue" (ibid.).

[3]Joseph Allegretti, *The Lawyer's Calling* (New York: Paulist, 1996), p. 1.

Desire and Daily Work

The premise of this book is twofold. First, most Christians in the legal profession earnestly desire a deeper, more integrated approach to serving God in their work. By *integrated,* I mean an approach that takes into account the Christian as a whole person—not disintegrated, compartmentalized, and divided by conflicting demands in different roles. The Christian of integrity is a man or woman who serves God with heart, soul, and mind in every calling in life—as husband or wife, lawyer, parent, parishioner, employer, or employee. While these callings assist us in knowing our duties, which change based on our responsibilities within each, we are not double-minded—split in our allegiance. There is true continuity between Sunday and the work week. By God's grace we serve God as whole, integrated human beings in every area, through faith doing the good works he has prepared for us to do (Ephesians 2:10). Christian law professors, law students, judges, and practitioners want their work to be fully part of the life of faith.

Second, despite this desire, most Christians in the law do not know what following Christ really means as a practical matter to their daily work. Some struggle with the concept of vocation as Christian calling in the first place, or are unable to accept that law is an appropriate arena in which to serve God and neighbor. Others believe that law can be a high calling, but nonetheless stop short of appropriating the historical resources of the church for the benefit of their law teaching, study, or practice. These lawyers, like me and my law school colleagues, may be simply ignorant of the wealth of these resources—or too hurried and busy to apply themselves to the task. Finally, there are still others who desire to serve God in their work but have no idea that faithful, deeply fulfilling Christian service is possible in the ordinary practice of law.

A good example of the state of affairs is a note I received from Sally, a young woman preparing to enter a major law school: "I'm a Christian, and I am a bit confused about how I will be able to use a career in law to grow in Christ and work for Him, while at the same time serving our legal system." Again, there are those who have never even considered the possibility of growth in Christ through a legal career. But many, like Sally, are simply confused about how to go about it.

Can I serve God in a big law firm? What about representing guilty clients? Do I need the rules of ethics if I have a Bible? How could someone practice family law and serve God? Can I be a good lawyer and a good Christian?

These questions are good and important. And it's not just students asking the questions—practicing lawyers struggle with the basics too. Of course, when we're well into our careers, still looking for answers to some of the basic questions of our chosen profession—that's a sign that not all is well. Sally's case, too, raises a concern: why would she decide to go to law school in the first place without knowing whether she could serve Christ in the legal profession? But of course it's more complicated than that. Usually, it's not that we don't have a general idea that we *can* serve God and others in the legal profession but that we are confused about *how*. In addition, along the way, further doubts gain a foothold through what we experience between entering law school and finding full stride in our work.

Desire and Disillusionment

Our initial desire to follow Christ in the legal profession is often extinguished, or at least dampened, by the law school experience. The dominant jurisprudence of the legal academy treats law as merely a human artifact, and it subtly undermines our early pursuit of the transcendent in the law and the lawyer's life. Later, in the formative years of practice, the desire for a deeper understanding of ourselves and our vocation is further discouraged by the roles we believe we must assume. Both the bar and the public see lawyers as hired guns, sharks, or friends, the role changing with each changing circumstance. In the early years of our life in the law, there is no integrated approach in sight, and we continue to wonder if this job is really a calling from God. Our spiritual advisers and counselors express the same doubts, unable to provide a biblical perspective on the complex issues we struggle with.

More than one practicing lawyer has confided to me that he would not go to law school if he had to do it all over again: "It's just too hard to serve God and your clients." Others have voiced similar sentiments. "It's lonely trying to do what's right—half the time I'm not even sure that I know what *is* right." A Christian lawyer I know who works closely with law students jokes that law school is just "boot camp for Satan."

Moreover, I know believers who have practiced law for ten, fifteen, and twenty years, who have not given more than a superficial thought to whether the substance of their law practice—what they do every day—is pleasing to God. I asked one lawyer, who had practiced eminent-domain law as a specialty for more than ten years, whether the very idea of the state taking private property through eminent domain was biblically supportable. "Wow," she said. "That's a good question. I've never thought of that."

We've got a problem all right, and much of it due to our own apathy and neglect—but there are external factors that exacerbate our problems too. For example, many pastors and church leaders are suspicious of lawyers. Brilliant law professors tell us that there is no such thing as "moral" legal theory and that metaphysics is irrelevant to the law. Add to that the negative perceptions of the general public, on the one hand, and the prideful presumption of many lawyers, on the other, and it's no wonder there is confusion and disillusionment within the ranks of Christian lawyers.

Stumbling Blocks

There is no single reason why so many fail to experience the joy of Christian calling in the ordinary life in the legal profession—there are as many reasons for disillusionment as there are lawyers applying to teach Shakespeare (and there are plenty these days). But I will suggest three related stumbling blocks that Christians face when seeking to serve Christ in the study and practice of law. These potential obstacles do not directly *cause* ignorance or bewilderment, but lawyers who fail to address and overcome them may spend their careers spinning their wheels in frustration.

1. American legal education subtly conveys the concept that law is simply a tool and lawyers are social engineers. Spiritual apathy is therefore the norm since students believe they must be a-theistic to approach law properly.

Lawyers, like everyone else, are pressed on all sides by views opposed to a biblical vision of their duties and calling. For lawyers it begins in law school, where the culture subtly lays a foundation of sand. The prevailing jurisprudence teaches that law is simply a tool for engineering human action and lawyers are social engineers.[4] Because this presupposition is a mostly unstated assumption, subtly presented in an environment in which students are competing at the highest levels, learning for the first time the language of the law and being grilled by drill instructor professors in order to build think-like-a-lawyer skills, it is difficult to challenge. In fact, this false worldview is adopted as if by osmosis by all but the most alert students. Then they

[4]See, for example, Robert Samuel Summers, *Instrumentalism and American Legal Theory* (Ithaca, N.Y.: Cornell University Press, 1982).

begin to build on this sandy foundation and it shifts.

2. The church, for the most part, no longer has a well-developed doctrine of vocation and is therefore unable to provide instruction on the topic or to build community that fosters Christian service in the professions.

The local church has provided little assistance, if not outright hindrance, to professionals in working out biblical solutions to issues that arise in their lives. These issues often take the form of the false roles already mentioned. Because there is no teaching on vocational duty, some Christian lawyers fall, as if by default, into the prevailing identity of the lawyer as "hired gun" or the inflated ideal of the lawyer as social engineer. Neither view is helpful to a vision for Christian service. And many of the Christian lawyers who consciously or subconsciously reject the hired-gun or social-engineer models still see their life in the law as "just a job." While the church has recently realized that a "marketplace ministry" is needed, its focus has not been on the doctrine of vocation.

Even Christian leaders who are optimistic about Christian service in the law cannot provide positive theological guidance on important issues like the lawyer's calling, justice, advocacy, or the workplace. This is to say nothing of lawyers who need theological guidance on more specific ethical or theological dilemmas posed by the substance of their work. They have even fewer places to turn for answers within the church.

3. Lawyers no longer think theologically about the substance of the law and therefore are blind to the goodness (or wickedness) of their daily work, which might otherwise be apparent in light of Scripture and the teachings of the church through the centuries.

The failure of attorneys and students to think biblically about the law and their daily work opens the door for confusion about the lawyer's calling and the goodness of the lawyer's work. Does God have a purpose in tort law? What is a contract? Is there a biblical reason for corporations, and should I participate in creating one? For the most part lawyers don't ask these questions about the meat of the law; that is, they fail to develop a theology of their work. This is a failure in the life of the mind, and it is a problem running through the entire church, not just the bar. A decade ago Mark Noll documented this failure in *The Scandal of the Evangelical Mind:* "The scandal of the evangelical mind is that there is not much of an evangelical mind."[5] Of course, this failure of ser-

[5]Mark Noll, *The Scandal of the Evangelical Mind* (Grand Rapids: Eerdmans, 1994), p. 3.

vice to God in the life of the mind runs through the first two obstacles as well.

Gene Veith calls the law a "culture-making profession."[6] By this he means that lawyers have the potential to serve in ways that matter to those around them. For all its difficulties, life in the law summons us to full-time Christian service to God and neighbor. In that service a lawyer can find true satisfaction—the satisfaction that flows from following the call of Christ in every area of life.

Yet following Christ in the law requires our attention to potential distractions and obstacles as well. We'll discuss the stumbling blocks beginning in chapter two with the American law school culture.

[6]Gene Edward Veith, *God at Work* (Wheaton, Ill.: Crossway, 2002), p. 67.

2

The American Law School Experience

Law school is like a tree that has fallen across your driveway: it threatens to block the way before you can even get on the road.

It is possible, of course, to overstate the potential barriers that law school poses to Christian service in the legal profession, and I don't want to blame legal education for every problem in the profession or make it appear that students are helpless in its grasp. Many Christians do thrive in the law-school environment, and some emerge understanding what it means to serve God with their hearts and minds in the law. But it is a potential stumbling block since the entire law-school experience tends to push students away from contemplation of the transcendent—of the good—as it relates to what it means to be a Christian in the legal profession. This happens because law school usually gives students the impression that good legal minds do not think in theological or moral terms about first principles in law.

The Law School Climate

Students gain this impression simply by breathing in the atmosphere of the typical American law school. A combination of two related conditions in that atmosphere—climatic phenomena, if you will—have a decidedly detrimental affect on the aspiring Christian scholar. The first condition is the absence of a serious historical, religious, or moral center in the classroom. A seismic shift in assumptions about the nature of humans, the law, and truth has completed the legal academy's divorce from the pursuit of transcendent truth. The second condition is that the first is accomplished under the radar of most students. The prevailing presuppositions about law, humanity, and reality are largely part of an underlying framework that is never expressly identified in the classroom. In addition, due to the demands of the unfamiliar material and methods of instruction, the typical law student inhabits a pressure-cooker atmosphere that deters contemplation or study beyond the standard rations. It's tough, in other words, to notice the pattern in the wallpaper while you're being grilled by your professor on four hours' sleep.

I'll close this chapter by discussing the most harmful fruit of prolonged exposure to these climatic phenomena: spiritual apathy—what medieval thinkers called *acedia*. To set the context for that discussion, let's first examine the two climatic conditions in some detail.

Climatic Condition 1: Lack of Spiritual Center

First, as George Marsden has noted, contemporary university culture is "hollow at its core," because it "lacks a spiritual center."[1] Because law is rooted so firmly in religion, morality, and history, it is particularly troubling to see the academy's rejection of these and other first principles in favor of the merely pragmatic. The law schools' "lack of spiritual center" manifests itself in an unspoken assumption that law is rooted in nothing more than power politics, the latest economic theories, and pragmatism. These things are important to the study and practice of law. Yet today's law students are denied introduction to the great thinkers of the millennium in favor of diverse pragmatic theories of last week. The rejection of the historical, moral, and religious nature of law means that students go through their training completely unaware of the very resources that might assist them in making sense of their duties to God and neighbor.

The shift. In 1215 when Archbishop Stephen Langton and a group of English nobles coerced the signature of King John onto the dotted line of the Magna Carta, they were simply acting on a principle that had been known to the Western world since Moses descended Mount Sinai with the Ten Commandments: even human rulers are under the law. The reason that the king is under law is that he is a human being—and, after all, every human being is subject to law. But why should that be? Kings, though they are kings, are subject to law because law itself comes from outside of humanity—outside of human

[1]George Marsden, *The Outrageous Idea of Christian Scholarship* (New York: Oxford University Press, 1997), p. 3.

rulers—from the moral order inherent in the created universe. Without a sovereign Lawgiver, there is no reason that kings should be "subject" to a greater law. This elementary principle is affirmed by the great thinkers of the West, from Augustine, Aquinas, and Sir Edward Coke to William Blackstone, James Madison, and Martin Luther King Jr.

Of course, while the principle that "no one is above the law" is still given lip service, the foundation for that principle is truly out of fashion. Today, when judges and law professors speak of "the law," they understand it to be solely a creation of human rulers, simply a set of commands backed by the coercive power of the state. This law is independent of any moral order apart from what men deem good or right—and are able to enforce. To paraphrase law professor Phillip Johnson, when it comes to current beliefs about the nature of law, the enlightened have come to realize that God is really dead and we are therefore on our own.[2] This is the American legal academy.

Harvard law professor Harold Berman describes the current state of affairs as hinging on beliefs about the nature of law:

> It is widely accepted in our law schools that law is essentially something that is made by political authorities, including legislators, judges, and administrators, to effectuate their policies; that law is essentially a means of social engineering; that law is essentially a pragmatic device, an instrument, used by those in power to accomplish their will. Of course, law *is* all that. But it is not solely that—it is not *essentially* that. What is omitted from the prevailing view is a belief that law is rooted in something bigger than the people who hand it down—that law is rooted in history and in the moral order of the universe.[3]

This view has resulted in a radical shift, says Berman, a shift "from a religious to a secular theory of law, from a moral to a political or instrumental theory, and from a historical to a pragmatic theory."[4] This shift from a religious, moral, and historical theory of law exposes the lack of spiritual center in the legal academy. We'll use it as a place to begin considering the missing foundation for a Christian calling in law.

Whatever happened to William Blackstone? It was not until the late 1800s,

---

[2]Phillip E. Johnson, *Reason in the Balance* (Downers Grove, Ill.: InterVarsity Press, 1995), p. 67.

[3]Harold J. Berman, "The Crisis of Legal Education in America," in *Faith and Order: The Reconciliation of Law and Religion* (Atlanta: Scholars Press, 1993), pp. 333-34.

[4]Ibid., p. 335.

when formal "law school" was a relatively new development, that American legal education began to abandon the idea that law was based on something eternal.[5] Until the middle of the nineteenth century, lawyers were trained mainly by reading for the law in the context of lengthy apprenticeships. Because lawyers believed that law was an integral part of the universal moral order of things, reading for legal education involved a broad exposure to ethics, philosophy, theology, the arts, and rhetoric as well as what we now think of as more traditional subjects, such as corporations, real property, and criminal law.

David Hoffman's 1846 *Course of Legal Study* is one of the most well-known syllabi for reading the law. The syllabus and commentary—not the actual cases and works that the student is to read—run 825 pages and lists readings "for students as have time and inclination to study thoroughly every branch of legal science before they engage in its practical duties." The full course would take a student about seven years, but a four-year course could be completed by excluding some of the suggested readings. The "short" course is divided into thirteen titles, each containing an average of ten major works each.

Hoffman's *Course of Legal Study* definitely does *not* lack a weighty spiritual center. In the *proem,* or preface, he eloquently outlines the nature and purpose of law:

> He who aspires to a thorough acquaintance with legal science, should cultivate the most enlarged ideas of its transcendent dignity, its vital importance, its boundless extent, and infinite variety. As it relates to the conduct of man, it is a moral science of great sublimity; as its object is individual and national happiness, it is, of all others, the most important; as it respects the moral actions of men, and of nations, it is infinitely varied; and as it concerns all his rights and obligations, either derived from, or due to his God, his neighbour, his country, or himself, it must necessarily be a science of vast extent.[6]

Hoffman's outline of instruction to the student reinforces the "transcendent

[5]For general orientation and some history, see Herbert W. Titus, *God, Man, and Law: The Biblical Principles* (Oakbrook, Ill.: Institute in Basic Life Principles, 1994), pp. 1-22; Anthony T. Kronman, *The Lost Lawyer* (Cambridge, Mass.: Harvard University Press, 1993), pp. 17-23, 165-270; Mary Ann Glendon, *A Nation Under Lawyers* (New York: Farrar, Straus, & Giroux, 1994), pp. 177-229; and Berman, "Crisis of Legal Education in America."

[6]David Hoffman, *A Course of Legal Study* (1846; reprint, Buffalo, N.Y.: William S. Hein, 1968), p. 23.

STUDENT'S PRAYER BEFORE THE STUDY OF LAW

Dr. Samuel Johnson—1765

Almighty God, the giver of wisdom, without whose help resolutions are vain, without whose blessing study is ineffectual, enable me, if it be thy will, to attain such knowledge as may qualify me to direct the doubtful, and instruct the ignorant, to prevent wrongs, and terminate contentions; and grant that I may use that knowledge which I shall attain, to Thy glory, and my own salvation; for Jesus Christ's sake. Amen.

DAVID HOFFMAN, *A COURSE OF LEGAL STUDY*

dignity" of the law. He notes in his introduction that the works must be read in the order designated because each title builds on those preceding it. The first work to be read, in the first title of the course, is the Bible. This is not unusual or surprising, unless one is a product of post-1920 legal education. In Hoffman's day and before, the great lawyer was a person of great virtue. This was not because the profession was elitist or that it even had the character requirements that it does today. The study of law was reserved for the person of virtue and character because *the law was a subject of dignity and import.* Moral reality—distinguishing between right and wrong, conserving natural rights and duties—is central to its very nature. That is why the student was expected to study Scripture, philosophy, writings on human nature, rhetoric, and ethics.[7]

Hoffman is not some aberrational legal "fundamentalist" who stumbled into the nineteenth-century legal academy. On the contrary, he stands firmly in the middle of the stream of Western jurisprudence, a stream whose source is at Mount Sinai and beyond.

For example, one of the important works in the Hoffman syllabus, required alongside Justinian's *Institutes* in the course's second title, is William Blackstone's *Commentaries on the Laws of England,* completed in 1769. Blackstone was perhaps the most influential text for early American lawyers. Though the *Commentaries* are primarily a technical and painfully detailed primer on the particulars of every common-law subject, the work featured several famous essays that articulated a robust Christian view of the nature of law. The Founders knew the *Commentaries,* and, with the Bible and theological writings of the

[7]For example, Hoffman's "Title I" (of thirteen) includes sixteen assigned works, including the Bible, Cicero's *Offices,* Paley's *Philosophy,* Montesquieu, Aristotle's *Politics,* Grotius and Puffendorf, among others.

Reformers, it had a formidable influence on the shape of early American law.[8]

Blackstone defined law as "a rule of action dictated by some superior being," which the inferior was bound to obey. It follows that "man, considered as a creature, must necessarily be subject to the laws of his Creator, for he is an entirely dependent being." And because "man depends absolutely upon his Maker for everything," human beings must conform to the Maker's will. Given the nature of God and the nature of humanity, then, the bottom line is that this "will of the Maker is called the Law of Nature."[9]

This conception of the law of nature did not originate with Blackstone, of course; he was simply articulating basic truths well known to the common law, and he was building on a pretty sound foundation. In the early seventeenth century the writings of Edward Coke, one of the most important lawyers in the history of the common law, already assumed the truth of this view. In 1610, in *Calvin's Case,* he identified its source:

> The law of nature is that which God at the time of creation of the nature of man infused into his heart, for his preservation and direction; and this is *lex aeterna,* the moral law, called also the law of nature. And by this law, written with the finger of God in the heart of man, were the people of God a long time governed, before the law was written by Moses, who was the first reporter or writer of the law in the world.[10]

This view of the law of nature is expressly biblical, a virtual citation of Romans 2: "When Gentiles . . . do instinctively what the law requires, these, though not having the law, are a law to themselves. They show that what the law requires is written on their hearts, to which their own conscience also bears witness" (Romans 2:14-15). Coke's biblical approach was an articulation of mainstream Anglo-American jurisprudence.[11]

Natural law. The Western legal tradition has always been dependent "on belief in the existence of a body of law beyond the law of the highest political

---

[8]See Jeffrey A. Brauch, *Is Higher Law Common Law?* (Buffalo, N.Y.: William S. Hein, 1999), p. 37. "Until the Civil War, Americans who studied the law learned it from Blackstone. He is thus foundational to America's legal development" (ibid.).

[9]William Blackstone, *Commentaries on the Laws of England,* vol. 1 (1769; reprint, Chicago: University of Chicago Press, 1979), p. 39.

[10]*Calvin's Case,* 7 Coke's Reports 1 (1610).

[11]On this historical claim, see Edward S. Corwin, *The "Higher Law" Background of American Constitutional Law* (Ithaca, N.Y.: Cornell University Press, 1955).

> **EDWARD COKE'S SUMMARY OF *CALVIN'S CASE***
>
> 1. **That ligeance or obedience of the subject to the Sovereign is due by the law of nature**
> 2. **That the law of nature is part of the laws of England**
> 3. **That the law of nature was before any judicial or municipal law in the world**
> 4. **That the law of nature is immutable, and cannot be changed**

authority, once called divine law, then natural law, and recently human rights."[12] C. S. Lewis, in the *Abolition of Man,* says, "This thing which I have called for convenience the *Tao*, which others may call Natural Law or Traditional Morality or the First Principles of Practical Reason or the First Platitudes, is not one among a series of possible systems of value. It is the sole source of all value judgments."[13] In the Western legal system, its foundation was the natural law thinking of Aquinas.

Blackstone, Coke, and others built on the legal foundations of Magna Carta and the theological footing of Thomas Aquinas. In his *Summa Theologica,* in the "Treatise on Law," Aquinas speaks of four types of law: eternal law (the *lex aeterna* that Coke cites), natural law, human law, and divine law. He held that all law flowed from the eternal law—which Blackstone would later call the law of nature, the will of the Maker. All natural law and human laws are subject to the eternal laμw. As Professor Ralph McInerny puts it, "Natural law has eternal law as its measure. Human law has natural law as its measure. In short, there is an unwritten law that stands in judgment on human ordinances."[14] "Natural law" is the human participation in this eternal law: it is what human reason can discern regarding the will of the Maker.

Thomas lived in the midst of a world that believed in this power of reason and utility to define and to bring about the good life. But if reason and utility are enough, what need is there for faith? How is the Christian to live in such a world? Thomistic natural law answers these questions: it is the link between reason and revelation; it identifies the grace that permits us to participate in divine reason—the will of God that governs the universe. "Natural law is the

[12]Harold Berman, *Law and Revolution,* p. 45.
[13]C. S. Lewis, *The Abolition of Man* (San Francisco: HarperSanFrancisco, 2001), p. 43.
[14]Ralph McInerny, introduction to *Treatise on Law,* by Thomas Aquinas (Washington, D.C.: Regnery, 1996), pp. xv-xvi.

token of the fundamental harmony between human and Christian values."[15]

> Now it is evident, granted that the world is ruled by Divine Providence . . . that the whole community of the universe is governed by the Divine Reason. . . . And since the Divine Reason's conception of things is not subject to time but is eternal, . . . therefore it is that this kind of law must be called eternal. . . .
>
> Now among all others, the rational creature is subject to Divine providence in the most excellent way. . . . Wherefore it has a share of the Eternal Reason, whereby it has a natural inclination to its proper act and end: and this participation of the eternal law in the rational creature is called the natural law.[16]

Yet without the opening condition ("the world is ruled by Divine Providence") and the closing definition ("participation in the eternal law"), natural law is not natural law. It is "unintelligible unless we realize its close link with the eternal divine order on which the whole creation ultimately rests."[17]

Scripture teaches that this eternal order is revealed in the creation itself—and is apparent, at least partially, to all humankind (see Romans 1:18-24). God reveals himself to us through the Bible, his creation, his work in history, experience, and conscience.[18] These last nonbiblical sources of norms are called general revelation, because they are available to all people generally.[19] General revelation has an important relationship to human law. Even the pagans understood this. Cicero, for example, had a familiar conception of natural law:

> True law is right reason, harmonious with nature, diffused among all, constant, eternal; a law which calls to duty by its commands and restrains from evil by its prohibitions. . . . It is a sacred obligation not to attempt to legislate in contradiction to this law; nor may it be derogated from nor abrogated. Indeed by neither the Senate nor the people can we be released from this law; nor does it require any but ourself to be its expositor or interpreter. Nor is it one law at Rome and another at Athens; one now and another at a late time; but one eternal and unchangeable law binding all nations through all time.[20]

---

[15] Alessandro Passerin d'Entreves, *Natural Law* (London: Hutchinson University Library, 1957), p. 45.

[16] Thomas Aquinas *Summa Theologica* 1-2, 91.1-2.

[17] Passerin, *Natural Law*, p. 39.

[18] See Wayne Grudem, *Systematic Theology* (Grand Rapids: Zondervan, 1994), p. 122.

[19] Ibid.

[20] Cicero *Republic* 3.22.16, quoted in Edward S. Corwin, *The Higher Law Background of American Constitutional Law* (Ithaca, N.Y.: Cornell University Press, 1955), p. 10.

Aristotle called it natural justice: "Political justice is of two kinds, one natural, the other conventional. A rule of justice is natural that has the same validity everywhere, and does not depend on our accepting it or not."[21]

From Cicero to C. S. Lewis, then, the natural law has been recognized as the cornerstone by which to square human laws and social norms. Yet the American legal academy, the training ground for our judges, legal scholars and lawyers, plows on as if Aristotle, Aquinas, Coke and Blackstone had nothing to say worth considering. Granted, the idea of natural law is quite a stretch for moderns. The Thomistic system "cannot be called a 'rationalist' system. The proud spirit of modern rationalism is lacking. There is no assertion of man's self-sufficiency and inherent perfection. There is no vindication of abstract 'rights,' nor of the autonomy of the individual as the ultimate source of laws and of all standards."[22]

On the other hand, it should not be a stretch to see, even in the modern world, that there is in fact an objective moral order to which human beings are subject and in which we participate. More importantly, we act as if human beings can know something about this moral order and as if we have responsibilities—things we *ought* to do—within it. We all seem to have some ability to pursue the good life and to agree on some of its essentials. And further, it seems that we are able to make decisions about the common good—and even about law—by use of our reason and powers of observation, regardless of our profession of faith in a supreme being or lawgiver.

The Mount Sinai law reports. There are, of course, practical difficulties involved in discerning our participation in the eternal law (that is, determining the specific content of the natural law). Blackstone, building on Aquinas, sees special revelation as central to the task. If our reason were perfect, the task of discerning the law of nature would be "pleasant and easy," according to Blackstone. Yet our reason is corrupt and our understanding "full of ignorance and error." Therefore, God has made "gracious provision" by giving us the Bible:

> In compassion to the frailty, the imperfection, and the blindness of human reason, [Divine Providence] hath been pleased, at sundry times and in diverse manners, to discover and enforce its laws by an immediate and direct revelation. The doctrines thus delivered we call the revealed or divine law, and they are to found only in the Holy Scriptures.

---

[21]Aristotle *Nicomachean Ethics* (trans. Harris Rackham) 7.1.
[22]Passerin, *Natural Law,* p. 45.

This revelation is of course part of the law of nature. "Upon these two foundations, the law of nature and the law of revelation, depend all human laws; that is to say, no human laws should be suffered to contradict these."[23]

Coke was right then to call Moses the "first reporter" of the law. If revelation is the direct statement of portions of the law of nature, it is a sure footing on which to build human laws and legal institutions. Until the late 1800s, this was obvious to most people. Russell Kirk makes the connections from Moses to Anglo-American order:

> The tap-root of American order runs deep into a Levantine desert; it began to grow some thirteen centuries before the birth of Jesus of Nazareth. Through Moses, prophet and law-giver, the moral principles that move the civilization of Europe and America and much more of the world first obtained clear expression. . . .
>
> "Revelation" means the unveiling of truths that men could not have obtained from simple experience in this world. It is a communication of knowledge from some source that transcends ordinary human perception. To the Israelites, Moses made known that there exists but one God, Jehovah; that God made a covenant or compact with His people; that he had decreed laws by which they should live. From that revelation have grown modern ethics and modern social institutions and much besides. . . .
>
> What we call "biblical law" was not the first code of justice. . . . Yet it is the Law made known through Moses that has survived, and which still works upon the society in which we live.[24]

These foundations, then, are rooted deep in the history of orthodox Christianity and built into the common law itself. The great minds of the West were not seeking to establish a theocracy, as is sometimes claimed. To the contrary, they believed that legal order, including liberties such as the right to worship as one deems right, follows from a universal moral order.

The views of Blackstone, Coke, and Aquinas, as they found expression and flourished in America, deserve close examination, even rethinking and debate, as we work out their social and legal implications for our democratic polity. My purpose is not to hold up either the Thomistic or Blackstonian formulation of the nature of law as unerring. Neither do I discount the influence on jurisprudence of Enlightenment rationalism and humanistic notions of per-

---

[23]Blackstone, *Commentaries on the Laws of England*, vol. 1, p. 42.

[24]Russell Kirk, *The Roots of American Order* (Washington, D.C.: Regnery Gateway, 1991), pp. 11-13.

sonal autonomy. I simply mean to demonstrate the very basic historical, religious, and moral richness of the American legal tradition, a tradition that is today ignored or suppressed in legal education.

In place of these rich historical treasures on which yesterday's lawyers built their teaching and practice, today's legal scholars have substituted politics and pragmatism as the first principles of legal theory.

The root. The root of this break with classical legal thought is an "instrumental" approach to law. An instrumental approach sees legal rules and other forms of law as most essentially *tools* (or "instruments") intentionally "devised to serve practical ends, rather than general norms" laid down by officials in power, natural law, or social phenomena.[25] Law, in this view, is primarily a tool to be used to reach particular social ends. Because those ends are always changing, based on the views of the society, the larger culture, or judges, it is essentially a political theory: the only real issue is who has the political stroke to decide the ends to which law shall be used.[26]

Instrumentalism was the product of many cultural and legal forces, but its most famous proponent was Oliver Wendell Holmes Jr., a law professor whose pragmatism and moral skepticism landed him a seat on the Supreme Court of the United States, where he served from 1902 to 1932. Holmes's view that law was a tool to effect the evolving goals of modern society, coupled with his scientism, led him to reject historical approaches in favor of what society needed. His already shaky religious faith was shattered by his experience as a Union soldier, and his low view of humanity is infamous: "I see no reason for attributing to man a significance different in kind from that which belongs to a baboon or to a grain of sand."[27] Followers of Holmes in the legal academy, in one

---

[25]Robert Samuel Summers, *Instrumentalism and American Legal Theory* (Ithaca, N.Y.: Cornell University Press, 1982), pp. 28-29. Summers coins the term *pragmatic instrumentalism* to describe the American jurisprudence of Holmes, the legal realists, and others in the early twentieth century strongly influenced by pragmatist philosophy. Pragmatic instrumentalism is "a dramatic reorientation in American legal thought," which occurred between "1881 when Oliver Wendell Holmes published *The Common Law* and the 1930s" (ibid., p. 19).

[26]A good source regarding instrumentalist legal theory, in addition to Summers, is Brian Z. Tamanaha, *Law as a Means to an End: Threat to the Rule of Law* (New York: Cambridge University Press, 2006). See also my "Oliver Wendell Holmes and the Decline of the American Lawyer: Social Engineering, Religion, and the Search for Professional Identity," *Rutgers Law Journal* 30 (1998): 143-208.

[27]*Holmes-Pollock Letters: The Correspondence of Mr. Justice Holmes and Sir Frederick Pollock,*

form or another, have thrived. Among the influential movements in legal theory that count Holmes as their intellectual predecessor and instrumentalism as a central tenet are legal realism, critical legal studies, law and economics, and critical race and gender studies.

After Holmes, the law was ever a tool—an engine—and lawyers and judges were the social engineers. The engineers are important for their role in *shaping* the ends and in *directing* society toward them. This was the initial shift that changed the face of legal education. This new vision is at war with Aquinas, Coke, Blackstone, and Hoffman on several fronts, but the shift that formed the basis of the war can be distilled to its essence: Pragmatic or political calculations have precedence over moral, historical, and religious ideas.

Scholars from every era of human history have taught that law is much more than a human tool. Flowing from the divine law, it is a reflection of the Creator—it is primarily the Creator's tool, only secondarily ours. As Phillip Johnson puts it, "there is a moral order independent of what human rulers may from time to time prefer, and law is just to the extent that it comports with that moral order."[28]

Instrumentalist theory, taken for truth in law schools across the nation,[29] has serious consequences for Christian law students. Instrumentalism's rejection of the law's rootedness in the created order hinders the law student novice from seeking the good and true in his or her studies.

Practical consequences. The rejection of moral, historical, and religious theories as the primary basis for law results in a very particular sort of legal education. I'll try to identify its consequences in light of our attempt to spot barriers it might pose to the aspiring Christian lawyer.

First, the lawyer of virtue so important to Hoffman is no longer valued in legal education. No one today speaks of the law's "transcendent dignity" or its moral sublimity. The call to virtue and character in its study is therefore no longer necessary. Rather than a broad education in philosophy, literature, and

---

1874-1923, ed. Mark DeWolfe Howe, vol. 2 (Cambridge, Mass.: Harvard University Press, 1961), pp. 251-52.

[28]Johnson, *Reason in the Balance,* pp. 138-39.

[29]See for example, Tamanaha, *Law as a Means to an End,* p. 1. "An instrumental view of law—the idea that law is a means to an end—is taken for granted in the United States, almost a part of the air we breathe."

theology, the lawyer simply needs a bit of technical education and an acquaintance with how to find the positive law on the books. A passing knowledge of basic economics or sociology doesn't hurt either. Technical proficiency and sociological knowledge have replaced virtue as the most important indication of fitness to study the great moral science that is law.

Some confusion may arise regarding this last point because there is now, perhaps more than ever, paper after paper published in law journals and magazines calling out for virtue among lawyers. "Can a good lawyer be a good person?" they ask. Where is the moral center of the profession? Why are there so many substance abuse problems? How can we solve the lack of professionalism and civility in litigation? This hand-wringing may lead observers to conclude that virtue is on the very top of the wish list for law schools as they seek students. But the observer would be wrong.

The reason for the outcry is that the profession is full of engineers who care little for virtue and much about outcomes. In addition, it is the law schools that are turning out the lawyers who are unethical, struggling with addictions, and playing "ends justifies means" games in the courtroom. They have matriculated, trained, and graduated them. How can they now complain? Law schools have taught, by example, that virtue is less important than activism.

The second practical consequence of the shift to an instrumental foundation in the law schools is that religious belief is expressly discouraged as irrelevant to the study of law. It's okay to be religious—at home—but it has nothing to do with what we study in the classroom. Law schools are generally not hostile to religious people, but they have no use for religious views about law. Judge Richard Posner, a prolific and eloquent writer at the forefront of law and economic theory, is quite clear on this issue. He argues that philosophical pragmatism is the best foundation for pragmatic legal theory, and he finds certain fundamental theses "most congenial" to his approach:

> Since we are just clever animals, with intellectual capabilities oriented toward manipulating our local and physical environment, we cannot be optimistic about our ability to discover metaphysical entities, if there are any (which we cannot know), whether through philosophy or any other mode of inquiry. We cannot hope to know the [metaphysical] universe as it really is. . . . Renouncing the quest for metaphysical knowledge need not be cause for disappointment, however, because it means that . . . there is no deep mystery at the heart of existence.

Or at least no deep mystery worth trying to dispel and thus worth troubling our minds about.[30]

It couldn't be plainer. Renounce the quest for moral truth. Pragmatic theory is all that matters in the law since we are unable to prove or discover anything outside the physical world. Nonmaterial reality is irrelevant.

How can mere law students stand and seek truth about law in the face of famous, brilliant law professors telling them to quit? Students who enter the legal profession only vaguely interested in the possibility of how one might serve God and neighbor never have a chance. Their vague desire gives way easily, and thoughts of the transcendence of law never form. And those seeking a law degree because they had a real desire to serve a supernatural Creator by loving their neighbor through law and justice are faced with discouragement right out of the box.

As Posner's position makes clear, pragmatists must adopt their own "religious" presuppositions. For example, with the stated purpose of rejecting metaphysical inquiry, Posner, as if by faith, adopts two metaphysical presuppositions. First, he claims that humans are "just clever animals." This leads to a second assumption, that humans are better at solving practical problems than in "handling abstractions." He says, "Our intelligence is primarily instrumental rather than contemplative." This is a bold step of faith for a scholar who writes shelves of awe-inducing contemplative and abstract books. He is "exhibit A" for the proposition that a benevolent Creator "added mind to the clay."[31]

The problem is not, of course, the *existence* of false presuppositions about the nature of human beings. It's that the truth of the presupposition—the assumption opposed to the historical theological view of the law—is taken for granted. No debate, no discussion.[32]

Third, the instrumental view of law detaches students from the roots of legal theory. When legal theory is discussed in the classroom, it still basically falls in line with the prevailing pragmatic views. Students do not read Aquinas, Coke, or Hoffman; history has taken a back seat to the pragmatism

[30]Richard A. Posner, *Law, Pragmatism, and Democracy* (Cambridge, Mass.: Harvard University Press, 2003), pp. 4-5.

[31]Ibid., p. 4.

[32]Although Posner does not allow that his presuppositions may be faulty, he at least clearly and eloquently admits them. In this, he is the wonderful exception to the rule. We'll discuss the stealth nature of the instrumentalist presupposition later in this chapter.

of today's academy. This means that Christian students—or any students, for that matter—seeking the religious implications, foundations, or applications of time-honored legal theories are left in ignorance. This might also stunt a law student's normative understanding. How can one learn about natural law theories if the very basis of the theories is called illegitimate? How can we argue from first principles about what the law ought to do when first principles are limited to a tiny subset of economic and sociological calculations, and the great moral and religious ideas about the law are off-limits?

Finally, this regular exclusion of religious, moral, and historical approaches to law also leads students to believe that there is no serious Christian thinking on the problems of law. The legal academy hides at the back of the shed the tools that students might use to help themselves. Of course, well-grounded and educated students may recognize the existence of these tools, but even they will receive no help in discerning their relevance and import. As a result, the great treasures of the saints of the church—and all who have borrowed from them—are left buried.

To close our discussion about the consequences of the great nineteenth-century shift regarding the nature of law and lawyering, we'll turn to Alexis de Tocqueville, a man who discussed the American lawyer's calling in some detail more than half a century before the shift began. His description of the American lawyer's virtues will highlight some of the fundamental harm caused by the shift to instrumentalism.

Habits and taste. Tocqueville toured America in the 1820s to observe its culture, institutions, and habits. The fruit of his observations, *Democracy in America,* published in 1835, remains one of the most insightful political commentaries ever written.

Tocqueville believed that responsible social institutions, such as strong families, religious groups, and local communities, would preserve America's liberties. In addition, he believed that American lawyers and their "love of regular and lawful proceedings" would ensure that "the judgment of the multitude" would not degenerate into mob rule.[33] Tocqueville valued the safeguards of religion and law, but worried that without an aristocracy there would be no

[33]Alexis de Tocqueville, "The Temper of the Legal Profession in the United States, and How it Serves as a Counterpoise to Democracy," in *Democracy in America,* trans. Henry Reeve, ed. Phillips Bradley, rev. ed. Francis Bowen (1835; reprint, New York: Colonial Press, 1900), 1:278-81.

check on arbitrary power of governing majorities or the unreflecting passion of the people. In American lawyers he found that check:

> In America there are no nobles or literary men, and the people are apt to mistrust the wealthy; lawyers consequently form the highest political class and the most cultivated portion of society. They have therefore nothing to gain by innovation, which adds a conservative interest to their natural taste for public order. If I were asked where I place the American aristocracy, I should reply without hesitation that it is not among the rich, who are united by no common tie, but that it occupies the judicial bench and the bar.[34]

Tocqueville was optimistic about lawyers' value to the American system, primarily because of their "training and tastes." Because of their habits, lawyers are "attached to public order beyond every other consideration," and they unite "a taste for and reverence for what is old" with "a love of regular and lawful legal proceedings."[35] "Men who have made a special study of the laws derive from this occupation certain habits of order, a taste for formalities, and a kind of instinctive regard for the regular connection of ideas, which naturally render them very hostile to the revolutionary spirit and the unreflecting passions of the multitude."[36]

One reason that lawyers ultimately failed to maintain these virtues was the erosion of lawyers' traditional habits and tastes. The flood that caused this erosion was legal education: instrumentalist theory significantly altered the training that Tocqueville praised as central to the lawyer's temperament. There is no doubt that lawyers no longer value "what is old," and, with pragmatism and the social sciences displacing history, theology, and virtue, the habits and tastes of which Tocqueville spoke are no longer nurtured in the classroom. Today, lawyers do not simply "direct the blind passions of parties," they cultivate and enflame those passions. Rather than "contempt" for the judgment of the "multitude," lawyers seem more and more to be in the business of manipulating the judgment of the multitude by way of the media, pop psychology, or showmanship.

Tocqueville believed that lawyers' training informs their view of themselves and their role. Training brings about certain habits of mind, values, and tendencies that lawyers share in common based on their education. In short,

---

[34]Ibid., p. 283.
[35]Ibid., pp. 280, 281.
[36]Ibid., pp. 277-78.

training matters. The shift in assumptions about the nature of law, now simply part of the wallpaper of the American legal academy, helps to confuse or discourage the thoughtful student hoping to discern how to accomplish good works in the legal profession.

Climatic Condition 2: Stealth

The second condition indigenous to the law school climate is the method by which the first condition is sustained. The deprivation of historical, moral, and religious context we've just discussed is infused into the law school culture by stealth. Rarely do law professors discuss in the classroom the presuppositions of the prevailing jurisprudence of materialistic pragmatism. This relatively new article of faith goes unspoken and unacknowledged, yet it forms the foundation of every subject taught. In addition, due to the environment under which students receive their training, the first condition is more easily absorbed by harried scholars with little time or energy to look elsewhere for help.

The ordinary religion. In 1978, the dean of the Cornell law school, Roger Cramton, created a small stir with an article in the *Journal of Legal Education* called *The Ordinary Religion of the Law School Classroom.*[37] The article examined "the unarticulated (and usually unexamined) value system of legal education." He called this unspoken value system the "ordinary religion" of the law school classroom. His evaluation of the content of the ordinary religion is consistent with our discussion regarding its lack of spiritual center and its sacrifice of historical and moral approaches in favor of pragmatic, instrumental theories. Its "essential ingredients" include a "skeptical attitude toward generalizations, an instrumental approach to law and lawyering," and "a faith that man, by the application of his reason and the use of democratic processes, can make the world a better place."[38]

Again, these characteristics cause their own far-reaching problems. But Cramton's premise involved not only the *content* of the ordinary religion but also its stealth delivery: The content of the ordinary religion is almost never articulated. Cramton notes that a sophisticated observer to the typical law school classroom would detect "certain fundamental value assumptions un-

---

[37]Roger Cramton, "The Ordinary Religion of the Law School Classroom," *Journal of Legal Education* 29 (1978). Cramton's observations are more relevant today than they were twenty-five years ago when he made them.

[38]Ibid., p. 248.

consciously presupposed" by most faculty and students:

> This intellectual framework is almost never openly articulated, but it lurks behind what is said and done. [F]undamental assumptions "appear so obvious that people do not know what they are assuming because no other way of putting things has ever occurred to them."[39]

Because the value system is taken for granted, including in large part the leaps of faith about the nature of law and the nature of humankind that we see articulated by Richard Posner, it is difficult for the novice to detect its presence. Its truth, like the flu, is caught, not taught.

Of course, some professors are better than others at bringing out discussion of first principles or identifying otherwise unspoken assumptions. Some law schools are better at assisting faculty to do so. Some professors are not even consciously aware of the ordinary religion, and others who are may be intentionally fighting it. Nonetheless, the vast majority of the teaching and discussion that takes place in the classroom does so without acknowledgment of the underlying framework. The discussion about what the law "is" forges ahead, while what the law "ought" to be is ignored. This is both the proof and the consequence of the legal academy's unspoken assumptions.

Cramton's admissions about the state of the academy also expose what he calls "surface goals" that appear to substitute for value judgments. "Efficiency, progress, and the democratic way are taken at face value," yet their worthiness as goals is never questioned or even addressed directly.

This puts the dissenting—or seeking—student at a distinct disadvantage. Perhaps the instrumental view of law is worth pursuing and its redeeming qualities embraced in a fallen world. Perhaps, even if the pragmatic approach is relatively new, it is best. But even if it is best, it is not the *only* view. It is not the histor-

JUST FOR LAW STUDENTS

Are you alert to the unstated assumptions of the ordinary religion of the law school classroom?

These assumptions are not wicked—or even intentional. But what we assume as "given" about the nature of the law or the nature of human beings influences every decision we reach.

As you discuss cases in class, identify the underlying assumptions made by your professor and your colleagues.

---

[39]Ibid., pp. 247-48.

ical view. It is not the moral view. It is not the view of orthodox Christians through the ages. The unsuspecting student should at least get a crack at appraising these perspectives before being led by the nose into the weeds without warning. The Christian student, who is to measure all things against a biblical standard—to take every thought captive in order to demolish arguments (2 Corinthians 10:3-6)—is put in the position of having to ferret out the assumptions before he or she can evaluate them. As a novice in a difficult learning environment, the Christian student has very little practical hope of engaging in sustained, thoughtful dialogue that respects a Christian perspective.

This point leads us to a compounding factor. The difficult learning environment makes "catching" the flu of the prevailing jurisprudence very likely. Pressure and stress are not unreasonable hurdles in themselves, but they are an added burden to the student who seeks meaning and depth in the law school curriculum and beyond. In this way, the emotional, physical, and mental stress experienced in law school is akin to sleep deprivation techniques used in prisoner interrogation: it doesn't kill you, but it makes you more susceptible to the tactics of the adversary. The crisis that law school creates in students is not a problem in itself, except that it is accompanied by the covert worldview shift we have just discussed.

A crisis by design. Due to the pressures faced by law students as they seek to learn a new subject, with a new language, by new methods, the law school worldview is easily caught. The thin gruel of amoral pragmatism, preserved by stealth, is served up in the context of a hyper-competitive, high stress environment, which distracts, deadens, or exasperates the student to the point of capitulation. Those who cared in the first place, who sought the good and the true in the law when they initially came to law school, are often disabused of their idealism fairly quickly. This is to say nothing of those who entered the paper chase only for money, prestige, or power in the first place.

This is not to say that the methods or techniques of the typical law school classroom are evil or even harmful in themselves. In fact, most of the time-honored methods of instruction—the burdensome schedule, the hefty reading assignments, the Socratic method—are designed to help the student become a person who thinks analytically and objectively about legal issues. Yet when overwhelmed with an oppressive sense of inadequacy, the typical student will have little time to contemplate the greater issues not raised in the classroom.

A foreign language. The first year of law school shifts most students into emergency crisis-management mode. It is nothing like they expected, and the experience is not like any other educational experience.

There is more reading in a law school week than most undergraduate semesters. In fact, much of the time it is nearly impossible for the average student to read and comprehend all the assigned materials for each class. In the first year the materials are primarily reported cases, containing written legal opinions. Most students have never studied these before, and if they have, it wasn't in such large doses. How does one discern rules from a decision of a judge? Was he right or wrong? And what does a case from 1723 have to do with the law today? To compound the problem, the cases are written in a foreign language, the language of the law, spoken by a judge. It takes a semester just to get used to the different terms for the parties taking part in a case, let alone the arcane legal terms of art that sprinkle each of the hundred pages per night.

On my first day of law school in the very first class, the professor called on one of my classmates and asked him what *assumpsit* means. "Bill" turned pale and stuttered that he didn't know. The professor, pointing out that *assumpsit* is the very first word of the very first case studied for the very first class on the very first day of law school, chewed him up and then spit him out. Bill was white as a sheet when he finished. I got out my *Black's Law Dictionary* that night (and every night thereafter) as I read my cases. The prof's foreign language lesson had hit its mark. Of course, if we had taken the time to look up every word that we didn't quite understand in those cases the first year, it might have taken six months to read the first week's assignments.

The hot seat. In addition to the language issues, the method of instruction is a whole new world. In order to encourage students to exercise their analytical reasoning skills in addition to their memorization skills, professors conduct dialogue with students about the cases, playing devil's advocate, challenging conclusions, and pitting student against student on the issues raised by a particular case or cases. The mortal fear that the professor will call on you keeps you involved in the discussion and provides a somewhat intense motivation for class preparation each day. To add to the pressure, the exam at semester's end is generally the only feedback for each course.

Again, much of this is actually designed to assist the student in analytical problem-solving and thinking on his or her feet. Providing legal counsel requires analysis and process more than legal knowledge. "What you're learning is different," Dean Dana Underwood of St. Louis University Law School explains to prospective students on the school's website. "You're not memorizing and regurgitating facts, you are learning a process. In the first year the training is not so much in the course material but in the analytical process."[40]

This new way of learning does, however, stress out most students. David Nammo, director of Law Student Ministries for the Christian Legal Society, says that law school "squeezes the student, emotionally, physically, mentally, and spiritually." The desire for a competitive edge, he adds, coupled with the rigors described, "breaks down" many students, who don't take the time to study Scripture, pray, enjoy fellowship, or worship. In short, it wears down students' spiritual and intellectual sensitivity in subtle ways. Not that every student feels intense pressure, of course. I had a student a few years ago who had been a Navy fighter pilot before coming to law school. He wasn't stressed out by professors or exams: "Once you've been shot at," he told me, "law school's just not that stressful." So law school stress isn't universal. But the point is that for most students the competitive, performance-based law school environment compounds the smoke screen behind which the wallpaper of pragmatism lurks. It's tough to keep focused on what is important. The failure to keep an eye on the ball causes many students to be blindsided by the legal academy's misleading approach to justice, service, and calling.

We've seen that the law makes truth claims, including claims about the nature of human beings, the purpose of civil government, and the nature of law itself, just to cite the obvious ones. The fact that these claims remain unspoken in the classroom means that while the student is focused laserlike on the elements of a criminal assault, he or she is never prompted to wonder about the purpose of punishment or how it relates to justice. The "air" of the law school helps that happen. We simply catch the prevailing worldview, without really learning it or evaluating whether it is consistent with reality. Again, this is not necessarily the intent of all law professors. Some mock and trash the law; others esteem it. Some take great joy in deconstructing legal theory; others see great meaning and dignity. Yet most profs, intentionally or not, participate in the propagation of the instrumentalist climate under the radar of their students.

In sum, the harried student is screened from the full force of the underlying religion of the law school classroom, a religion that is based on unspoken assumptions about reality starkly at odds with the historical jurispruden-

[40]Accessed at <http://law.slu.edu/overview/expect>.

tial worldview of legal thinkers. The screen works to keep uninformed students in the dark about the reality of first principles, and to keep alert students from availing themselves of resources that might point them to a competing orthodoxy.

Acedia

The real problem posed by the law school culture is the insidious fruit of the two conditions discussed. After exposure to the unspoken amoral assumptions inherent in the law school climate, students are often deadened to the potential for Christian service in the law. They leave law school with a profound inclination toward a sort of spiritual apathy, fostered by the law school experience. It is a sluggishness about the pursuit of first things, about pursuit of ultimate goodness, truth, and beauty. Medieval scholars used the Latin term *acedia* for this spiritual sloth.

We are created to pursue the One who is good, who is the truth, and who is beauty. Our chief end, according to the Westminster Shorter Catechism, is to glorify him and enjoy him forever. This includes seeing his hand in the natural world, its laws and our duties. In our pursuit of the highest good, we pursue the good things and the noble and the true in the world, in our lives, and in our calling. Our stewardship of this material world is related in part to understanding that we were "created in Christ Jesus for good works, which God prepared beforehand, that we should walk in them" (Ephesians 2:10 ESV). Our good works are in *this* world; they are here and now. Our great joy is to seek and knock, to search with our hearts, to discern our calling to serve God and others in what we do with our daily work. To abandon this quest is to reject the very privilege that comes with being created in God's image. Yet *acedia* steals that joy and wrests the privilege of seeking and knocking from our hands.

This is the joyless state in which many lawyers find themselves. One reason they're in this position is that, as law students, they gradually came to understand that any desire for eternal truth in the law should be suppressed as irrelevant. This is a form of spiritual sloth.

Thomas Aquinas discusses this *acedia* in the context of the sin of despair: "The fact that a man considers an arduous good impossible to obtain, either by himself or by another, is due to his being downcast. . . . [I]t seems to him that he will never be able to rise to any good. And since sloth [*acedia*] is a sadness that casts down the spirit, in this way, despair is born of [*acedia*]."[41]

In other words, *acedia* arises when we look at some worthwhile good thing as impossible to achieve. It is this very despair of achieving a worthwhile good that is fostered in law school. Recall that Judge Posner tells us that we should *not* despair when we renounce the metaphysical quest, because there is no mystery at the heart of existence "worth troubling our minds about." Yet because we know that we were created to pursue that mystery and that our happiness depends on it, we do despair. And if we are told enough times that the good is unattainable or irrelevant, we adopt Posner's *acedia* as our own and experience the despair that arises from it.

The German philosopher Josef Pieper describes the implications, based on an "older" view of reality:

> [*Acedia*], for the older code of behavior, meant especially this: that the human being had given up on the very responsibility that comes with his dignity: that he does not want to be what God wants him to be, and that means that he does not want to be what he really, and in the ultimate sense, *is*.[42]

The law school climate encourages us to reject the responsibility inherent in our image-bearing nature. We are encouraged, not always directly but at least through the atmosphere we breathe, to do the one thing, the only thing, that we cannot do—stop pursuing that which is good, true, and beautiful. If we abandon that calling, we might as well not study law.

Lawyers are called to the law to serve, to care, and to seek. We pursue God's purposes in the natural world and in human laws as they reflect the Creator's glory. We seek to understand our own bent and gifts in light of the needs of others as we learn to serve them through the law as counselors and advisers. And we seek the truth in law—about the moral order of the world—as it *is* reflected in human systems and as it *ought to be* reflected. The opposite of *acedia* is simply "the cheerful affirmation by man of his own existence, of the world as a whole, and of God."[43]

That's our job as lawyers and law students: to pursue the true, the good, and the beautiful in our studies, scholarship, and practice. Not because we will be

---

[41]Thomas Aquinas *Summa Theologica* 2-2.20.4.

[42]Josef Pieper, *Leisure, the Basis of Culture* (South Bend, Ind.: St. Augustine's Press, 1998), p. 28.

[43]Ibid., p. 29.

better lawyers—though we will be—but because we were created to pursue the One who is truth, goodness, and beauty.

Conclusion

In our practice, teaching, and study of law, we should cheerfully affirm our calling as human beings to pursue God. Yet there are stumbling blocks, potential barriers that threaten to distract or discourage us as we attempt to discern practical ways to serve God and neighbor. From the beginning of our training, law school is a potential detour from the path. Right from the start, two conditions in the cultural climate of the academy push us toward despairing of our calling as stewards in the law. One, the rejection of the moral, religious and historical center, leads us away from discerning first principles critical to our initial approach to law. The other, the law school learning environment itself, masks the assumptions that we need to recognize and, at the same time, distracts us from addressing them.

Together these two climatic conditions can lead us to apathy—to sluggish complacency about our duty to pursue truth and goodness in the law. I have hinted at some ways around these barriers, and I will pursue solutions in more detail in part two.

First, however, I'll address two additional barriers that build on the law school experience.

For Further Thought

1. Are you more or less cynical than you were when you entered law school? Are you more or less idealistic? More merciful or less? Consider the reasons that law school affects us in the ways that it does.
2. Brainstorm a list of the various religious resources your law school professors brought (or bring) to bear on legal study. How were they helpful?
3. What might you do as a lawyer or a law student to pursue the goodness—or even the beauty—of law and legal study? Consider practical ways to carry out a long-term plan to do just that.
4. Do you believe that historical religious approaches to law and lawyering are relevant to your law study or practice? If so, how? How might you or your clients benefit from these approaches?

3

Vocation and the Local Church

There can be no true Christian life without the church. That is, without the fellowship of the saints, the hearing of the Word, and participation in the sacraments we are dead. Perhaps this is why so many Christian lawyers feel lifeless in their work: they are cut off from the reality of the local congregation. Our remaining stumbling blocks are related to this "disconnect" between Christian lawyers and the "pillar and bulwark of the truth," the church (1 Timothy 3:15).

Not every lawyer feels cut off from the church, and not all churches fail to disciple lawyers. But it *is* difficult, for a number of reasons, for churches to equip lawyers in the way they need to be equipped to pursue their calling. This problem is not unique to lawyers, of course. Many parishioners seeking guidance in their nine-to-five work find that the local church offers little encouragement or instruction in that area. Often this is simply the result of the nature of the professions in general, since the ethical choices facing doctors and lawyers, for example, stem from issues and require knowledge beyond the common experience of most pastors. Whatever the cause, the fact is that Christians, lawyers and other laypeople, do not often experience the joys of discipleship regarding ordinary work and calling.

In this chapter, I suggest that the problem—the second major stumbling block to Christian service in the law—is the Western church's flawed approach to ordinary work and its relationship to divine calling. Regardless of whether it flows from apathy on the part of church leaders, outright theological error, or simple lack of knowledge, *much of the church has forgotten or abandoned the doctrine of vocation.*

The Second Stumbling Block: Work and the Local Church

Vocation comes from the Latin word *vocatio,* "a calling." The crux of the doctrine of vocation is that God has called us to particular roles and equipped us with his gifts to perform the good works associated with those roles. He has prepared good works for us to do—in fact, he created us *to* do them (see Ephesians 2:10)—and he literally "loves our neighbors" through (i.e., by means of) us. In other words, vocation is God's calling out to us to love those whom he has placed in our lives. And because he is the one who has placed us in the stations in which we find ourselves in the first place, we can be confident that faithful service at those stations is faithfulness to him. We therefore have a variety of divine vocations or callings: in our family, our occupations, the local church, as citizens, and as neighbors.[1]

The church has not always taught this. Medieval churchmen believed that only those in the institutional church "professions" were truly called by God. This "elevation of the spiritual at the expense of the secular" meant that most people were a sort of second-class spiritual citizen.[2] Contemplation was the highest calling, and those who were not so called, though necessary to the world, were less important to God's work on earth. The fourth-century historian Eusebius famously summarized the medieval view, writing of "the two ways of life given by Christ": the "perfect form" and another, more "humble," way:

> The one is above nature, and beyond common human living. . . . Wholly and permanently separate from the common customary life of mankind, it devotes itself to the service of God alone. . . . Such then is the perfect form of the Christian life. And the other, more humble, more human, permits men to . . . have minds for farming, for trade, and the other more secular interests as well as for religion. . . . And a kind of secondary grade of piety is attributed to them.[3]

This is the *locus classicus* of the two-tiered Christian life. The top tier, a sacred calling, consists of the contemplative, monastic, or priestly life, and the

---

[1]Most understand the words *vocation* and *calling* to be synonyms. See Douglas J. Schuurman, *Vocation: Discerning our Callings in Life* (Grand Rapids: Eerdmans, 2004), p. 2.
[2]Os Guinness, *The Call* (Nashville: Word, 1998), p. 32; see also Leland Ryken, *Work and Leisure in Christian Perspective* (Portland, Ore.: Multnomah, 1987), p. 66.
[3]Eusebius *Demonstratio Evangelica* (trans. W. J. Ferrar, 1920) 1.8.

second tier is the necessary secular life of work in and of the world. In the words of Os Guinness, the medieval view of calling "flagrantly perverted biblical teaching by narrowing the sphere of calling and excluding most Christians from its scope."[4]

The Doctrine of Vocation

In contrast to this dualism stands the doctrine of vocation, which developed in its full flower with the Reformation,[5] particularly in the teachings of Martin Luther and John Calvin.[6] The Reformers taught that all spheres of life, including home, politics, church, social, work, and leisure, are "religiously and morally meaningful" because they are "divinely given avenues through which persons respond obediently to the call of God to serve their neighbor in love."[7] The Reformers, in other words, "affirmed the essential spirituality of the everyday, ordinary life."[8]

It bears noting here that although it was the Reformers, primarily, who recovered a faithful view of calling, in more recent years, it has been Roman Catholic thinkers who have emphasized the spiritual importance of ordinary work and roles outside the institutional church. In fact, at least since the early 1900s, it appears that the Roman Catholic Church has been much more effective at holding the line against the medieval approach, while mainstream evangelicalism pulls in the opposite direction. Pope John Paul II, in particular, was very clear in his writings that ordinary work is a spiritual activity flowing from the *imago Dei* and participating in the ongoing creational work of

---

[4]Guinness, *Call,* pp. 32-33.

[5]Schurrman, *Vocation,* p. 4. That it was the Reformation alone is not uncontroversial, and there is much to be seen in Roman Catholic writers during the Renaissance. For example, in the late fourteenth century, William Langland's epic *Piers Plowman* contained an extended passage on the gifts of the Spirit given by personified Grace to men in various callings in order that "idleness, envy, and pride" would not overcome men. The gifts of craftsmanship and skill are listed in a handful of other professions besides the clergy, who are also listed. See William Langland, *Piers Plowman,* Passus 19.11. See also Ryken, *Work and Leisure*, p. 68.

[6]See, for example, Gustav Wingren, *Luther on Vocation* (Eugene, Ore.: Wipf & Stock, 2004); and John Calvin *Institutes of the Christian Religion,* especially 3.10.6.

[7]Schuurman, *Vocation,* pp. 4-5.

[8]Charles Taylor, *Sources of the Self* (Cambridge, Mass.: Harvard University Press, 1989), p. 227, quoted in Paul Marshall, *A Kind of Life Imposed on Man* (Toronto: University of Toronto Press, 1996), p. 102.

God.[9] Both Protestants and Catholics suffer from the leavening of the cultural perversions of the vocational thinking, while groups and teachers within both traditions seek to restore a biblical view of calling.

Primary and secondary callings. The doctrine of vocation centers on our various stations in life through which we serve God in daily living. Yet vocation, in this "secondary" sense, is entirely dependent on a primary, first-cause call: our call to follow the Caller himself. Os Guinness describes the relationship between primary and secondary calling:

> *Our primary calling as followers of Christ is by him, to him, and for him.* First and foremost we are called to Someone (God), not to something (such as motherhood, politics, or teaching) or to somewhere (such as the inner city or Outer Mongolia).
>
> *Our secondary calling, considering who God is as sovereign, is that everyone, everywhere, and in everything should think, speak, live, and act entirely for him.* We can therefore properly say as a matter of secondary calling that we are called to homemaking or to the practice of law or to art history.[10]

As we discuss the important principles in the doctrine of vocation, we should never lose sight of its only foundation: the call *to* God.[11] Yet there are important secondary concepts running through the doctrine of vocation that demand our attention if we are to fully integrate our lives and our ordinary work.

Key concepts in vocational thinking. *The masks of God.* The first element in the Reformers' thinking is the idea that God acts *by means of* human beings.[12] It is true that we are his servants, but we are also his *instruments.* We are "channels" of God's love to the world.[13] We receive by faith what God gives, and then we

---

[9]See John Paul II, *Encyclical Laborem Exercens,* paras. 24-25. In addition, Opus Dei, a Roman Catholic group, understands the calling of the laity in ordinary work to be a high calling. Despite some controversy surrounding the organization, its stated goals regarding work as sacred calling are sound.

[10]Guinness, *Call,* p. 31.

[11]Paul Stevens would go so far as to say that we err by focusing too much on a "particular call" or "station." We should look, instead, to the various *means by which* God calls us to himself, which includes the specific tasks of everyday life and ordinary work (Stevens, *The Other Six Days* [Grand Rapids: Eerdmans, 1999], pp. 75-80).

[12]My purpose is not to examine the full history and complexity of the doctrine of vocation but simply to bring a theological and historical perspective to our discussion of serving God in the law. For a full treatment, see Schurrman, *Vocation;* Ryken, *Work and Leisure;* Stevens, *Other Six Days;* Gene Edward Veith, *God at Work* (Wheaton, Ill.: Crossway, 2002); Marshall, *Kind of Life;* and Guinness, *Call.*

[13]Wingren, *Luther on Vocation,* pp. 126-27. See also Veith, *God at Work,* pp. 25-45.

"give forth" to our neighbors in love according to our callings.[14] Luther spoke of God's creative work being accomplished through those who yield to him in their stations in life. "Creation, the work of God, is carried out through the person, who being faithful to his vocation, is a coworker against the Devil. . . . God continues his creative work on earth where man's vocation lies."[15]

God, in other words, uses human beings in their various callings to do his work. In our cooperation with God's work on earth, says Luther, we are his "masks"—a costume or disguise, really—under which he is hidden while he works his purposes, demonstrating his love (or his wrath). For example, God could create children without the "help" of husband and wife, but he "hides himself" in marriage, through which he creates children, his creative person "disguised" by a husband and a wife.[16] To put it slightly differently, husband and wife are God's instruments in his creative ministry.

This principle is illustrated most starkly and, for the lawyer, aptly, in the discussion of the wrath of God at the end of Romans 12 and the beginning of Romans 13.[17] In Romans 12, Paul instructs us to leave vengeance to God and to love our enemies; it is God's own province to repay. "Vengeance is mine, says the Lord." Yet, not a hundred words further into the passage, he describes the means for "leaving it" to him: God calls *a human being* to administer his wrath. The civil magistrate is "the servant of God to execute wrath on the wrongdoer" (Romans 13:4). Undeniably, the civil ruler described here is an "instrument" of God, which God uses to execute his wrath and demonstrate his love (to the people protected by punishing evildoers).

No accidents. Second, perhaps the most basic strand of the doctrine of vocation is that the circumstances and boundaries of our lives are not accidents but are ordered by God. If our Creator has prepared the good works that we are to do, then it follows that he has created us with the desires and talents necessary to those works.[18] In addition to those more "inward" giftings, God has also created the platform on which they play out: our social circumstances, geographic limitations, family background, and resources. These prepare us for the life to

---

[14]Wingren, *Luther on Vocation,* p. 126.

[15]Ibid., pp. 126-27.

[16]Ibid., p. 138.

[17]For an excellent exposition of this principle through these passages, see Veith, *God at Work.*

[18]This is the crux of Ephesians 2:10: "For we are God's workmanship, created in Christ Jesus to do good works, which he has prepared in advance for us to do" (NIV).

which he calls us *and* set the conditions under which we work it out.

Inherent in this basic concept are hints about discerning our vocation and experiencing God's call to us. Paul Stevens, for example, admonishes that we should not focus on discerning a "particular" call, but instead, as part of the life of discipleship, we must learn "how to live in every dimension to please him." In addition to the effectual to call to become a disciple, Stevens identifies three distinct means by which God calls. First, God directs through all the *circumstances* of life (the "providential call"). Second, God summons us through the *gifts* he has given us (the "charismatic" call). And third, God directs us through the *desires* created in us by his Spirit (the "heart call").[19] As we live to seek God, he calls us.

Multiple callings, multiple duties. In addition, vocational thinking recognizes that we have multiple callings—more than one "station" in our multifaceted lives. We are called by God to be at our posts in all areas: in our family, at work, as citizens, and in the local church. Knowing that we have been called as brother or sister, husband or wife, citizen, and worker provides purpose in daily living in each area, and through our activities in each sphere, we participate in God's providential care for creation and his continuing work in the world.[20]

This principle too is illustrated in Romans 13. The civil ruler is also a private citizen and perhaps a husband or father as well. In those vocations, his duty is to love his enemies and repay evil with kindness. Yet, on the other hand, he must administer punishment in his role as civil servant. In this context, we see that vocation assists us in determining our duties in our various roles, even under the same circumstances. "The same man is, for instance, father of his children, husband of his wife, master of his servants, and office holder in the townhall."[21] To Luther, it was a matter of "office." We hold the office, God does the work, we love our neighbor.

The particular way we are to live out the offices of parent, spouse, lawyer, or farmer is determined by discernment of obligations germane to the particular post under the circumstances at hand. We are called to carry out the duties of our "posts," no more, no less.[22]

---

[19]Stevens, *Other Six Days,* pp. 75-80.
[20]Schuurman, *Vocation,* pp. 40, 50-52; Veith, *God at Work,* pp. 35-45.
[21]Wingren, *Luther on Vocation,* p. 5.
[22]Schuurman, *Vocation,* pp. 4-5. See also Calvin *Institutes* 3.10.6.

Who is my neighbor? Vocation, in this sense, is very practical. Not only does it assist us in discerning our duties, it helps us focus our limited resources in the areas to which we are called. The implications of vocational thinking are practical as well. For example, a vocational view of God's hand will keep us faithful to our "real" neighbors—those whom God has placed in our lives—rather than serving "humanity" in the abstract or "saving the world." Calvin expressed this idea in his teaching that "the Lord knows the boiling restlessness of the human mind, the fickleness with which it is born hither and thither, its eagerness to hold opposites at one time in its grasp, its ambition."[23] We can't do *every* good thing at once, so "lest all things should be thrown into confusion by our folly and rashness, he has assigned distinct duties to each in the different modes of life."[24]

This way of looking at our world does not permit me to debate whose parents I am to honor, which boss deserves my respect, or what country to which I owe my allegiance. We honor the parents God has given us. We respect our employers and obey the authorities in the jurisdiction God has planted us. We recognize that God has placed us in particular circumstances to love particular people in particular ways. "Every man's mode of life, therefore, is a kind of station assigned him by the Lord, that he may not be always driven about at random."[25]

To allow God to direct our lives in this way is very freeing. We can pursue our work to the glory of God instead of searching for more "spiritual" outlets for gifts. We can love the neighbors in our own family, at our office and on our street rather than searching for strangers to whom we should "minister." Our various vocations are the ministry we are called to, and when we recognize that God has laid on us the burden to do what we do, wherever we are, we will by faith endure the difficulties and toil associated with that burden.[26] Not only that, but we will realize that no matter the world's opinion of us and our work, we know that if we follow our callings, even the meanest task has, in the words of Calvin, "a splendour and value in the eye of God."[27]

---

[23]Calvin *Institutes* 3.10.6.

[24]Ibid.

[25]Ibid.

[26]"Again, in all our cares, toils, annoyances and other burdens, it will be no small alleviation to know that all these are under the superintendence of God. . . . Every one in his particular mode of life will, without repining, suffer its inconveniences, cares, uneasiness, and anxiety, persuaded that God has laid on the burden" (Calvin *Institutes* 3.10.6).

[27]Calvin *Institutes* 3.10.6.

In short, all of life is sacred when lived in faith, and the stations to which God has posted us are "callings" *from him* in a very real sense. Contrary to the teaching of the medieval church, vocation infuses all of life—even mundane activities—with religious significance, and the duties that our stations in life impose upon us are governed by God's will and judged accordingly. In fact, all our actions are "estimated in His sight" under the test of his calling. "In everything the call of the Lord is the foundation and beginning of right action. He who does not act with reference to it will never, in the discharge of duty, keep the right path."[28]

Dallas pastor Randy Marshall says that the problem with life is that "it is so *daily*." At the heart of the doctrine of vocation is the solution to that problem! Vocation orders our daily lives and work. The concept is simple: God loves our neighbors—our clients, our children, our friends, our brothers, and sisters in Christ—through our faithful service in every element of our ordinary lives.

The application for lawyers is obvious. Lawyers serve God as instruments of his love to our neighbor clients. Law professors are God's means of equipping neighbor students to in turn love their neighbors and do justice with the love of God. Judges love the community by administering justice. Prosecutors and defendants serve not only their own clients but assist the civil government as it seeks to punish wrongdoers—and only wrongdoers—and reward those who do right. Estate planners assist and encourage their neighbor clients' stewardship—loving their families and neighbors according to God's call on their lives. And on and on.

Yet lawyers, like others in the church, do not usually think vocationally, and the church does not generally teach vocation. I suggested at the beginning of this chapter that much of the church has abandoned the doctrine of vocation altogether. This abandonment did not occur in a vacuum, and the church's tendency to be shaped by the prevailing culture has contributed to its weak approach to ordinary work.[29] The doctrine, in short, has been largely twisted, co-opted, and perverted out of existence over the past four-hundred years. As Professor Stevens notes, the "theology of work held by most Christians" comes from a variety of sources often "unconsciously absorbed" through historical and cultural developments in the "marketplace of ideas."[30] For example,

---

[28]Ibid.; Schuurman, *Vocation,* pp. 5-7.
[29]Ryken, *Work and Leisure,* pp. 45-59, 69-77.
[30]Stevens, *Other Six Days,* p. 110.

the secularizing influence of the Enlightenment was bound to infest Christian attitudes about work. Leland Ryken calls the Enlightenment "the saddest chapter of all in the history of attitudes about work."[31] The rationalizing and secularizing forces of that period removed the theological and spiritual foundations of the Protestant doctrine of vocation, and perverted it into a "creed of personal success."[32] Likewise, the industrial revolution and the rise of a rampantly consumerist society fueled other distortions of the doctrine of vocation.[33] Whatever the root causes, we are often faced, even in the church, with deviant offspring of the doctrine of vocation.

The Deformation of Vocation

In the remainder of this chapter, we'll examine contemporary manifestations of the deformed doctrine, suggesting the particular contribution of each to our current stumbling block and the consequences for Christian lawyers. We'll consider four approaches to work that we have "unconsciously absorbed" over the years and their consequences to our theologies of work.

The decline of the Protestant work ethic. The Protestant work ethic is the name given to the particular brand of vocational thinking of the Puritans, intellectual descendants of Luther and Calvin with regard to their high view of ordinary work. In the waning years of the Renaissance, as Enlightenment thinking took hold, the Protestant ethic gave way to a counterfeit to vocation.[34] Because the Enlightenment placed ultimate faith in progress and in rational man while embracing the Reformation's high view of work, it effectively bulldozed vocation's foundation—faith in the sovereignty of God in all areas of life. The doctrine of vocation all but eroded, leaving nothing but self-sufficiency and financial security as building blocks. For Luther, vocation was about love of neighbor, and the station to which we are called is simply "a

---

[31]Ryken, *Work and Leisure,* p. 69.

[32]Ibid.

[33]Schuurman, *Vocation,* pp. 8-14; and Ryken, *Work and Leisure,* pp. 72-75.

[34]Whether the Puritan work ethic was faithful vocational thinking is apparently a matter of some debate, thanks in large part to Max Weber's *The Protestant Ethic and the Sprit of Capitalism.* Ryken holds that the Protestant ethic had to be perverted first in order for the spirit of capitalism to flourish. Whatever the historical truth, the fact remains that the Reformed doctrine of vocation, whether by the Puritans or despite their best efforts, was perverted by the secularizing spirit of the Enlightenment (see Ryken, *Work and Leisure,* pp. 87-115).

channel for God's love to the world and his care of human beings."[35] In sharp contrast, by the end of the eighteenth century Adam Smith could baldly state that it is "not from the benevolence of the butcher, the brewer, or the baker that we expect our dinner, but from their regard to their own interest. We address ourselves, not to their humanity, but to their self-love."[36] In the perversion of the Protestant work ethic, all hint of motivating love of neighbor and providential station is gone. Ordinary callings in the home, church, or workplace were no longer elevated as sacred in themselves, reflecting God's particular call in the life of the believer. Rather, they were elevated because work seemed good, even apart from divine providence, since it was useful, producing goods, culture and, most of all, money. Just as the medieval church created a dualism that elevated the sacred over the secular, so the distorted Protestant legacy was a dualism with the converse result: "elevating the secular at the expense of the spiritual."[37]

Leland Ryken calls the Enlightenment "a dark shadow" over the Christian view of work.[38] He notes that "survival of the fittest, thrift, social climbing based on economic interest, self-denying work, and self-reliance" were hallmarks of the "enlightened" view.[39] The Enlightenment influence continues to infest the culture and the church that has absorbed it. In fact, with the continuing march of secularization and the relegation of religion to the private realm, the situation is even worse today. Douglas Schuurman wonders whether it is even possible to sustain "a vital sense of God's call among mundane activities" today in a society that "systematically privatizes religion in splendid isolation from the secular social orders."[40]

Incidentally, this will not be the last time we identify the conditions of modernity itself as a troubling stumbling block to faithful witness in the law. The hallmarks of modernity, including its faith in reason alone, the primacy of science, human self-sufficiency, and individual autonomy as the source of all norms, will present themselves in our discussion as persistent pitfalls for the unwary traveler.

---

[35]Wingren, *Luther on Vocation,* p. 125.

[36]Adam Smith, *Wealth of Nations,* cited in Ryken, *Work and Leisure,* p. 71. Marshall notes that Luther was "scandalized" by talk of wealth-building and so forth (*Kind of Life Imposed on Man,* chap. 8).

[37]Guinness, *Call,* p. 39.

[38]Ryken, *Work and Leisure,* p. 71.

[39]Ibid., p. 70.

[40]Schuurman, *Vocation,* p. 8.

One subtle consequence of the secularized work ethic in the church is the idea that in our daily work we are "doing something useful for God." Of course, in all that we do we serve God, and in that sense we are working for (that is, under) him. Yet the idea that I hear so often among Christians is that in our work we perform tasks that help him. I think this flows from the modern regard for utility and productivity. While there is absolutely nothing wrong with productivity, it is not the primary concern in the doctrine of vocation at all—and it is not a biblical view of the God we serve. We are not temporal butlers, doing menial tasks that help God run his earthly operations. Nor are we his personal assistants, carrying out the work that he is too busy to accomplish. In fact, he does not need us. To be sure, he delegates authority to us to work, but he is still the Prime Mover, the Ultimate Worker, giving us the privilege of being the tool in his hand or the mask that hides his face. To think otherwise is to ignore the sovereign greatness of the King of the universe:

> Heaven is my throne
> and the earth is my footstool.
> Where is the house that you will build for me? (Isaiah 66:1 NIV)

Vocation helps us remember that our ministry to others is not something we "do for God" but something that is part of God's eternal and ongoing ministry. God is love, and our love for our neighbors is simply the overflow of God's love for us. Yet this love is not simply God's disposition toward his people but part of his character. The ministry of God has no beginning and no end. We know that his love existed before the foundation of the world, expressed in the inter-trinitarian ministry of the Godhead. We know, for example, that the Father loved the Son "before the foundation of the world" (John 17:24). While the love of God was manifest in the ministry of the Son (1 John 4:9), God *is* love, apart from any manifestation of it to us. His love of our neighbor, then, is simply an expression of his character and work. We join with him in the ministry that began before the foundations of the world.

These two ideas, love of neighbor and participation in trinitarian ministry, will help guide our thinking as we sort out the issues at the heart of the lawyer's calling in later chapters.

Work and the Fall. Though less prevalent than some other perversions of vocation, the classical view that work is a curse has returned in new forms.[41] While it retains vestiges of a biblical view of the fall of man, its faulty premise completely eliminates the foundation of "calling." We have somehow unconsciously absorbed the idea that work is part of God's punishment of humanity—a consequence of the Fall. Given the clear narrative to the contrary in Genesis 1, it seems hardly worth mentioning, but some Christians do have the impression that work itself is the result of sin. If work came from sin, then it is merely a necessary evil. We work only to live, and the reason we must work to live is Adam's sin. Work is a problem, in other words, but at least it permits us to live our *real* lives, in pursuit of leisure and the good life. Although most probably do not learn this in church, their churches do not do much to rebut the notion. Not surprisingly, those who see work as a curse do not usually view God as the one who calls them to their ordinary work. If work is a curse, the doctrine of vocation makes little sense.

> GENESIS 1 AND WORK
>
> **"And God saw that it was good."**
>
> **This description of creation, which we find in the very first chapter of the Book of Genesis, is also in a sense the first 'gospel of work.' For it shows what the dignity of work consists of: it teaches that man ought to imitate God, his Creator, in working, because man alone has the unique characteristic of likeness to God. Man ought to imitate God both in working and also in resting, since God himself wished to present his own creative activity under the form of work and rest.**
>
> JOHN PAUL II, *LABOREM EXERCENS*

There are many Christians today, regardless of their view of work and the Fall, who see work only as a necessary evil. At best, those who endure work as a means to something else, whether it be "the good life" or merely food on the table and a means to the roof over one's head, see work not as an expression of the *imago Dei* or an opportunity to participate in divine ministry but as a tool. This tool exists to procure leisure, wealth, early retirement, or pleasure, but it certainly has no inherent value.

Toil and difficulty in work are in fact the result of the Fall—"by the sweat of your face / you shall eat bread / until you return to the ground" (Genesis 3:19)—and to ignore these elements in any discussion of work is a mistake. All

[41]Stevens, *Other Six Days*, p. 112; Ryken, *Work and Leisure*, pp. 64-65.

of human work is infected by the curse of Adam and Eve's sin. But *work itself* is not a result of the Fall, only the sweat and toil now associated with it. God is a worker himself, and we are created in his image. He placed Adam in the garden, in his perfect world, "to till and keep it"—to work, before the Fall.[42] God's great and creative work is continually on display, although, like Adam's seed, it is now marred by the fall of humankind. While we can't ignore the elements of the curse in our work, work is not merely the result of sin; it can be at least partially redeemed.[43] The half-truth that work is a curse stymies workers who seek to walk out God's calling.

Self-actualization and the invention of meaning. Alongside these other popular approaches to work and faith stands the new humanism: cultural views of human autonomy and self-actualization have contributed to a vocational theory based on a self-directed search for meaning that relegates God to the sidelines in all of ordinary life, including daily work. We live, as Paul Stevens has pointed out, in a "post-vocational" age in the truest sense. We are formed and guided no longer; now we form and guide ourselves, being even so powerful as to create our own meaning and reality. Stevens explains:

> Without any theology of vocation, we lapse into debilitating alternatives: . . . [including] the most common alternative today, self-actualization (in which we invent meaning and purpose of our lives, making us magicians). In contrast, the biblical doctrine of vocation proposes that the whole of our lives finds meaning in relation to the sweet summons of a good God.[44]

In 1992, the United States Supreme Court famously expressed the logical end of this foolishness: "At the heart of liberty is the right to define one's own concept of existence, of the universe, and of the mystery of human life."[45] Ryken and others trace this thinking through the Renaissance to Karl Marx. "For Marx," writes Ryken, "work 'is the very touchstone for man's self-realization,' and the thing 'which should make him happy.'"[46] Likewise, Stevens points out that Marx proposed an "alternative to contemplating God"—finding "fulfillment in contemplating ourselves through the work of our hands."[47]

---

[42]Genesis 2:15; Ryken, *Work and Leisure,* pp. 128-29.
[43]Ibid., p. 131. See also John Paul II, *Laborem Exercens,* pars. 24-25.
[44]Stevens, *Other Six Days,* p. 72.
[45]*Planned Parenthood v. Casey,* 500 US 833 (1992).
[46]Ryken, *Work and Leisure,* p. 73.
[47]Stevens, *Other Six Days,* p. 112.

The most dangerous consequence of this kind of antivocational thinking is that it turns work into the means of spiritual fulfillment. This is idolatry. And let's face it, among many lawyers today, work is indeed an idol. It defines our self-worth and is the very center of our existence. Ordinary work is the centerpiece, at least in the Western world, of the life of purpose. "Work is good for you, a remedy for pain, loneliness, the death of a dear one, a disappointment in love, or doubts about the purpose of life."[48] When we want to get to know someone, the first question we ask is, What do you do for a living? And how often have we heard from the self-help gurus that "emotional fulfillment comes from career success"? Work is the primary factor in our personal identity and even social status.

This idolatry flows from selfishness. Doug Sherman notes that when people believe that the "ultimate purpose of work is to fulfill yourself," what follows is a "morbid preoccupation with one's 'needs.'"[49] We focus on our emotional needs, spiritual needs, sexual needs, need to grow, need to be assertive, need to be challenged. It's as if we believe that "the process of filling [our] unmet needs is like filling a set of wine glasses at a dinner party: the more needs filled, the greater the self fulfillment."[50] Work, then, is simply an "intoxicating spirit with which to fill up the glasses" and liven up the party—our lives.[51]

And it is not only those *seeking* to substitute work as a means of spiritual fulfillment who risk the danger of elevating work to an idol. Those who have a high view of work and seek to participate in divine ministry may go too far: "If vocation is twisted so that human activity usurps divine activity in creation and redemption, it must be challenged."[52] In other words, our high view of work as sacred vocation may itself tend toward its elevation as fulfillment or redemption.

In addition, when vocation becomes simply a justification for seeking power or prestige, we miss the point and abuse our calling. This may be a particularly acute temptation for those involved in law and politics. As my friend Bill Brewbaker points out, it's pretty easy to justify our job as a senator or a

---

[48]Sebastian de Grazia, *Of Time, Work, and Leisure* (New York: Twentieth Century Fund, 1962), p. 46.

[49]Doug Sherman and William Hendricks, *Your Work Matters to God* (Colorado Springs: NavPress, 1987), p. 25.

[50]Daniel Yankelovich, cited in Sherman and Hendricks, *Your Work Matters to God,* p. 26.

[51]Sherman and Hendricks, *Your Work Matters to God,* pp. 25-26.

[52]Schuurman, *Vocation,* p. 85.

hot-shot lawyer as "sacred calling." Of course we want to justify our comfortable lifestyle and position! Would we feel the same if we had less "prestigious" work? We need to take care that we don't use the doctrine of vocation as an excuse for seeking our glory rather than God's. As Schurmann points out, vocation is abused when we use it to hide behind a corrupt status quo or enjoy our place at the top of an unrighteous or artificial hierarchy: "It is a pernicious evil when persons in positions of social power abuse that power to cause suffering, and then recommend that their victims turn to the cross as a remedy for their suffering."[53]

Meaning, creation, fulfillment and redemption come from God alone. We work because he created us to work. We are called; he is the Caller.

A New Dualism

None of the preceding ideas is nearly as prominently featured in American pulpits as the view that there are two tiers of work, one "called" and the other not. This new dualism has its root in this false distinction between "spiritual" and "secular" occupations; that is, in our failure to recognize the inherent spirituality of ordinary work done in faith before God. This error has been just as effective as medieval priests in relegating ordinary work to the spiritual sidelines. To put it bluntly, the phrase *full-time Christian work* is simply a newfangled expression of the medieval distinction between the "perfect" life and the "more humble" secular life. In an ironic return to the medieval view, today's evangelicals have embraced a new sacred-secular dualism reminiscent of Eusebius.

Surrendering to "full-time" ministry. I watched as Stephen, who had just turned nineteen, stood before his church at a Sunday evening service. "The Lord has gotten hold of my heart," he said, "and I just want to publicly announce that I have surrendered to the ministry." By this, Stephen meant that he believed that he would spend his life in "full-time Christian work," that is, in the clergy. Stephen's announcement reflects common practice at many conservative Protestant churches: young people who feel a call to a deeper level of submission in their faith are encouraged to "surrender to the ministry." Thus they begin informal preparation for a career as a youth pastor, evangelist, preacher, or missionary. In these circles, there is little consideration—at least no direct discussion or instruction—that "surrendering to God" might best be accomplished through

[53]Schuurman, *Vocation*, p. 115.

full-time Christian work as a physician, teacher, writer, or lawyer.

Most often, an announcement like Stephen's comes from a young person whose heart has been stirred to deeper submission to God. This stirring may have little or nothing to do with career or secondary calling issues. More likely, it is the longing to respond to God's primary calling to surrender one's life, in every area, to God.[54] Stephen and his church leaders simply assume that his secondary calling in everyday work, based on gifts, talents and ability—will be professional ministry in the church. At a time in their lives when students should be encouraged to broaden their education and perspective on the world, this "surrendering to the ministry" has the opposite result. The student narrows his or her focus to biblical studies or youth ministry, narrowing the options and focus during an important formative period of discovery. Rather than gaining a broad education and wisdom in applying the things of God to real-world experience, the student is often isolated from the opportunities to develop various gifts and talents. Even in churches where the encouragement to "surrender to the ministry" is not phrased in those terms and where the narrowing effect is less obvious, Christians often think of a serious call by God as a call into "full-time" Christian work.

A friend told me about his son-in-law, who at the age of seventeen announced to his local congregation that he was "surrendering to the ministry." As the young man grew in wisdom, however, he saw that the gifts God gave him did not precisely fit the pastorate or youth work. His talents were in a serving profession, to be sure, but not pastoral care, administration, or preaching. Only when he overcame his guilt for not entering "the ministry," did he begin to pursue training as a nurse—a calling in which he will minister the love of Christ to many. His ideas about "surrendering to the ministry"—his doctrinal stance on vocation, if you will—actually hindered his *doing* ministry!

"Secular callings" and church work. A prominent Christian pastor tells the story of being asked why he doesn't feel guilty asking tired, busy parishioners to volunteer at the church. His response illustrates another aspect of the new dualism:

> You're going to meet car dealers and stockbrokers and brick layers and police officers and plumbers, who despite their commitments to their careers and jobs,

[54]For an excellent discussion of primary and secondary callings, see Guinness's *Call,* and Stevens's *Other Six Days.*

> are honest enough to admit that their secular vocation does not offer enough meaning to satisfy the deeper needs that stir in their souls.
>
> Some of them love their jobs; they feel stimulated and energized by their work. Some of them even leave their workplace each day knowing that they have honored God by their work and their love for people. But few of them would say: *This is what life is all about.*

He concludes:

> Whenever we wonder if the daily eight-to-five grind or our round-the-clock parenting tasks are all there is to life, the divine desire nudges us. Whenever we feel restless and unsatisfied, the desire whispers in our soul. Whenever we wonder what a life of real purpose would feel like, the desire calls us to be something more.[55]

While this pastor is dead right that people founder for lack of purpose in their work, much of this aimlessness and dissatisfaction comes from our failure to understand and preach the reality of God's divine call in everyday work. He is wrong to offer another false dualism as the church's solution to the drudgery of work. Rather than emphasizing a sense of God's presence *in one's ordinary calling*—the "eight-to-five grind" or "round-the-clock" parenting—we are encouraged to find "real meaning" *outside* of our callings by—surprise!—volunteering for tasks in the local church! This is like "running around" a poor backhand in tennis. Rather than fix the real problem, we ignore it and substitute something good but not entirely appropriate: a strong forehand or "part-time lay ministry." This is simply a radical two-tiered Christian life: serving God and loving neighbor through everyday work and family life cannot provide "a life of real purpose." *True* meaning in life comes only through jobs created by the local church. Eusebius is alive and well.

Note how this modern dualism works to discourage faithful Christian service in the professions. If secular work is indeed irrelevant to Christian service unless it is geared toward expressly religious ends, then the doctor's, lawyer's, or accountant's work can *never* satisfy our longing to serve God. Our ordinary work cannot fulfill his "calling" in any meaningful sense of that term—no "secular calling" can. The church's doctrine of vocation has so decayed in recent years that we no longer recognize "secular calling" as an oxymoron.

---

[55]Bill Hybels, *The Volunteer Revolution: Unleashing the Power of Everybody* (Grand Rapids: Zondervan, 2004), pp. 12, 14.

Whether rooted in the fallacy of "full-time" Christian work or of the primacy of church sponsorship, this false dualism is simply unbiblical.

Platforms, money, graffiti and other cheap substitutes. A common mindset of many Christians who have fallen into this false dualism is the belief that their secular jobs, while mostly worthless in themselves, are best seen as tools to more "spiritual" ends, such as evangelism. The most common theologies of "secular" work that arise as a consequence are what I call the *platform* theory, the *finance* theory, and the *graffiti* theory.

> **WHAT IS GOD LOOKING FOR?**
>
> **What is God looking for in the world, then? Assistants? No. The gospel is not a help-wanted ad. It is a help-available ad. Nor is the call to Christian service a help-wanted ad. God is not looking for people to work for Him but people who let Him work mightily in and through them: "The eyes of the Lord run to and fro throughout the whole earth, to give strong support to whose heart is blameless toward him" (2 Chron. 16:9). God is not a scout looking for the first draft choices to help His team win. He is an unstoppable fullback ready to take the ball and run touchdowns for anyone who trusts Him to win the game.**
>
> JOHN PIPER, *BROTHERS, WE ARE NOT PROFESSIONALS*

The platform theory. Under the platform or soapbox approach, a job is worthwhile spiritually if it provides exposure or opportunities for the worker to evangelize.[56] A worker's credibility and reputation are highly valued in this view, since potential audiences will be more receptive to the preaching of the gospel. Workers who believe that their platform is the paramount consideration are usually very careful about the ways they present themselves to their coworkers and others so they don't put stumbling blocks in the way of their hearers. As a consequence, the platform approach to work encourages pious, spiritually alert workers.

We can learn plenty from these Christians how to make "the most of the time, because the days are evil" (Ephesians 5:15). Yet for all their piety, they often miss the inherent spiritual richness of the ordinary tasks they perform every hour of every day. Loving one's neighbor involves much more than just evangelism. In fact, the Great Commission, on which most adherents base the

---

[56]Sherman and Hendricks, *Your Work Matters to God,* p. 63. They call the soapbox theory the "mainstream model."

platform theory, is primarily about making disciples. And discipleship involves obedience to God in a life lived completely to God's glory, including working out the second Great Commandment to "love your neighbor as yourself" (see Matthew 22:37-40).[57]

Young lawyers and law students find the platform approach attractive because we are attracted to the worldly status and credibility that the title "attorney" brings. In fact, there is some truth to the impression that people do respect individual lawyers—how many teachers, elders, and deacons in your congregation are lawyers? The temptation is to think that since God provides that position for a reason, we need to take advantage of it. The trick is, of course, to remain humble in order to discern how God is calling us to serve others rather than exalt ourselves.

The finance theory. A second theological theory of work that has come to replace the doctrine of vocation is the finance theory, whereby workers evaluate the spiritual worth of their jobs by how well they are able financially to support the local church or world missions. These are fantastic goals—in fact, they are primary duties of Christians. But God desires much more than just our money—he makes a claim on all areas of our lives. Because he doesn't need our money, especially, he is likely to be just as concerned with our submission to him in the things we do with our hands, our minds, and our talents. If we think about our work solely in financial terms, the richness of God's provision and love poured out through us to our neighbors in everyday, ordinary work is forfeited in favor of a spiritualized materialism.

The finance theory is particularly popular among lawyers who have been practicing long enough to know that they really dislike their everyday work, yet they are afraid to leave the comfort and security of the lifestyle to which they've grown accustomed. Likewise, young lawyers and law students attracted by the money are apt to use the finance theory as an excuse to avoid the hard work of thinking vocationally about what they do at law school or in the firm.

The graffiti theory. A final theological theory of work might be called the graffiti approach: we want to "make a mark" on the world around us. The fallacy of this theology is that true influence—real mark-making—comes only as a byproduct of loving neighbors one at a time rather than changing the

---

[57]See ibid., pp. 66-72.

world through some high-profile activity—figuratively painting on a prominent brick wall for all to see. "Changing the world" or "making a difference"—leaving a mark—cannot really mean anything at all in the abstract. In fact, there's a word for leaving a mark where we are not called to scrawl: *graffiti*. God changes the world as the church leavens the culture, and the church leavens the culture by being God's people in each place we are called to. We bloom, so to speak, where we are planted, and the work of the church takes root. The church changes the world by feeding the hungry, clothing the naked, discipling the nations, loving the fatherless, cheering the downcast, confessing our sins, taking dominion, being good stewards, and in a million other specific acts. We change the world by loving our neighbors—wife, children, client, boss, coworker, civil authority, pastor, law partner, fellow parishioner and, yes, even our physical on-the-street neighbor—as God calls us to. More often than not, changing a diaper is more likely to change the world than appearing on CNN.

The making-a-mark mindset may be best illustrated by the explicit career goals of most Christian law school applicants: "I want to fight for religious liberty," they say. "I want to do first amendment religious freedom litigation when I graduate." This is no mean career goal, and I thank God that there are hundreds of men and women in public interest firms and private foundations around the world doing just that. Yet not one in a hundred of these students will have the opportunity—or even the desire, by the time they graduate—to pursue such a practice full time.[58] It's not the career planning that's amiss: it's the motivation. All students want to "do something big" with their law degrees. And why not? The church really doesn't disciple men and women to be motivated to love God and neighbor in ordinary ways. But what better way to love my neighbor than to assist him or her in stewardship duties by setting up a corporate entity for a family business? What better ministry than to help parents leave an inheritance for their children by working up a will set and financial plan? What more important religious service than to represent an injured person who needs to be compensated for disabling injuries in order to provide for his or her family? If students and lawyers understood the spiritual worth of the lawyer's ordinary work across the

[58]I'll discuss some other potential problems with the religious-rights-equals-Christian-lawyer motivation in chap. 8.

board, they would be better equipped to pursue it with all their hearts in law school and beyond.

In addition, the gravitation of Christian lawyers to political organizations may be a sign of our narrow view of culture-changing vocation. Political activism is often a knee-jerk response to the cultural drift away from moral truth. Yet the culture is almost never changed by politics; the culture must change first, and then political solutions will follow. It's not that political activity is wrong—indeed, we are called to participate in and influence our political institutions—but we need to beware of our own brand of social engineering, in which we seek to remake the culture in our image through political means. This is the very instrumentalism I criticized in chapter two for being at the root of a shift away from our religious moorings.

Conclusion

Again, the problems caused by the current state of the doctrine of vocation in the church are not unique to lawyers. But one of the main reasons that lawyers fail to pursue their Christian vocation in their ordinary work is in fact the lack of encouragement and instruction on the kingdom value of ordinary work. (This may be said of doctors, plumbers, and accountants too.) The church needs to do a better job at teaching vocation, and lawyers need to wake up and work with the local church to educate pastors and to disciple other workers foundering in their professions.

Lawyers stumble in their search for the integration of faith and practice, and I have here suggested that one problem is that the church has all but forgotten or abandoned the doctrine of vocation. In its place we have seen a secularized work ethic, viewing of work as a necessary evil, a variety of self-centered "actualization" theories, and the new evangelical dualism. We have an uphill climb within the church if we are to overcome this stumbling block to Christian service in the law and other professions. As we'll see in further detail in part two, we could do worse than to begin to recover the basic principles of the Reformers' thinking on sacred calling in ordinary work.

In this chapter, we've discussed the church's flawed approaches to the nature of work and the doctrine of vocation. In chapter four, we'll address the final stumbling block: the legal profession's own failure to understand the nature of the practice of law theologically.

For Further Thought

1. Do you ever think of your volunteer work at church as more important than your ministry to your clients? If so, why? Think about ways that you serve in the local congregation and the ways that you serve your clients. How are they similar? How do they differ? Think of ways that God has used you to love others in each situation.
2. Have you ever thought of the legal profession as ministry? Does it matter what you call it if you do in fact serve your clients and allow God to love them through you?
3. Do you tend to view spiritual things as irrelevant to work? Do you view work as valuable only insofar as it serves some "more spiritual" end? What can you do to resist these dualistic tendencies?
4. Spend five minutes praying, then make a list that will help you think of your law practice (or study or work at the bench) as having spiritual relevance even in the "daily grind." Then discuss it with another lawyer or law student.

4

Thinking About Lawyering

I know a Texas pastor who understands the doctrine of vocation and has a heart to minister to lawyers. He pastors a very large metropolitan church with more than 250 lawyers on its membership roll. To get some advice on how to better disciple the lawyers in his congregation, he approached a retired lawyer and asked him what Christian lawyers needed from their church leaders. "I don't know," replied the attorney, "no one has ever asked me that before." Later, the pastor took this lawyer to see another lawyer in the church to discuss the same issue. "I couldn't even get them to understand the question," says the pastor. "So I gave up."

There in a nutshell is the problem: a church without tools and lawyers that can't help. In chapter three we discussed the trouble in the church. This chapter is about the lawyers, the third stumbling block to Christian service in the law. We stumble because we do not faithfully think about who we are and what we do.

In chapter three, I noted that a questionable theology of work within the church may hinder Christian service in the law. But common sense tells us that theologians and pastors, without at least some insight from "insiders," will be unable fully to address issues that require particular knowledge in a field such as law or medicine. While the typical problems of balancing professional and domestic duties, ethical quandaries, and stress are experienced in common by almost everyone, there are issues that are unique to lawyers. As one pastor told me, "I don't know exactly what you [lawyers] are facing out there every day." In addition, answers to some larger theological questions—the role of the civil government, the nature of human law, or the functioning of the court system, for example—are addressed more easily with the expertise of legal minds in the church. The church needs Christian lawyers to work within the body to identify issues and struggles on which the church and the profession should speak. Yet we cannot expect our pastors to instruct us in the intricacies of the law. We need to rise to the challenge. Pope Paul VI put it this way:

> For guidance and spiritual strength let [the laity] turn to the clergy: but let them realize that their pastors will not always be so expert as to have a ready answer to every problem (even every grave problem) that arises; this is not the role of the clergy: it is rather up to the laymen to shoulder their responsibilities under the guidance of Christian wisdom and with eager attention to the teaching authority of the Church.[1]

What is at stake here, as it concerns Christian lawyers, is one of the church's central functions: equipping the saints (Ephesians 4:12). Lawyers must participate more intentionally if the church's equipping ministry is to function within our profession. It's not that lawyers aren't involved in their local congregations; they are. The point is that lawyers must be just as concerned about kingdom issues relating to the courts and their clients as they are about teaching Bible study classes. We are stymied by our own inability to define the issues and formulate questions about the details of our calling, even when we happen to have church leaders who think clearly about vocation and the kingdom.

In Ephesians 6, the first piece of the armor of God that Paul mentions is the belt of truth. He admonishes that, before putting on the rest of the armor, we are to "gird our loins with the truth" (v. 14 NASB). The Roman soldier "girded up" by gathering his uniform about his thighs and waist, and fastening it with his belt, thereby removing anything that might cause him to stumble in battle. The belt—the truth—holds it all in place. We stumble, in part, because we fail to gird ourselves with the truth—the truth about God, about ourselves, about work—even the truth about lawyers and the practice of law. Failing to think about who we are and what we do causes us to stumble in being and doing.

The crux then of our third stumbling block is pretty simple. We have trouble *acting* like Christians in the law because we do not make the effort

---

[1]Paul VI, *Gaudium et Spes: Pastoral Constitution on the Church in the Modern World,* par. 43 (1965). I owe this reference to Robert K. Vischer, "Catholic Social Thought and the Ethical Formation of Lawyers: A Call for Community," *Journal of Catholic Social Thought* 1 (2004): 430.

to *think* as Christians in and about the law. In this chapter, we'll discuss some specific indicators of this failure and some further barriers to biblical thinking for lawyers.

Before moving to those specifics, however, we should address the context for our own failure faithfully to think about law and law practice. Lawyers are not alone in their failure to think Christianly about their daily practices and the institutions they regularly interact with. American evangelicalism suffers a general failure of the life of the mind, of which our own failures are a symptom, or perhaps simply an avoidable consequence.

The Scandal of the Evangelical Mind

Mark Noll evaluated this more general failure within the evangelical church in his 1994 classic *The Scandal of the Evangelical Mind.* He defined the scandal as the failure

> to think like a Christian—to think within a specifically Christian framework—across the whole spectrum of modern learning, including economics and political science, literary criticism and imaginative writing, historical inquiry and philosophical studies, linguistics and the history of science, social theory and the arts.[2]

Noll demonstrated that the scandal—which I am suggesting is alive and well within the legal profession—arose from a combination of historical factors within American evangelicalism, such as an inordinate emphasis on individual conscience and "personal" salvation, which resulted in a largely ahistorical and anti-intellectual approach to the church's mission. The consequence is an evangelicalism that is not engaged in kingdom work across the board—particularly within American universities and the academic culture.

Noll's specific focus is American evangelicalism's approach to scholarly and intellectual pursuits, primarily within academia; he does not expressly address the mindset of individuals in the working world. His diagnosis, however, explains many of the intellectual methods and attitudes of American Christians in all facets of their lives, including the way we think—or fail to think—about our daily work and the role of our work in the mission of the church in the world. Many American Christians think of their faith as a personal matter—

[2]Mark A. Noll, *The Scandal of the Evangelical Mind* (Grand Rapids: Eerdmans, 1994), p. 7.

"between me and God"; we think of missionary evangelism as the highest calling; we look upon "book knowledge" as counterproductive unless it leads immediately to changed "hearts"; and rarely do we consult Christian opinion outside of our times and culture. We give very little thought to what it means to do work that advances the kingdom of God in the arts, the sciences, and the professions.

As we saw with vocation (see chap. 3), the problem is our theology. The theological environment today is apt to lean toward the individualistic and therapeutic rather than toward the corporate and historical.[3] The church's response to modernity has led many Christians away from historical church resources and kingdom theology toward self-improvement, individuated faith, and sensateism.[4] Theology, and therefore the applied theology of the Christian life, has been usurped by the subjective self. The Christian mind has been eroded by this self-absorbed therapeutic theology, and, in the words of David Wells, this "psychologizing of life undermines the desire and capacity to think, without which theology is obviously impossible."[5]

When we think like the world—the culture that surrounds us—it should

Moralistic Therapeutic Deism

Namely, we suggest that the de facto dominant religion among contemporary teenagers in the United States is what we might call "Moralistic Therapeutic Deism." The creed of this religion, as codified from what emerged from our interviews with U.S. teenagers, sounds something like this:

1. **A God exists who created and orders the world an watches over human life on earth.**
2. **God wants people to be good, nice, and fair to each other, as taught in the Bible and by most world religions.**
3. **The central goal of life is to be happy and to feel good about oneself.**
4. **God does not need to be particularly involved in one's life except when he is needed to resolve a problem.**
5. **Good people go to heaven when they die.[a]**

[a]Christian Smith, "On 'Moralistic Therapeutic Deism' as U.S. Teenagers' Actual, Tacit, De Facto Religious Faith," *2005 Princeton Forums on Youth Ministry* (Princeton, N.J.: Princeton Theological Seminary Institute for Youth Ministry, 2005), pp. 46-47.

[3]The best place to begin on this topic is David F. Wells, *No Place for Truth: Or Whatever Happened to Evangelical Theology?* (Grand Rapids: Eerdmans, 1993).

[4]These movements are, of course, reactions to other abuses and problems within the church, and some elements of each have positive results for the life of the mind.

[5]Wells, *No Place for Truth*, p. 181.

come as no surprise that we act like the prevailing culture rather than like God's people. A recent Barna Group study found that there is no real difference between the daily conduct of nonbelievers on one hand and believers who do not have a Christian worldview on the other.[6] We see different lives only when we compare those who hold a biblical worldview with those who don't. In other words, "having a biblical worldview makes a more dramatic difference in your life than does simply embracing Jesus Christ as your savior."[7] When we say we belong to Christ yet do not allow him to transform our thinking about our daily life and work, our relationship with Christ is irrelevant in the world.

Part of the reason for our failure is that, living in the world, we are pressed to fit into its mold, to see reality through the lens of the prevailing culture. I recognize that even as I write this book, I write as a participant in early-twenty-first-century American evangelicalism and culture myself, and to the extent that I listen to and think like the surrounding culture and the contemporary church, I unconsciously absorb—and parrot—many of the attitudes and ideas that prevail.[8] The reader, then, must read critically, in light of Scripture, the teachings of the historic church, and the guidance of the Holy Spirit.

That must likewise be our approach to legal study and law practice. We *can* seek by the power of the Holy Spirit to think theologically—Christianly—about who we are what we do. But we need to see through the lens of biblical, historical Christianity in order to see aright. In fact, even that is not enough. We need, as Lesslie Newbigin says, a "more radical kind of conversion," a conversion "not only of the will but of the mind, a transformation by the renewing of the mind so as not to be conformed to this world, not to see things as our culture sees them, but—with new lenses—to see things in a radically different way."[9] This is of course what Paul teaches in Romans 12:2: We must be transformed by the renewing of our minds.

The State of the Christian Legal Mind

Judging by my experience, Christian lawyers have not experienced that "more

---

[6]George Barna, *Think Like Jesus* (Brentwood, Tenn.: Integrity, 2003).
[7]Ibid., p. 26.
[8]On the many barriers to the gospel of what he calls "modern Western culture," see Lesslie Newbigin, *Foolishness to the Greeks: The Gospel and Western Culture* (Grand Rapids: Eerdmans, 1986).
[9]Lesslie Newbigin, *The Gospel in a Pluralist Society* (Grand Rapids: Eerdmans, 1989), p. 38.

radical conversion" of the mind any more than most other Christians. Most lawyers, like most Americans, *do not* think theologically about their work. We generally do not see our work through a lens different from that of our non-believing colleagues. In my observation of the state of the Christian legal mind, I have noticed that we Christians lack a principled apologetic of the lawyer's work.

An apologetic apologetic. A sure clue that we have failed in our thinking is the attitude of Christian laity toward their legal brothers and sisters. Have you noticed that Christians are suspicious of their brothers and sisters who are lawyers? This surely tells us something about our own thinking—even our friends don't know who we are! They are a testament to the unimpressive apologetic of Christian lawyers of life in the law. Apparently, we are ill-equipped to present ourselves as ministers of justice in the kingdom.

One Christian doctor has written that "according to God, lawyers are not allowed to be paid one dime for either defending or prosecuting anyone, whether this dime comes as a salary paid by the government, a lawyer's fee paid by the client, or an actual bribe paid by someone else."[10] He concludes: "Modern American lawyers present and advance their client's point of view with every legal means possible at the expense of the truth, and on occasion may even defend people who they know are guilty."[11] Of course this is poor exegesis. It also exhibits lack of clear thinking about the nature of the criminal law, the role of the state, and the lawyer's task in the criminal system, among other things. But when Christians speak this way, it is a sure sign that there is something deeply wrong with Christian thinking about lawyers and the legal system. And we lawyers don't know how to respond.

While these folks might be atypical in the extremity of their views, there are many Christians who view the legal profession with suspicion, even among those who would say that a good Christian *can* practice law. It is no wonder that law students and lawyers struggle with how to serve Christ in the legal profession when other Christians are hostile to the very idea of a "Christian lawyer." But Christians who misunderstand the lawyer's role take their cue from lawyers themselves, who labor under the same misconceptions. If Christians in the pro-

---

[10]David James King, *Creating a Nation Under God: Rebuilding America with Biblical Principles* 102 (Bellevue, Wash.: Prescott Press, 2000), p. 102. King cites the bribery passages of Exodus 23:8 and Deuteronomy 16:18-20 as the proof texts.

[11]Ibid., p. 103.

fession thought clearly about the profession, the church at large would think clearly as well. If we are to "take every thought captive to obey Christ" (2 Corinthians 10:5), and "be ready to make your defense [*apologian*] to anyone who demands from you an account of the hope that is in you" (1 Peter 3:15), then it is certainly our responsibility to provide a defense of the way we spend most of our waking hours, whether to God's glory or to our shame!

So why don't Christian lawyers think deeply about the nature of their work? I see at least two reasons that lawyers generally cannot provide such a defense: spiritual apathy and lack of historical grounding.

Time and energy? The most prominent excuse for lawyers' failure to think Christianly about lawyering is lack of time and energy. Let's face it, many of the practicing lawyers who have read this far are thinking that this is a bunch of theoretical twaddle that they don't have time to mess with. They are concerned about billable hours, emergency hearings, supporting a family by collecting from clients, and other lawyers looking over their shoulders, ready to capitalize on any mistake. The reality is that the profession "is what it is," life is a daily affair, and law practice is grueling. Discussions of the life of the mind and the role of the American lawyer are for law school. In short, real lawyers *don't have time* to contemplate the intricacies of their callings and their practices because they're too busy as grist in the daily mill of the law grind.[12] There is some truth in this, but the reality is that if lawyers saw biblical thinking about their practices as important, they would be pursuing it, regardless of the cost.

So when it comes right down to it, the real problem is not lack of time or energy, it is apathy. Lawyers have time to do all sorts of things that are important. We golf, hunt, fish, ski, play sports, exercise, coach our kids, shop for rare books—why not stop to think about what we do and who we are? Because we don't believe it is worth the effort. We have decided that engaging our minds about what we do to the glory of God—an important and worthwhile "good"—is not worth doing. Again, Aquinas called this *acedia*—the spiritual sloth discussed in chapter two. We are giving up on the duty that comes with being made in the image of God—the duty to pursue what is good, right, and true.

The first cause of our failure to think Christianly is that we are spiritually

[12]Incidentally, pre-law and law students also believe they are too busy with the grind of school and other urgent matters to pursue discipleship in the life of the mind.

apathetic about our calling and the biblical basis for what we do every day. We just don't care.

Richard Posner and Atticus Finch. Second, we are largely ignorant of the historic Christian resources on law and government through the ages that would shed light on the contemporary problems in the law. Of course, the fact that most lawyers have never read William Blackstone or Thomas Aquinas is not necessarily a sign of the apocalypse, nor is it an insurmountable obstacle in itself to serving Christ in the law. After all, much of Blackstone's *Commentaries* and Aquinas's "Treatise on Law" are philosophy and theory, bearing only indirectly on the daily work of most American lawyers. Yet when we are cut off—or cut ourselves off—from our own intellectual roots and Christian foundational thinking about the nature and purpose of law, we force ourselves to build on other foundations or become susceptible to false narratives of what law is and who we are. Of course, the very nature of legal education today contributes to the severance of historical ties and introduces an alternative—and false—narrative of the end of and means to justice. As I suggested in chapter two, the antimetaphysical, instrumental legal education we receive *really does* have consequences. Lawyers are cut off by most legal education from the roots of Western thought on the nature and purpose of law. When the very preparation for our practice ignores most of the fundamental first principles of our calling, we lose that perspective, or by God's grace recover it elsewhere.

Whatever the cause, we are simply not connected to Christian thinking about law. It is telling that the theories of Richard Posner and Richard Rorty are more influential, even among Christian students and lawyers, than are those of Blackstone, Augustine, or Aquinas.

Moreover, it's not just in theory that we shun the Christian past. There are great lawyers in history, from all parts of the political spectrum, that have something to say about the right and wrong way to go about the very particular details of the lawyer's life. If you ask a Christian lawyer today about a famous Christian lawyer of the past that has influenced his thinking on the law, the most common answer you'll get is Atticus Finch. Fortunately, Thomas More rates a close second in this unscientific survey, thanks largely to student groups on campus that bear his name. This is an encouraging and necessary sign. But how many lawyers or students have heard of David Hoffman, William Stringfellow, or Daniel Webster, or have read the writings of Lincoln, Joseph Story, or James Kent on the legal profession?[13] Try a quick test. Brainstorm as many Christian lawyers as you can think of from history that you might suggest as role models for current law students or to adopt for yourself. Now, see if you can identify this Christian lawyer on your list: Faithful husband and father, devoted national leader in his denomination, an influential founding father, many writings on law and government, president of the Continental Congress; chief justice of the United States, president of the American Bible Society. Do you recognize this prominent role model for aspiring Christian lawyers? Most Christian lawyers would not recognize John Jay and his contribution to Christian thinking about law and government, but they know Alan Dershowitz, Richard Posner, Gerry Spence, and Johnny Cochran. We have forgotten the past.

C. S. Lewis discusses the dangers of preferring the modern over the "ancient" in his introduction to *St. Athanasius on the Incarnation:* "Every age has its own outlook. It is specially good at seeing certain truths and specially liable to make certain mistakes. We all, therefore, need the books that will correct the characteristic mistakes of our own period."[14] The only solution to our own prejudice is "to keep the clean sea breeze of the centuries blowing through our minds, and this can be done only by reading old books."[15] This, modern lawyers have failed to do.

Who Am I and What Am I Doing?

If we lawyers were able to overcome our apathy and historical disconnectedness to work toward an effective apologetic of our work, we would need to begin by addressing our identity confusion and then work to establish a biblical approach to the substance of our law practices. Let's address each of these problem areas in turn.

Hired guns and sharks. The first issue that requires a sound biblical approach is the nature of the lawyer's work. How do we know that the lawyer's

---

[13]For examples of some lesser known but principled approaches to the law in earlier generations, see John Dos Passos, *The American Lawyer* (1907; reprint, Littleton, Colo.: Fred B. Rothman, 1986); David Hoffman, *A Course of Legal Study* (1846; reprint, Buffalo, N.Y.: William S. Hein, 1968); James Pike, *Beyond the Law* (Westport, Conn.: Greenwood, 1973).

[14]C. S. Lewis, introduction to *On the Incarnation* by St. Athanasius (Crestwood, N.Y.: St. Vladimir's Seminary Press, 1993), p. 4.

[15]Ibid., p. 5.

calling is—or can be—legitimate love of and service to neighbor rather than simply respectable prostitution? The premise of this book is that life as a lawyer or judge, when lived in faith, has the potential to be fruitful service before God and love of neighbor. Yet we must face the fact that most Christian lawyers don't think of their work in this way. Even those who take the time to think about it in the first place have some real doubts about the nature of the practice of law and its potential.

In the movie *Regarding Henry,* Henry (Harrison Ford) is shot and loses all memory of his life as a hard-charging lawyer. He tries to recover and resume his old life. As he recovers, however, he is not so sure about his "old life." He tells a friend, "I don't like who I was back then." His physical therapist encourages him: "Let me tell you something Hank. Don't listen to nobody trying to tell you who you are. It might take a while, but you'll figure yourself out."[16] Henry is a picture of the profession. This isn't just a movie about a lawyer; it's a movie about *lawyers.* We're not sure who we are, and we have all manner of experts trying to create an identity for us, devoid of meaningful history or moral context. We haven't "figured ourselves out," and we listen to all sorts of crazy ideas as we seek to define ourselves in our lives in the law.

Many Christian lawyers, like most lawyers, embrace artificial identities and role-playing as an acceptable model for practice. Rather than thinking biblically, we enter the murky waters of role-based morality and the tensions of unqualified "zealous advocacy," all the while lamenting the much-advertised "identity crisis" among lawyers. This results in a sort of schizophrenia in Christian lawyers. We identify with Christ, based on religious understandings of the human person and moral responsibility, but also with a "hired gun" or "shark" or some such character. And yet we know that our game-playing is false! A pastor once commented to me that he never knew a group so apologetic about their profession as Christian lawyers. "Every time I hear a lawyer speak to a group of fellow believers," he said, "he apologizes for being a lawyer." What a telling observation!

The problem is exacerbated by the fact that clients are also immersed in the culture that values and promotes "hired gun" lawyering. Some are blunt: "I don't want a Christian lawyer to represent me. I want a shark that will chew

---

[16]*Regarding Henry,* written and produced by J. J. Abrams, directed by Mike Nichols (Paramount Pictures, 1991).

up my opponent." Of course, these same folks are surprised if the shark treats them roughly too.

The legal profession at large has wrung its hands over this issue for decades, and lawyers and professors are forever addressing an ongoing "identity crisis" in the legal profession.[17] Article after article in the professional magazines detail the unhappy state of the life in the legal profession and our failure to come to grips with it. In 1993, the dean of the Yale Law School wrote that the legal profession's problem was a "spiritual crisis," the "product of growing doubts about the capacity of a lawyer's life to offer fulfillment to the person who takes it up."[18] He worried that the profession was "losing it's soul." Over the past three decades, lawyers and law-related public interest groups have analyzed this "crisis" in graphic detail.

One obvious reason for the crisis is that law schools teach and lawyers believe that we can compartmentalize ourselves into two beings: a human being and a lawyer being. This is the dualism we discussed in chapter three. The human being has obligations, responsibilities, and roles determined by complex and interrelating moral values, societal norms, family heritage, community practice, history, and religious faith. The lawyer being has responsibilities and roles determined by the client that are, in some instances, tempered by the rules of ethics. Normally, a person who believes he or she is two distinct beings is called schizophrenic or delusional. Not in the legal profession.

The good news is that not all lawyers buy into this set up. One Christian lawyer I know says that it's all an invention of academics: "There's no identity crisis. We know perfectly well who we are." Even much of the recent academic literature recognizes the inherent impossibility of the two-being system. The best such literature goes so far as to encourage the sorts of complex moral evaluations that are necessary when thinking vocationally and morally. Some of the best work in this area is often done by Christian scholars who take diverse roles and complex moral reasoning seriously.[19] For example,

---

[17]"ABA Journal Round Table: *Identity Crisis*," *American Bar Association Journal* 80 (1994): 74 (experts discussing the theory that professionalism is giving way to commercialism, causing dissatisfaction in lawyers' work).

[18]Kronman, *Lost Lawyer*, p. 2. Kronman suggests a "lawyer-statesman" model as a solution to the crisis.

[19]Thomas L. Shaffer and Robert F. Cochran, *Lawyers, Clients, and Moral Responsibility* (St. Paul, Minn.: West, 1994), L. O. Natt Gantt II, "Integration as Integrity: Postmodernism, Psychology, and Religion on the Role of Moral Counseling in the Attorney-Client Rela-

one such text identifies the issues clearly:

> We suggest that lawyers have a moral responsibility for what they know and for what they do. Their responsibility is complicated by the responsibility (also a moral responsibility) that lawyers have to clients, but lawyers should not hide from the complications of the moral life behind the illusion that the adversary system will yield the just result.
>
> The issue is not whether moral soundness in life is easy. It is whether lawyers are disabled from pursuing moral soundness. Certainly, determining the directions indicated by justice and mercy may be difficult.[20]

This admission that moral soundness is not easy and that self-identity across roles is complex is a huge first step to clear thinking about our callings.

There are two related issues at work here that we ought to distinguish in order properly to address them in the context of the Christian legal mind. First, there is a fairly popular idea that an identity crisis, perhaps a "spiritual crisis," pervades the profession. Its causes and consequences are difficult to pinpoint, as the vast literature from a variety of perspectives attests. Yet the received wisdom is that lawyers' general dissatisfaction with work and morally ambiguous practices are part of this identity crisis. Christians lawyers, though not completely caught up in this "crisis," need to exhibit clear thinking, wisdom, and sound guidance toward deciphering the confusion in the contemporary profession.

For example, we ought to be able to speak to the perceived crisis without furthering a doom and gloom mentality. In order to do this, we should be bold to name the causes of the prevailing professional schizophrenia. The split between public and private truth inherent in instrumentalist legal education and lack of vocational thinking will of course disintegrate the lives of lawyers and law students. We ought to say so. In addition, we should address our own complicity as Christians in the crisis mindset. I cannot count the number of meetings of Christian lawyers, law professors, or students I've attended where the prevailing sentiment was "it's so hard to be a Christian in this profession,

---

tionship," *Regent University Law Review* 16 (2003-2004): 223; Robert K. Vischer, "Heretics in the Temple of Law: The Promise and Peril of the Religious Lawyering Movement," *Journal of Law and Religion* 19 (2003-2004): 427; Teresa Stanton Collett, "Speak No Evil, Seek No Evil, Do No Evil: Client Selection and Cooperation with Evil," *Fordham Law Review* 66 (1998): 1339.

[20]Shaffer and Cochran, *Lawyers, Clients, and Moral Responsibility*, pp. 11-12.

let's huddle together and share our tales of woe." This bunker mentality is at odds with the truth that the good news has something to say to lawyers about what we do every day. When Christians huddle together in despair, we fail to engage the profession in a most significant area.

Second, broad acceptance of the gunslinger persona is a related problem. Again, many simply reject this persona as an artificial human being/lawyer being split. On the other hand, this vision of the lawyer's work is taken as the model by many. And even for those who do not fully accept it, the model serves as the baseline from which other models are discussed. For example, Professor Joseph Allegretti, a Christian law professor, highlights the issue by structuring his book about the lawyer's calling around the "varying self-images" adopted by Christian lawyers in response to this "standard vision" of the lawyer's work. He identifies this adopted persona with "the proverbial hired gun of the old west" in which the "lawyer brackets his own moral values and serves as the amoral instrument of his client":

> The lawyer is the *neutral partisan* of his client. He is neutral, in that he does not let his personal values affect his actions for clients; and he is partisan, in that he does whatever he can to achieve his client's objectives, whatever they might be, limited only by the law itself.[21]

That is at least very close to how we learn it in law school, and that's the picture the public has too. It's tough to believe that it's not reality. Even many of the ethical texts simply explain that there are different approaches that a lawyer may take based on what role he or she wishes to play. To Christian leaders (and even in our own minds) we're hired guns, prostitutes, sharks, or snakes.

We will discuss both of these issues and the importance of complex moral reasoning for professional identity in much greater detail in chapter ten. But for now, we simply must acknowledge that there is some confusion about the lawyer's role generally and a clear need for Christian thinking on identity issues. These identity issues vary, but the primary confusion seems to stem from the lawyer's moral responsibility to his or her client.

It's just a job. The second area that requires sound biblical thinking is the substance of our daily work. We don't take much time to develop a useful apologetic for the particular *kind* of practice we engage in every day. Even if *being*

[21]Joseph Allegretti, *The Lawyer's Calling* (New York: Paulist, 1996), p. 9.

a lawyer is different than being a pornographer or a mob assassin, how exactly is what I do different, and why? Are there some practice areas more inherently Christian than others? Is it okay to sue people or to write children out of a will? With few exceptions there is little or no discussion of biblical approaches to the various areas of law practice among Christian attorneys. When was the last time you heard a lawyer discuss the theological basis for his or her area of practice? Only criminal defense lawyers are regularly called on to defend their work—and it has resulted in an edifying discourse on exactly why it's okay for Christians (or moral lawyers, etc.) to "defend guilty people." Otherwise, lawyers just don't talk about it much (or think about it, either). Because rarely do we take the time to think seriously about them, these kinds of doubts also hinder Christian lawyers seeking to live out their callings in faith.

Here again the instrumental bias of our legal education hinders faithful thinking. It's not just first principles on which we are shortchanged in most American law schools. Our education provides little if any metaphysical justification for tort practice, contracts, criminal defense and prosecution, or any other practice area. In short, we are trained to ignore the most important questions of our calling. Of course, we can develop biblical thinking on our own, but the efforts of novices at coming to grips with a theological approach to practice are just not as productive as comprehensive instruction. Ironically, we come out of law school thinking *less clearly* on first principles than when we went in.

The problem is acute for Christian lawyers. Very few of the lawyers and Christian law students with whom I discuss this issue have ever thought about law practice as anything more than "just a job." And it's not just the lack of vocational thinking that we addressed in chapter three. Not only do lawyers fail to think of their work as ministry, they have usually not given a moment's thought to whether their particular work is good work by God's standard. Professor Allegretti observes, "Most lawyers I talk to, even those who are devout Christians, see their religious values as irrelevant to their work or as providing only vague and minimal guidance (don't lie, don't cheat)."[22] I have found the same thing in my conversations over the years with hundreds of lawyers and students. When I ask practitioners how their specific practice—whether it be drafting wills, representing injured parties, or prosecuting—fits into God's

---

[22]Ibid., p. 22.

work in the world, they usually reply to the effect that it helps them feed their family. "It pays the bills" is a poor theological justification for one's life work.

Perhaps what we see among Christian lawyers is the fruit of the evangelical emphasis on individual conscience and the primacy of personal piety that Mark Noll discusses. When institutions that once provided meaning, role, and relationships are fragmented or abandoned, clear thinking about vocation and professional identity are sure to suffer too. When the idea of vocation is no longer viable as a doctrine and the church is no longer embraced as a meaningful institution, an identity crisis takes place throughout the culture.[23] This is compounded by the rise of postmodern thought, which has created a culture in which it is difficult—or perhaps even socially illegitimate—to integrate moral reasoning into professional roles.[24]

In such a world, the typical Christian lawyer practices law "by conscience." Is there a Christian way to practice? Sure. "Do what feels right and don't lie, and you'll be fine," is the way one evangelical leader told a group of my law students. We take an ad hoc approach—one phone call, one case, one client at a time, evaluating each by its own gut feel, perhaps praying regularly about each one. One Christian law professor goes so far as to say that there is no systemic moral evaluation possible—one must "be led by the Spirit" to take cases, then represent the client's interest fully, tempered only by the Holy Spirit's on-the-spot direction and the ethics rules to guide our zealous representation. I have a colleague who calls this the "Spirit-led shark approach" to litigation.

Don't misunderstand me here: we must be led by the Spirit, by conscience, and by regular prayer about each case and client! These are *essential* to the Christian lawyer's practice. But there must be more. Personal piety alone is insufficient to the task of bringing one's law practice under the headship of Christ. A sincere, devout lawyer cut off from the body of Christ and traditional thinking on the nature of his task will have a difficult road.

By now, the fundamental relationship of the identity crisis to the doctrine

---

[23]On this topic, see James D. Hunter, *American Evangelicalism: Conservative Religion and the Quandary of Modernity* (Piscataway, N.J.: Rutgers University Press, 1983), pp. 94-95.

[24]I owe this insight to my colleague Larry O. Natt Gantt II, "Integration as Integrity: Postmodernism, Psychology, and Religion on the Role of Moral Counseling in the Attorney-Client Relationship," *Regent University Law Review* 16 (2003-2004): 240-45. In chap. 10 we'll discuss this work further and seek to apply our integrated lives to our professional identity.

of vocation should be evident. Because we don't think vocationally, we by default latch onto the prevailing identity of the lawyer as hired gun, aspire to the inflated ideal of the lawyer as social engineer, or undervalue our work as "just a job." Each view falls short as a vision for Christian service. If we don't understand that our work can be sacred before the Lord when pursued in faith as worship to him, then we simply won't evaluate it in that light. If we don't evaluate it in that light, we aren't thinking about it in a fully Christian way. We may be moral, ethical, and well-respected, but we are not intentionally pursuing the ends of our Creator through the means that he provides. In short, we're missing out on the true meaning of practicing law.

Kinder, gentler, nicer social engineers. There is another danger of misguided Christian thinking about law that lurks even among lawyers who might tend toward an integrative approach to law practice. As we saw in chapter two, the root of the move away from transcendent thinking about law was instrumentalist legal theory. Today, that view prevails, and most scholars and judges believe—or act as if they believe—that the law is primarily an instrument or tool to be used for the broader social good,[25] and it is taken for granted then that lawyers, judges, and professors are the law's engineers. Law itself is really no different from power politics, a politics in which the elites of the lawyer class are the unelected arbiters of the common good. No wonder so many believe that lawyers are arrogant!

The problem is that this temptation to social engineering is no less evident among Christian lawyers. This tendency toward Christian social engineering rears its head in the consequentialism of much of the Christian thinking about law. We want the right "result" in the world or in a case, and we are happy to "engineer" the law to that end. We desire to "do justice" or pursue "social justice" in a vacuum apart from procedure, parties, and individual human beings.[26] For example, there appears to be no higher injustice these days than to let a criminal off on a "technicality." But technicalities *are* the moral fiber of justice. We "do justice" not by engineering cases and laws

[25]See chapter two. "American pragmatic instrumentalism . . . is our only indigenous general theory of law and was our most influential legal theory during the middle decades of this century" (Robert Samuel Summers, *Instrumentalism and American Legal Theory* [Ithaca, N.Y.: Cornell University Press, 1982], p. 35).

[26]See Thomas Sowell, *The Quest for Cosmic Justice* (New York: Free Press, 1999), and J. Budziszewski, *What We Can't Not Know* (Dallas: Spence, 2003).

and theories to benefit groups or "society," we do justice by doing right between two litigants, or between the state and the accused, or between two contracting parties. The way we accomplish this goal is through a series of procedural and evidentiary rules designed to protect against doing wrong to one party or the other. Sometimes this requires that "true" evidence is not admissible, or that past conduct is not disclosed to the jury, or that some documents are not trustworthy enough to prove a point. These so-called technicalities are rooted in the moral basis of a system that recognizes the limits of human impartiality and fairness. In the Mosaic legal system, one of these technicalities was that two witnesses were required to prove a crime or offense. If only one witness, no matter how reliable, spoke to the crime, the accused was let free, on a technicality.

But even when *human* justice is unable to do *perfect* justice to an accused and the guilty go free or the victim goes uncompensated, God's justice prevails. If we really believe that the King of the universe is sovereign, then we know that there are no gaps in ultimate justice. God judges the deeds of all humans. It is this relationship between divine justice and human justice that has led one political scientist to observe that faith in a just and sovereign God is the only source of confidence in imperfect human legal systems. Not only that, but our desire for global perfection is a recipe for disaster: "One of the strongest motives to do wrong is to make everything go right."[27] Any attempt to fully do God's work of society-wide justice—cosmic justice—is unfaithful social engineering.[28]

Our misunderstanding of this tempts us to engage in our own brand of power politics as a substitute for law. That is why it is so troubling to hear so many Christian students speak as if "religious liberty litigation" were the sole manner in which the life of the Christian lawyer can be lived. Religious liberty work can be good and faithful service, but the human justice system is but a small part of the realm in which we struggle to see truth prevail. Ultimate justice is not about the courts or legislation or religious "rights." We should seek to bring God's truth to bear *upon* and *in* these systems, but to use systemic power to engineer our desired results is just kinder, gentler social engineering that flies in the face of the transcendent nature of law.

---

[27]Budziszewski, *What We Can't Not Know,* p. 67.
[28]On this topic, see also Sowell, *Quest for Cosmic Justice.*

Pluralistic Civility

Several years ago, I gave a talk to a student group in which I raised some of these indicators of our failure to think Christianly about the law. I also suggested that there was a right way and a wrong way to read the Constitution, to draft a contract, and to deal with clients, and that we could learn how to practice law as worship before God. I suggested that in order to do these things, we needed to be intentional in seeking truth as part of a body as we were designed to be, that we needed to apply Scripture and the teachings of the church to our daily work, and that we needed to submit all areas of our lives to God, including our callings, which come from him. Afterward, a law student approached me and told me that it was impossible to do what I suggested. "We are not the majority, and our way of thinking about things is okay in our Christian group, but not out there in the classroom or the courtroom." I asked her if we needed to abandon the truth of the Christian faith in order to be a law student or practice law. She wasn't certain, but she definitely considered it a viable option!

Most believers don't want to speak or act as if there are "Christian" answers to the questions of how we should live, in light of the varying traditions within the church and the broader pluralist American culture. It may be that we are afraid of being intolerant or arrogant. Humility is a good thing, and our approach to the world should be filled with grace—but truth as well. As Randy Alcorn puts it, "Truth without grace breeds a self-righteous legalism that poisons the church and pushes the world away from Christ. Grace without truth breeds moral indifference and keeps people from seeing their need for Christ."[29] So while there is something to be said for humble hesitation, our lives must reflect both the truth and grace of the gospel. But this young lady did raise an important issue: in light of the vast array of opinions and theories that exist in the culture, how can we be faithful to speak the truth as we think about truth? I'll close our discussion of the call to the renewed mind by addressing her question.

First, we need to understand that "religion" and religious beliefs are not simply private opinions, worthy to be embraced in the privacy of home or church building but otherwise irrelevant. Yes, our beliefs and practices are rooted in the

[29]Randy Alcorn, *The Grace & Truth Paradox* (Sisters, Ore.: Multnomah Publishers, 2003), p. 18.

> **CHESTERTON ON PROGRESS**
>
> **We have mixed up two different things, two opposite things. Progress should mean that we are always changing the world to suit the vision. Progress does mean (just now) that we are always changing the vision. It should mean that we are slow but sure in bringing justice and mercy among men: it does mean that we are very swift in doubting the desirability of justice and mercy. . . . We are not altering the real to suit the ideal. We are altering the ideal: it is easier.**
>
> G. K. CHESTERTON, *ORTHODOXY*

revealed Word of God, and not everyone recognizes it as such. Yet we all have religious grounds for our opinions. As Lesslie Newbigin puts it: "There are not two separate avenues to understanding, one marked 'knowledge' and the other marked 'faith.' There is no knowing without believing, and believing is the way to knowing. The quest for certainty through universal doubt is a blind alley."[30]

At bottom, something is right, something is wrong. At some stage of the discussion the justification for what is preferred or not preferred, what is good and what is bad will come down to a "belief." Of course, even the position that religious conviction is an unsound basis on which to discourse publicly is itself an unprovable belief. Almost every public issue involves beliefs about what is right and wrong, what is moral and immoral. We needn't cave in to those who would relegate truth claims to the sidelines on the basis of their source.

Second, pluralism may be a good thing, but it does not mean that all ideas are equally good, important, or true. Moral relativism, in other words, is not necessary to pluralism. Some ideas are dumb. Some are harmful. Some theories lead to bad consequences. A pluralistic culture allows us to argue about ideas and theories and beliefs. But it does not require acceptance of bad ideas, wrong conduct, or harmful theories. On the contrary, it should lead us (in theory at least) to the true, the good, and the beautiful. Moral truth, argue relativists, changes from culture to culture, from time to time, from person to person, and from place to place. Christians know that it doesn't—but that cannot close the discussion! We are called to *demonstrate* the truth of our convictions and live out truth. Incoherent moral philosophies eventually crumble under their own weight. Moral relativism always fails when you steal the relativist's

---

[30]Newbigin, *Gospel in a Pluralist Society,* p. 33.

watch and argue that stealing isn't wrong "to you."

Third, Christian thinking must not intentionally politicize. Yes, the life of the lawyer's mind usually has important political or legal consequences—of course it does. And if clear, biblical, Spirit-led, body-centered thinking leads you to agree with the Republicans, then agree. If it leads you to agree with Democrats, agree. I am not warning against political involvement, which is one of the clear duties of the Christian. I am warning against equating truth with a particular political movement or goal rather than following the truth wherever it leads. One of the huge traps here is for Christians to follow leaders—presidents, professors or politicians—because they are "Christian," and therefore their ideas must be "Christian." We need to worry about the truth, follow the person of Christ and his revealed Word, and stop worrying about the labels on others. Look to their conduct—is it right? Look to their ideas—are they true? Look to the fruit of their leadership—is it morally sound? We need, for example, to stop worrying about whether the Founding Fathers were Christians or deists or pagans and start faithfully evaluating their ideas and the consequences of their ideas.

The bottom line, of course, is that the desire for civil discussion in a pluralist society is not a reason to abandon Christian thinking about the law and government. In fact, we should embrace it. To do that, we must overcome our spiritual sloth, pursue the teachings of the saints, reject artificial roles, be prepared to give a defense of our secondary callings as lawyers, and develop a coherent approach to the theology of our specific practices. I'll suggest more practical approaches to effecting these ideals in part two.

Conclusion

When Isaiah saw the Lord on the throne in the temple, he saw himself in a new light: "Woe is me! I am lost, for I am a man of unclean lips, and I live among a people of unclean lips" (Isaiah 6:5). When we see God for who he is, we understand ourselves, because he is our Creator, the One who calls us. When Isaiah understood himself in light of the glory of God, he was commissioned to do his work. This is exactly what lawyers need. We need to understand how God sees us and our work; then we will be prepared for *his* work.

Again, the failure to think Christianly—that is, to see all of life in light of God's revelation of himself to us—is not a problem among lawyers alone. Moral relativism, biblical illiteracy, heterodoxy, hypocrisy, and cultural Christianity rule the day. So it's not surprising in the least that Christian lawyers should fail to think biblically about who they are and what they do. We're simply like the rest of Western society. But that's no excuse. What we seek—and what we need—is an approach to lawyering that is at once pious, intellectually rigorous, theologically sound, biblical, historically informed, and charitable.

With rare exceptions, nothing in the ordinary life of the lawyer—not our law school training, not the local church, not our own experiences and thinking—prepares us for a law practice like that. To overcome—or to avoid—these stumbling blocks, we must first of all *be intentional* in the way we approach our lives in the law. If we aren't aware of the problems, we won't address them. In addition, we need to *cultivate alternative perspectives* on vocation, legal education, and the nature of law study and practice. We cannot expect spoon-feeding or pat answers as we seek to live fully as Christ followers in the law. Finally, we need to *submit* our lives—even our legal lives—to the rule and authority of God the Father and our Lord Jesus Christ. If law study and practice can truly be kingdom work, then it must be submitted to the King.

We'll discuss the fundamental commitments necessary to overcoming these stumbling blocks in part two, before closing with some practical suggestion in part three.

For Further Thought

1. How would you describe your own approach to the practice of law? Do you see yourself as a hired gun? Are you a social engineer? Is law just a job, perhaps even a good one in many ways, with some opportunities to serve others? Does it really even matter how you view yourself?
2. Can you think of theological foundations for your work? If not, how might you go about exploring that topic?
3. If you spoke to your pastor about the struggles involved in your daily practice, what would you want your pastor to know? Do you think your pastor understands what you do? How might your pastor be able to help you be a better lawyer?
4. How might you be able to help your church serve and challenge professionals?

PART TWO

INTEGRITY

5

Integrity

On July 17, 1981, more than a thousand people were watching a dance competition in the atrium lobby of the Hyatt Regency Hotel in Kansas City. Several hundred more watched from above, on three suspended walkways connecting the second, third, and fourth floors. Just after 7:00 p.m., everyone in the building heard a loud cracking noise. Two of the walkways crashed to the atrium floor, killing 114 and injuring 200 more. It was the deadliest structural failure in United States history. During the trial over the design and construction of these walkways, one of the main issues involved identifying the party responsible for their structural integrity. For all its beauty and visual charm, the walkway structure lacked integrity. After July 17, everything about the structure—the uniqueness of the design, the visual beauty, the stunning presentation—was irrelevant, except its integrity.

We have integrity problems too. Although we are creatures, we are multifaceted like our Creator, who is one though also three. We are body, soul, and spirit. We have mind, emotion, and will. We are worker, citizen, child. And we have various roles and responsibilities within our family, church, career, and country. How can we live in integrity when we are pulled in so many directions? There must be a good number of us wondering; the Associated Press reports that the word *integrity* was the single most looked-up word in 2005 by the seven million online users of the Merriam-Webster online website!

Integrity, while sometimes used simply as a synonym for *honest* or *good,* has much deeper connotations. Webster's tells us that integrity is "the quality or state of being complete; unbroken condition; wholeness; entirety." A quick look at its root confirms this central meaning. An *integer,* for example, is a whole number, and to *integrate* is to make "whole or complete by bringing together parts." Likewise, if something is *integral,* it is "essential for completeness." And *integrated* is the opposite of "dis*integrated*"—broken into fragments.

In other words, a person of integrity is whole, complete, and sound. Integrity in the human person is the integration of the spiritual life with the life in the world, the unity of our words with our deeds, and a consistency, rather than an inconsistency, between our thoughts and beliefs. Our profession and our confession work together rather than against one another. This is the integrated person, the sound man, the complete woman—the person of integrity.

We see this demonstrated in Job, the man described most often in Scripture as having integrity. Five times he is so described: once by his wife (who mocks him for it), twice by his friends, twice by Job himself, and once by God. What is it about Job that elicits such comment? For one thing, he steadfastly refuses to admit, first to his wife, then over and over again to his friends, that his faith is at odds with reality or that his practice has fallen short of his words and his beliefs. His wife recommends that he "curse God and die" rather than "hold onto his integrity." But to do that would be to abandon his core, his character. It would be to abandon his utter confidence that God, not circumstances, determines meaning in the universe and composes ultimate reality: "The LORD gave, and the LORD has taken away; blessed be the name of the LORD" (Job 1:21). This great confession is at the heart of integrity. Without it, we are inconsistent, disintegrated, two-faced. Job is the same man in trial that he is in prosperity. He is free from duplicity precisely *because* he does not at one moment believe that God is the great, beneficent Sovereign, and at the next curse him for the changing circumstances. He holds a coherent view of reality: faith in the sovereign Lord of the universe at all times, in all places, in all circumstances, in life and in death.

Job is a man moved by physical trials toward disintegration, but it is not always physical trials that threaten our integrity. Sometimes we are tempted to abandon a moral commitment; sometimes peer pressure persuades us to adopt a false role or identity; sometimes we believe that no one can see our private thoughts. Yet integrity holds us steadfast in all these circumstances. A person of integrity lives the complete life, wholly submitted to God in all areas, not compartmentalized, not withholding, not bursting into pieces. The pursuit of integrity is a worthwhile good in itself.

The Integrated Lawyer

Integrity, then, is essential to the pursuit of the fully Christian life in the law (or any other calling). We seek to make our lives in the law whole or complete by including something integral to it—faith in the Creator, on whom we are ultimately dependent. We seek to live an integrated life rather than a disintegrated one. We desire that our conduct flow from our beliefs, and that our thoughts, words, and deeds collaborate in service to our Savior. We explore how faith, which we profess to be central to our whole being, can be central to the shape of our law practice as well. The idea of Christian lawyers living in integrity, then, is nothing new or cutting edge: we are simply seeking to live completely submitted to the lordship of Christ in all things, including the study and practice of law. In short, the integration of faith and work is nothing more than basic Christian living.

In this chapter, I'll identify the foundations of this aspect of basic Christian living. I'll then apply these foundations to the world of the Christian lawyer in chapters six through eight, paying special attention to how integrity might help us hurdle the stumbling blocks to faithful discipleship in the law.

Commitments at the Heart of Integrity

The integrated law practice or study made "complete and whole" as part of service to God through love of neighbor will exhibit three characteristics or earmarks. These might be more accurately described as basic *commitments* necessary to integrity, because it is certainly possible to grow and mature in these areas. To be sure, no one will have perfect integrity in this world, though we desire, of course, by God's grace to grow toward completion or perfect integrity in Christ. My suggestion is simply that on the road toward completion in Christ, these three commitments will manifest integrity and encourage growth therein. These commitments, impossible without the empowering presence of the Holy Spirit, provide consistency and fullness in the areas where we are most likely to compartmentalize, or disintegrate, in the ordinary course of our lives.

1. The life of integrity requires assent to the essential unity of thought, belief, and action under the lordship of Christ.

The life of integrity is a life lived and perceived as a whole rather than as separate compartments, some of which are special to God. Life under the lordship of Christ is in its essence unified. It is neither a series of unrelated episodes nor a collection of compartments requiring varying levels of spiritual commitment. In him we live and move and have our being (Acts 17:28)—in all of life. We cannot compartmentalize our lives and expect to be fully submitted to Christ in our life and work. Assent and aspiration to this essential unity of thought, belief, and action, then, is by definition necessary to the integrated life.

Moreover, this assent requires a unified approach to reality—a coherent understanding of ourselves and the world in light of God's plan in space and time—and a consistent working out of that understanding every day. In other words, over and above our initial recognition that integration is better than disintegration, we need both a vision of reality and a consistent life.

2. Integrity requires a continual pursuit of life in and through community.

The second essential to the life of integrity is a commitment to life in community. Christians are called to work out our callings within the intimate community of *koinonia* fellowship in the body of Christ. This includes sharing in the reciprocal ministry of the diversity of spiritual gifts, the confession of sins one to another, and the accountability of familial love. It also involves recognition of the existence of the "communion of saints" in history. Most important, however, life in our present community flows from community with God: we are able to fellowship with one another only in, through, and from our fellowshiping, communing God.

3. The life of integrity demands truth: a commitment to the revelation of God of himself, communicated in creation, the incarnation, the Holy Scriptures, and the experiences and expressions of such truth in the various symbols, relationships, images, principles, teachings, and worship flowing from that revelation.

The life of integrity flourishes with a commitment to truth. First, of course, we must know the One who is the truth. Second, in addition to God's revelation of himself in the incarnation, we need to understand our daily practice or study in light of the eternal truth of the revealed Word of God in other ways: Scripture, the created order, the church, conscience, and God's work in history, for example. This too is the duty of all Christians, yet the depth and complexity of this task varies with the particular calling. Just as a composer has a duty before God to understand music, its uses, and its nature, to search the Scriptures and the teachings of the church on the calling of the life of the musician,[1] so we too have a duty to seek a biblical understanding of our law—and, particularly, our daily work in the practice of law. Third, we seek to develop truth within. "You desire truth in the inward being; therefore teach me wisdom in my secret heart" (Psalm 51:6). We must recognize the truth about ourselves, confessing our sin to God (1 John 1:9), exposing our inner darkness to the light. This is not only a matter of devotional piety but also the only way that the person of integrity *remains* integrated. We must *remain* in him, the true vine.

The three commitments of course overlap as we submit all areas of our lives to God and practice law as service to God and love of neighbor through Christ. As we do this we are encouraged to understand the content of our duties in the law, and we seek to apply the Word of God to our work, whether legal study, drafting wills or contracts, the merger of corporate giants, or the defense of an accused. And we pursue this truth in relational community to the glory of God. This is the beginning of the integrated life.

Integrity and the Stumbling Blocks

In chapters six through eight, we will examine in detail each of these commitments, beginning with the commitment to unity in chapter six. As we do so, I will attempt to develop solutions to the stumbling blocks we saw in part one. In evaluating these solutions, however, we need to remember that the solution is a life of integrity itself, not simply the practical approach that flows from our philosophical disposition toward it!

Because a life of integrity is the whole life, a nonbifurcated life, we will begin to see overlapping and interlocking patterns as I develop each of the characteristics and their implications for service in the law. For example, when I speak of unity and its reminder not to segregate our lives into compartments, we will also be reminded of the life of the mind as something that is not a separate compartment from our devotional lives. Likewise, this will lead us to consider the doctrine of vocation as it relates to our law school career, which will have further implications for living in community and so on. In other words, it would be foolish to talk as if a commitment to unity or community or truth will in itself provide a specific solution to a specific problem. As a result, then, we can expect to see repeating themes from chapter to chapter as

[1]See, for example, Christoph Wolff, *Johann Sebastian Bach: The Learned Musician* (New York: W. W. Norton, 2000).

we move to further articulate the characteristics of the integrated life. As I seek to be more practical, those themes will recur in my practical suggestions for overcoming the stumbling blocks as well.

Theology. One of the prominent themes in overcoming the stumbling blocks is the call to think theologically about all that we do. I was speaking with a group of law students not long ago, encouraging them to understand their law study as a sacred calling before God. I suggested that such an understanding might require a bit more explicitly biblical thinking about the nuts and bolts of the law than they had previously committed to doing. One student summarized the challenge: "to be theologians in all that we do." That is it, exactly. In its best sense, theology is the study of our Creator and his ways in the universe. Certainly this study is one to which we are all called.

Accountability. If it is true that we are called into community, there is some substance to that community life. The importance of accountability will be either implied or expressly developed in a variety of contexts in the discussions that follow.

The local church. While closely related to both theology and accountability, the central place of the local church cannot be overemphasized. Discipleship, doctrine, and growth flow from our place within the body, and we ignore it at our peril, despite some heavy undercurrents in evangelicalism that encourage the existence of the oxymoronic loner Christian.

Active intentionality. J. P. Moreland has defined the "empty self" as the life "constituted by a set of values, motives, and habits of thought, feeling, and behavior that perverts and eliminates the life of the mind and makes maturation in the way of Christ extremely difficult."[2] Moreland notes, among seven characteristics of the empty self, that it is both "infantile" and "passive."[3] The only way that lawyers and law students will hurdle obstacles is through active, intentional striving in the power of the Spirit. We cannot wait to be fed, as infants must, and we cannot expect to be carried through by others. We need to be alert to opportunities for growth, ministry, and service, and seize them.

Worship. Finally, the life of integrity is rooted in worship. Our commitments and struggles must always be seen in light of our chief end: to glorify God and enjoy him forever. All of ordinary work, all relationships with clients, all of our

---

[2]J. P. Moreland, *Love Your God with All Your Mind* (Colorado Springs: NavPress, 1997), p. 88.
[3]Ibid., pp. 89-90.

studies—all of life—is centered in proclaiming the worthiness of God back to him and to the world. This theme ties together all the other themes, subsumes all our desires to overcome obstacles, and underlies all of our commitments. Worship is at the root of our life in the law, or that life is nothing.

Before moving on to apply these ideas to life in the law, we should stop to consider what must be a critical preliminary point: It is possible to pursue and commit to integrity and its underlying commitments, yet still miss the richness of a life fully submitted to God. Again, our primary calling is not to the law or other important vocations; our primary call is to the Caller. Pursuit of God in, through, and around his callings is the only path to the abundant life in the law or anywhere else. Without the empowering work of the Holy Spirit, our efforts toward the integrated life will fail. Life without the empowering presence of the Holy Spirit and faith is no true life at all. As Peter put it, "Whoever serves must do so with the strength that God supplies, so that God may be glorified in all things" (1 Peter 4:11). As we consider commitment to unity, community, and truth, we must be mindful that these commitments flow from our preeminent commitment to God.

6

Unity and the Integrated Lawyer

We hear about it too often: a Christian family man, from all appearances loyal and devout, is found in an adulterous affair. An upstanding member of the community is discovered to have embezzled from his employer. A leader of the church youth group is caught in immoral conduct. We are surprised that appearances deceived, and we remark that these folks "led a double life"—one life to all appearances, the other life in secret. It's as if each were two different people, with two separate existences. Of course they weren't. The cheating husband led one life. It was a single disintegrated life that required plenty of work, deception, and repeated acts of the will to keep up the appearance of integrity. It's the treasonous will that makes that sort of disintegration so evil. Perhaps that's why Dante has the traitors—Judas, Brutus, and Cassius—in the innermost circle of hell, being gnawed eternally by Satan himself.

Of course, much of our ordinary disintegration does not involve an "evil will," as Dante called it. In fact, personal disintegration isn't usually planned and nurtured; it just happens. Yet one thing leads to another, and before you know it, you're "two different people." One reason for this may be that modernity itself encourages disintegration, and so disintegration is a "natural" state of modern man. So perhaps in the modern world (and even more so in the postmodern, which in some ways is an extension and acceleration of modernity) we tend toward disintegration, unless by an act of the will we pursue integration. This fact—the necessity of continual choices, intentional acts—is the starting point for our discussion of the three commitments necessary to integrity. In this chapter we'll address unity, the commitment to which is at the heart of avoiding the "double life"—whether it be grounded in treason or in sloth.

This first commitment is a broad one. By *unity* I mean an essential wholeness of life, in all its aspects, consistent throughout our varied relationships, our different callings, and our diverse interests. My argument here is that the life of integrity requires a commitment to an essential unity of life, thought, and conduct *in* and *across* every area of life. Given our definition of integrity, this unity is itself a defining characteristic: it is the central reality of integrity. In this chapter, however, we'll go a bit further in defining this unity and then close out the discussion with the implications of a unified life for the stumbling blocks we encountered in part one of the book.

One World, One System, One Mind

The commitment to wholeness has three presuppositions or philosophical starting points. First, the moral and natural worlds are the *same world*. We are "one-worlders" to use legal philosopher Michael S. Moore's term.[1] The truth or falsity of legal propositions, scientific propositions—any proposition—depends entirely on its correspondence to reality, which is independent of what human beings may believe about that reality. In short, there is a real state of affairs independent of what we may think.[2]

Second, in the words of Francis Schaeffer:

> The Christian system (what is taught in the whole Bible) is a unity of thought. Christianity is not just a lot of bits and pieces—there is a beginning and an end, a whole system of truth, and this system is the only system that will stand up to all the questions that are presented to us as we face the reality of existence.[3]

This is not to say that Christianity is simply a closed philosophical system but

---

[1]Michael S. Moore, cited in Dennis Patterson, *Law and Truth* (New York: Oxford University Press, 1996), p. 45.

[2]I recognize that there is merit to much of the postmodern critique of the correspondence theory of truth and even the concept of objective truth itself. For our purposes here, though, it is enough to say that reality—however poorly we are able to interpret it due to our relative situatedness—exists independently of the autonomous, rational person, and that there is no cosmic split between the "real" world and the moral world.

[3]Francis A. Schaeffer, *The God Who Is There* (Downers Grove, Ill.: InterVarsity Press, 1968), p. 178.

that our faith has meaning across all contexts and in all places.[4]

Third, there is unity in our belief and conduct. What we believe drives what we do. We are not compartmentalized beings—or two separate beings—one with thoughts and beliefs, and the other that acts. Similarly, our selves are not separate from our jobs or our obligations in the ordinary world, any more than we are different people at church and at work.

These three starting points, of course, are related. The universal order of things has implications for what we do in life and society. The created order, the whole counsel of scriptural truth, and our lives are bound up together in Christ. The essence of the integrated life is that in Christ "we live and move and have our being" (Acts 17:28). That living, moving, and being then is a unified life, not several separate mini-lives that are lived independently of one another (see chap. 3). Likewise, our beliefs have a direct bearing on our conduct, and our worship—whether of true or false gods—determines our priorities and desires. What we worship and what we believe—not what we *say* we believe but what we *actually* believe—is the centerpiece of the life of integrity. If we say one thing but act inconsistently with it, or if we worship something that is not worthy of worship, we will be torn, disintegrated, inconsistent. We will also tend to divide our lives into compartments, so as to hold off the obvious conclusion that our mini-lives are mismatched. Because this itself requires a certain commitment and force of will, this division can eventually lead to the treasonous conduct I noted at the opening of this chapter.

Here and There: Consistency from Place to Place and Calling to Calling

Our commitment to the essential unity of life involves, for lack of a better term, a *consistent* life. This may be the most common understanding of integrity—avoiding hypocrisy in everyday life and work. We often call it matching our walk to our talk or "practicing what we preach." The unified life essential to integrity is indeed marked by these characteristics.

---

[4]For an important critique of seeing Christianity as a system, see James K. A. Smith, *Who's Afraid of Postmodernism? Taking Derrida, Lyotard, and Foucault to Church* (Grand Rapids: Baker, 2006), pp. 26-29. Smith addresses the problem in light of what he sees as the very modern reliance on rationalism in classical apologetics. The issue for us here, however, is not the apologetic value of the system but the unity of thought, belief, and conduct across all areas of life, based on God's revelation of himself.

The Unity of the Human Person

Many nonlawyers (and some lawyers) are puzzled by consistent encounters with lawyers of faith who provide legal services by means or to ends that conflict directly with the values and principles of their faith traditions. In this view, the notion that one's faith can or should be disconnected from one's professional life defies the unity of the human person and the all-encompassing reach of faith.

Robert K. Vischer, *Catholic Social Thought and the Ethical Formation of Lawyers*

Place to place, calling to calling. Because integrity cooperates intimately with vocation, true integrity demands consistency among our multiple vocations. We are posted to various stations, yet we must be one integrated person from calling to calling and from place to place. Although a Christian lawyer is, for example, both a law partner and a wife, she is not a divided being. Both roles are lived as a unitary human person in submission to one God who is at work in her home and in her firm. Likewise, an integrated man is not a Christian in his calling as elder or deacon at church and a vulgar drunk at his country club. We are whole beings, like Job, holding fast to our integrity in prosperity and trials, at home and at work, eating with our cousins and praying with our pastor. Consistency from place to place, from time to time, and from role to role is one of the basic earmarks of the life of integrity. It's easy to say this, of course, but another matter altogether to live it in law school or in the firm.

Walk and talk. In addition, the life of integrity means a unity of belief and practice: our conduct matches what we say we believe. It certainly may be true that hypocrisy is simply a tribute that vice pays to virtue,[5] but too much of such a tribute—the work of vice in a person who knows of virtue—is a sure sign of disintegration, one way or the other. If it is true that we are transformed by "the renewing of [our] minds" (Romans 12:2), then hypocrisy is more than a simple matter of misbehavior; it is also a serious matter of misbelief. When our walk fails to match our talk, it may be that we don't *really* believe what we say we believe. Or, even worse, perhaps we don't even know what we are saying!

Peter Kreeft has pointed out that it may in fact be that modern humans have lost the very *knowledge* of virtue: "Christians, like other sinners, have al-

[5]Duc de la Rochefoucauld, *Réflextions ou Sentences et Maximes Morales* (1678), quoted in *Oxford Dictionary of Quotations* (Oxford: Oxford University Press, 1979), p. 310.

ways been susceptible to vice, but today we no longer seem to know what vice and virtue are."[6] To avoid the disintegration that comes with inconsistent living, we need to know what "Christian living" is. What is it that we are professing as professionals? Do we know what a virtuous lawyer looks like? It's one thing to know virtue, to sin against it, and to then repent. It's another thing to have lost our bearings as to virtue in the law, so that we no longer know what it means when we say "I'm a Christian lawyer." Do we even know the walk that matches that talk? That's certainly a very early step in the life of integrity.

"Walk in a manner worthy of the calling to which you have been called," the apostle Paul tells us as he begins the fourth chapter of Ephesians (Ephesians 4:1 ESV). Yet he has set the groundwork for this command in the first three chapters by fully defining the calling we are to walk worthily of. Before we can walk in it, we need to know the calling! Often Christian lawyers who fail to serve Christ in their daily work have never given serious thought to the relationship between Sunday and the rest of the week. Integrity demands at a minimum that we account for this reality as we live.

Sacred and Secular: False Disjunctions and Compartments

I have a friend who likes to say that "all we really need to know is John 3:16." There is a sense, of course, in which this is true: knowledge of God's love revealed in the redemption of sinners by Christ forms an umbrella that covers all of our daily lives and decisions. But there is a sense in which this claim is dangerous. What of our specific duties on earth? What about work, marriage, and the created world? How do we fit into God's plan for redeeming his creation and what role do we play in relation to his kingdom?

My friend's approach is in a way emblematic of American Christianity. Having been birthed out of revivalism, evangelicalism tends to keep the question of personal salvation uppermost, even at the expense of engaging cultural and social institutions we encounter every day, even—believe it or not—over and above ordinary legal work.[7]

American Christianity is beset with such false disjunctions. We tend to em-

[6]Peter Kreeft, *Back to Virtue* (Ft. Collins, Colo.: Ignatius Press, 1986), p. 20.

[7]On the history of American evangelicalism, its roots in revivalism, and its legacy, see Mark A. Noll, *The Scandal of the Evangelical Mind* (Grand Rapids: Eerdmans, 1994), pp. 59-145.

brace the hope of eternal life at the expense of the physical here and now. We value "spiritual" things—including work that we can call "religious"—more than earthly pursuits—and our "secular" jobs. We believe that faith trumps reason, and that a person's soul is more important than a person's mind. We therefore esteem devotional piety but are skeptical of the life of the mind. We listen for the call to "missions," but not to the unreached people groups in the jungles of corporate America.

The implications for the integrated life should be obvious. As Noll points out:

> The gospel properly calls the whole person. In keeping with the Bible's teaching concerning the various tasks given to different parts of the body, we may naturally expect Christians in different times and places to stress some things rather than others. The danger comes when the parts of the body, which are to complement each other—in this case, piety and the life of the mind—fall upon each other.[8]

Rejecting the compartmentalized life and embracing the larger context of God's creative and redemptive work breathes life into our pursuit of Christ. The commitment to the unity of thought and action involves a conscious rejection of false disjunctions. As a first step, integrity demands the recognition of the unity of the physical and spiritual world, an embrace of both devotional piety and intellectual development, and the rejection of unwarranted distinctions between sacred and secular. It rejects false disjunctions between reason and faith, fact and value, truth and moral imagination.

In some ways this seems to require a rejection of the very world around us. We are part and parcel immersed in the modern project, which worships individual autonomy and understands reality to be fragmentation and alienation. Modernity sees separate worlds, the physical and the spiritual, and holds that there is no connection between the two.[9] The focus of the unity of all things is no longer God, and nothing else can hold us together as a "whole." It doesn't help matters any that the church, having immersed itself in much of modernity, encourages its own kind of dualism. Nancy Pearcey, borrowing from

---

[8]Ibid., p. 46.

[9]See Colin E. Gunton, *The One, the Three, and the Many* (Cambridge: Cambridge University Press, 1993), p. 19; and Lesslie Newbigin *Foolishness to the Greeks: The Gospel and Western Culture* (Grand Rapids: Eerdmans, 1986).

Francis Schaeffer, calls this "two-story truth."[10] We live in a world where there is a public-private split, in which it is assumed that the large, public institutions, such as the state, academia, and corporations, are "value-free" or "scientific." Values are private, individual choice.[11] Pearcey calls the private sphere the upper story, and the public the lower story; values reside in the upper story, facts in the lower story. Facts are "binding on everyone"; values are "individual choice." This public-private separation, says Lesslie Newbigin, is a reflection of an unwarranted separation of "values"—which we are all free to choose—from "facts"—which are either true or false.[12]

The modern mindset makes it all the more important that we commit to pursuing a unified approach to the basic Christian life: the integration of thought and action around the lordship of Christ and God's creative and redemptive purposes in Christ. Important practical implications of this understanding spring to mind for our stumbling blocks flowing from law school, the local church, and the life of the mind.

Before moving to those implications, however, I want to suggest that our perspective on the kingdom of God has consequences for our commitment to unity as well.

The Kingdom of God

Jesus came to seek and save that which was lost (Luke 19:10). He died in order that we might spend eternity with him in heaven, but his death also works to redeem all that was corrupted by the Fall: he died to restore God's reign over *all* creation. And while that will not be fully accomplished until his ultimate return, his kingdom is in operation wherever he is king.[13] Jesus came to inaugurate the kingdom in which God will fix all that is broken. This means that God is at work, right now, to bring all that he has made under his kingship. This view of God's kingdom rejects any dualism between the sacred and sec-

---

[10]Nancy Pearcey, *Total Truth: Liberating Christianity from its Cultural Captivity* (Wheaton, Ill.: Crossway, 2004), p. 20.

[11]Peter Berger, cited in ibid., p. 20.

[12]Newbigin, *Foolishness to the Greeks,* pp. 16-20, 75-94.

[13]Good sources on the kingdom of God include Allen Mitsuo Wakabayashi, *Kingdom Come: How Jesus Wants to Change the World* (Downers Grove, Ill.: InterVarsity Press, 2003); Albert M. Wolters, *Creation Regained: Biblical Basics for a Reformational Worldview* (Grand Rapids: Eerdmans, 1985); and Russell D. Moore, *The Kingdom of Christ: The New Evangelical Perspective* (Wheaton, Ill.: Crossway, 2004).

ular in our approach to mission. Indeed we are called to work with God in his redemption of culture. "If the good news that Jesus proclaimed was that God was beginning to reclaim a lost creation and restore it to his creational intentions, does it not call us to live for and seek the love, truth and justice of God in *whatever way it is being challenged in our world?*"[14] Our devotional activities and our religious duties are but part of the larger call of the gospel: faithfulness to Christ at work, at home, at church, and on the golf course.

Some view the kingdom as coextensive with the church or religious activities, or perhaps even the life of the world to come. Yet the kingdom of God is at hand; it is among us (Luke 11:20; 17:21). God has rescued us from the kingdom of darkness and brought us into the kingdom of the Son he loves (Colossians 1:13). And a war wages over the territory of creation, where nothing is neutral:

> The chief protagonists are two kings, one legitimate and the other usurper, each having his own sovereignty and army, each waging war for the possession of the same territory. The kingship of the rightful sovereign is what the Bible calls "the kingdom of God" while that of his rival is called "the world" or the kingdom of darkness. The Scriptures call one of the armies "the people of God" ("the church" in the New Testament) and the other "those outside"—that is, all of mankind outside Christ and in bondage to Satan.[15]

We live in the tension of the kingdom "already here" and "not yet" at the same time. We live in the old age but already participate in the age to come, which is not yet here in its fullness. A commitment to unity—to the reality of one world—recognizes that while the kingdom of God and the kingdom of this world are both here at the same time, there can be only one ruler at a time over any one part of any contested territory. The implications for our call to integrity in the law are all-encompassing:

> Yes, we are to seek the salvation of men and women of all nations. No, that does not necessarily take precedence over feeding the poor, seeking justice for the oppressed or dismantling racism and corruption in society. As we individuals interact with our world, we need to consider how God's reign would be seen in all of our encounters and relationships.[16]

---

[14]Wakabayashi, *Kingdom Come,* p. 45.
[15]Wolters, *Creation Regained,* p. 84.
[16]Wakabayashi, *Kingdom Come,* p. 45.

Our call as lawyers is to minister God's truth, beauty, goodness, justice, mercy, compassion, or love wherever it is lacking, whether it be in our law office, our law school, the county courthouse, the adversary system, our client's family, our partner's life, or at the coffee shop.

Nancy Pearcey tells a story about a Christian lawyer that captures the issue very well. The lawyer was considering whether to take a job in the Washington, D.C., area, and he consulted with the leader of a D.C.-area ministry, who told him, "You can either stay where you are and keep practicing law, or you can come to Washington and *change the culture*."[17] Consider the implications: practicing law is not "culture changing" but politics is.

In the modern world and in the modern church we are all over the board on cultural engagement. Some evangelicals are still mired in separatist mindset, hoping for the Lord's return "before it gets too bad" and avoiding engagement with the surrounding culture as much as possible until then, except through evangelism. Others, who see the need for cultural engagement, like the ministry leader in Nancy Pearcey's story, believe that cultural engagement equals political activism. As Pearcey notes, this is backward. Political change comes *from* cultural change, not the other way around. The church's attempts at changing the culture through politics generally misfire as a result.

There must be some middle ground that avoids cultural isolationism, resists legal instrumentalism and top-down moralism, yet is open to Christ transforming culture through his people here and now. Perhaps a kingdom perspective solves these issues: we recognize that every square inch of creation is contested, but we are called simply to love our neighbors by engaging only the inch or two we've been called to.

An Integrated Perspective

So how will our commitment to unity help us in our pursuit of integrity in the law?

The sort of life that exemplifies unity rather than compartments, dualisms, and inconsistencies provides a foundation for overcoming the stumbling blocks we discussed in part one. At a minimum, as our understanding of the life of integrity grows, our perspective on the ideas, systems, and practices we encounter in the law will change.

---

[17]Pearcey, *Total Truth,* p. 18.

Unity and the law school classroom. A commitment to the integrated life will do much to combat the consequences of exposure to American legal education. At the very least, it will provide an increased awareness of the essential problem and then boldness to address it.

Awareness. First, it awakens us to the danger of failing to recognize fundamental connections between moral knowledge and conduct. A simple *awareness* will go a long way toward protecting law students and lawyers from the instrumentalist and materialist legal philosophy. A simple awareness that law is not merely a human artifact is an excellent first step toward a Christian perspective on lawyering.

Again, the lack of historical, moral, and spiritual center makes law school a "disintegrating" experience (see chap. 2). The intentional rejection of centering moral truth tends to dislodge students from the moral realities they are forced to live with every day as husbands, neighbors, and metro passengers. To anyone who lives in the real world, a detached amorality is simply impractical as a life system. Because unity in this sense is a perspective or an attitude as much as it is anything else, it is an excellent antidote to the moral vacuum of the American law school. Law students with the mindsets of the unity of life and knowledge will have their feet planted firmly in reality while pursuing truth in the law school environment. They will pursue the "ought" in the law as well as the "is."

Likewise, students committed to the existence of a coherent and consistent reality will recognize the unstated presuppositions of the ordinary religion of the law school classroom, and they will resist the cynicism that naturally arises from detachment from moral norms. These students will pursue a life of consistency at home, at church, at school, and in the life of the mind, which will naturally open their eyes to the skepticism, materialism, and instrumentalism that informs the disintegrated life in the law. Students who have a simple awareness that there are connections between the songs they sing in church and the things they discuss in torts class will naturally behave in ways that will reinforce the basic unity of life.

Boldness. Second, our commitment to unity will *embolden* us to rise to the challenge of those who would build a materialist mansion out of stolen, reprimed, repainted metaphysical lumber. In short, we'll stand up and shout when someone claims that there are no universal truths and then argues the point by relying on some universal truth. "However rude it may be to say so these days," remarks J. Budziszewski, "there are some moral truths that we all really know—truths which a normal human being is unable *not* to know."[18] Like the child who knew the emperor was naked and simply said so, we ought to speak the truth as well, though it appears to be rude.

Spiritual apathy—sloth—with regard to first things is an enemy of the Christian lawyer in this area (see chap. 2). Simple intentionality or "caring" about the religious truths at the heart of law and legal institutions is the necessary first response in resuscitating the Christian lawyer. Our teaching, scholarship, and practice will become more expressly religious once we wake up to the fact that religious assumptions—albeit false ones—already dominate the legal academy and courthouse. At the very least we should be able to mention that the emperor is naked as we face the parade of legal instrumentalism and those who pretend that metaphysical realities are irrelevant to the lawyer's task. In the first place, we ought to be able to engage such jurisprudence as if we are human beings with souls. In addition, and more specifically, we should be bold enough to confront that devious grandchild of the Enlightenment, the myth of the secular society, which flows directly from the modern materialist assumptions that rule the legal academy today.

Again, fundamental notions of the nature of humanity and its place in the universe, the nature of law, and the obligations of the state all flow from moral and religious convictions. For example, Judge Posner's defense of philosophical pragmatism as the best foundation for legal theory is based on his religious views on human nature, the end and limits of human knowledge, and the value of seeking the mystery at the heart of existence (see chap. 2). We should be invigorated by Judge Posner's approach. It is refreshing to read, for a change, an honest articulation of the importance of moral anthropology, epistemology, and theology as a foundation for legal theory! What a strong testimony to the metaphysical nature of our inquiry into the true purpose of the law. What a great invitation to discuss the nature of persons and our ability to grasp metaphysical problems and bring reason and faith to the law. What better example of the necessity of religious commitments to legal inquiry? This sort of legal scholarship should embolden our own scholarship to state and explore the metaphysical foundations of our work. It should embolden our study, causing us to dig deeper into the biblical implications of torts, contracts, or corpora-

[18] Budziszewski, *What We Can't Not Know*, p. 19.

tions. And it should embolden our practice, encouraging us to love our clients as eternal beings with temporal needs.

Yet many Christian law students I meet are convinced that religious language and convictions are inappropriate in the public discussion of law and politics. How many times have we heard, even from Christians, that religion and politics don't mix? After all, we live in a pluralistic society. Their error of course is that *pluralism* is not the equivalent of a *secular* society, where religious neutrality reigns. As Lesslie Newbigin eloquently established in his 1989 classic, *The Gospel in a Pluralist Society,* the idea of a secular society is a myth, and the pluralistic ideal is misunderstood. To begin with, the very nature of society renders impossible any meaningful separation of the private and public human being (see chap. 4). Public policies accepted by any given society, argues Newbigin, are "a function of the commitments the members of society have, the values they cherish, and—ultimately—the beliefs they hold about the world and their place in it."[19]

A faithful life in the legal profession starts with recognizing and rejecting the secularizing impulse to privatize virtue and faith commitments. The call into discipleship with Jesus Christ cannot mean "that one accepts the lordship of Christ as governing personal and domestic life and the life of the Church, while another sovereignty is acknowledged for the public life of society."[20] In rejecting the myth of the secular society, we emphatically reject the false compartmentalization between the public lawyer and the private person, and to do so, we must awake to the fact that we live not in a secular society without religious faith but in a religious society that has faith in other things—in "gods that are not God."[21]

In the law office the rejection of this secularizing myth might embolden us to treat clients as if they have souls and their problems as if they are not simply legal puzzles to be solved but moral and spiritual issues that need to be addressed in community. It may mean that we commit to certain financial boundaries or particular ways of organizing our law practices. It might mean that we pray with our clients and our secretaries, or that we take a public stand on legal or political issues about which we have some expertise.

For students, law school is certainly one of the most difficult environments in which to avoid compartmentalization. Aren't we virtually commanded to com-

---

[19]Lesslie Newbigin, *The Gospel in a Pluralist Society* (Grand Rapids: Eerdmans, 1989), p. 218.

[20]Ibid., p. 220.

[21]Ibid.

partmentalize? Bifurcation is surely implied when we argue both sides of every issue and represent views we disagree with. Yet my view is that argumentation and advocacy don't lead us into disintegration. Rather the habit of play acting—adopting false roles—encourages compartmentalization in our professional and personal lives. *Hypokritos* is Greek for "actor." From it we get the English *hypocrite,* one who acts, plays a role, is not real. Once we develop an integrated perspective on the unity of reality, taking on a hypocritical role as gunslinger or shark for the sake of a client becomes transparently unreal, akin to a Sunday deacon who is a womanizing carouser during the week. Not that those sorts of things don't happen, but once permission to compartmentalize has been denied, our spiritual eyes are open to the blatant inconsistencies in our lives.

Unity and vocation. A commitment to unity also helps to replace the artificial-role mindset with pursuit of biblical vocation before God, and in that vein, it directs us to our pastors as coworkers in the varied ministries of the kingdom of God.

Recovery of the doctrine of vocation. An early step for lawyers and law students who desire to walk as faithful Christians in the law is to recover a proper view of calling. To begin, we could do worse than to focus on the basic principles underlying the Reformation's recovery of the sacred in ordinary work that we discussed in chapter three. By way of review:

- When we surrender to God's call to become his, we surrender to full-time ministry in every area of life, including our studies, our scholarship, and our law practice. Even legal work is a religiously meaningful means to serve God and neighbor.
- We evaluate all that we are called to do in light of the second great commandment, "love your neighbor as yourself." An approach that seeks the good and goodness of our clients stands in sharp contrast to the gunslinger model so many lawyers adopt.
- We acknowledge that God doesn't need our work, but he will give us the privilege of serving as his "mask" as he reconciles, restores, and works his purpose in our lives and our clients' lives.
- Vocation gives both purpose and direction to our lives in the law. Rather than trying to do all good things at once, we can focus on this client, this case, this area of the law, and keep our noses out of issues and problems we haven't been authorized to examine.

- Calling reminds us to see vocation in multiple areas: home, church, work and country. We are called by the Caller to respond faithfully where we have been placed. Our law practice is only one of the many venues in which we love our neighbors.

Calling and God's sovereignty. Another application of the unified life as it relates to calling is, in the words of Gene Edward Veith, "We did not *choose* our vocations. We are *called* to them. There is a big difference."[22] This is most obvious in our primary vocation, the family. "We did not choose our parents. We did not pick our brothers and sisters." Marriage is less obvious but similar: we did not simply "choose" a mate from a wide range of options; we were called into the relationship. We did not choose the country to which we were born and to which we are called to serve as citizens.

But what about our litigation practice, our board certification, or our judicial campaigns? Certainly we have made choices and developed gifts and picked majors and chosen to take the LSAT. "Despite all this," says Veith, "it is simply not true in the ultimate sense, that we choose our lifework."

> God—making use of your family and your culture—created you as you are. The doctrine of vocation has to do with the mystery of individuality, how God creates each human being to be different from all of the rest and gives each a unique calling in every stage of life. Thus you have particular talents, which you are to understand are His gifts.[23]

I remember sitting in my office one day counseling a young law student. She was pleading with me to sponsor her petition for readmission to law school. She had been on probation for a semester after her grade point average had fallen below a 2.0. After the probationary period, her average was 1.2 on 4.0 scale. I had never seen an average that low. Yet she was convinced that she was called into law school, and she wanted another chance. She had worked hard but could not handle the course material and had no aptitude for analytical reasoning. No matter how much she wanted to choose law as her calling, God had not created her to "do" law school. "The human mind plans the way, / but the LORD directs the steps" (Proverbs 16:9).[24] Calling, by definition, comes from outside ourselves.

---

[22]Gene Edward Veith Jr., *God at Work* (Wheaton, Ill.: Crossway, 2002), p. 50.
[23]Ibid., p. 52.
[24]See ibid., p. 54.

As students, then, we should recognize God's hand in our financial resources (or lack thereof), our geographical limitations and desires, and our ultimate class rank and academic standing. If doors are closed, they're closed. God is in control. As practitioners, acknowledgment of God's sovereignty should encourage us to boldly decline cases that violate our conscience, pursue practices that fit our gifting, and pay attention to every story that "just shows up" on our doorsteps.

When I grow up. All of us have a tendency to postpone life. Until the day we die, most of us wonder what we will be when we grow up. We continue to look ahead to the day when the big break will come, when our life's work will be accomplished, when our life will really be lived. We begin as children, in grade school, believing that as soon as we get into high school life will begin. In high school we know that when we get our driver's license, then life will begin. After we're driving, we are certain that real life will really begin when we get out of the house. When we're in college, we know that as soon as we find a spouse or a job or a diploma, surely *then* life will begin. And it continues for the rest of our years. This tendency begins as a God-given internal mechanism for wisdom and discernment—planning for the future, vision and goals, drive to excel—all would be impossible without an inner yearning for what comes next. But too often we leave real life behind while we figuratively gaze out the window of our lives wondering what lies ahead.

I think James has this in mind in this famous passage:

> Come now, you who say, "Today or tomorrow we will go to such and such a town and spend a year there, doing business and making money." Yet you do not even know what tomorrow will bring. What is your life? For you are a mist that appears for a little while and then vanishes. Instead you ought to say, "If the Lord wishes, we will live and do this or that." As it is, you boast in your arrogance; all such boasting is evil. Anyone, then, who knows the right thing to do and fails to do it, commits sin. (James 4:13-17)

I have always seen this passage as a warning against presuming on tomorrow in arrogance. And that is the main point of the passage. But the final verse sets the presumption on tomorrow against something: failing to do what you are called to do today: "Anyone, then, who knows the right thing to do and fails to do it, commits sin" (v. 17). Vocation reminds us, if you'll forgive the cliché, to bloom where God has planted us. Failing to bloom while in search of other soil is sin.

Do you sit in your law office and wonder what God's plan is for your life? Do you spend hours each day thinking of what you might be when you grow up and life really begins? Do you look to fill your hours with fantasy football, church volunteer work, or bar association groups in order to bring meaning to your daily grind? For most of us, the meaning is right there in the daily grind if we'll forget about tomorrow and look for God's hand in today's clients, today's opportunities, today's motions, and today's depositions.

In James Joyce's classic short story *Araby,* the narrator, an adolescent boy, is infatuated with the older sister of one of his friends. He is enchanted by her and with the possibility of buying her something exotic at Araby, a bazaar some distance from his house. His anticipation of his fantasy-come-true wreaks havoc on his daily work:

> I wished to annihilate the tedious intervening days. I chafed against the work of school. At night in my bedroom and by day in the classroom her image came between me and the page I strove to read. The syllables of the word *Araby* were called to me through the silence in which my soul luxuriated and cast an Eastern enchantment over me. . . . I could not call my wandering thoughts together. I had hardly any patience with the serious work of life which, now that it stood between me and my desire, seemed to me child's play, ugly monotonous child's play.[25]

His expectations are eventually frustrated by the very Englishness of the "Arabian" bazaar, and he has an epiphany that the girl will probably never return his love. His return to reality is abrupt and depressing.

We are so often like Joyce's character! We spend today dreaming of the fantasy tomorrow, which is usually an invention of our imaginations. We should seek to understand the grind of daily life by God's plan and his present work through us, so that we'll have joy in the reality of faithfulness in the here and now.

The commitment to the unity of life esteems the doctrine of vocation as central to the Christian walk. We must understand that God calls us to love our neighbor in very specific ways, hedged about by particular callings to keep us from being "borne hither and thither," as Calvin put it.[26] God gives us vocations to guide us in serving others. Our duties and obligations are driven by our callings, yet we serve God and neighbor in all things. We recognize Christian calling in our marriage, just as we do at church. We serve God in recre-

[25]James Joyce, "Araby," in *Dubliners* (New York: Dover, 1991), p. 17.
[26]*Institutes* 3.10.6.

ation just as we do in singing praises. The baker, the CEO, pastor, or elder all minister, yet in different ways, according to their diverse gifts and duties.

In the law, we see God working through human hands to heal, protect, reconcile, feed, and encourage. God is at work, loving our neighbors through our law practice. He meets the needs of our clients through us. Do they need his mercy? His compassion? His wisdom? Must they be punished, vindicated, or reconciled one to another? Do they need assistance in leaving an inheritance for their children or taking dominion over the things God has entrusted to them?

In our approach to working with God in worship before him, we don't seek to fulfill ourselves, to "build him a house," or to find a platform to shout from. We worship him daily in all that we do: life is one piece, and that whole is centered in worship and obedience to our Creator and Caller.

To close out our discussion of unity's implications for vocation, we'll let Professor Schuurman demonstrate the close relationship of vocation, unity, and our next topic, theological thinking:

> The main effort of Christian theology is . . . to help Christians interpret the world in light of their faith in the God manifested in Jesus Christ who renews all of creation. . . . If Christians are to become faithful participants in the purposes and processes of creation and redemption, it is essential that they hold together both the "sacred" and the "secular," the "religious" and "non-religious" aspects of experience, and that they do so in a way that affirms the importance and integrity of each. The unity of life under God's reign is brought about by a vital sense of life as vocation.[27]

So let's proceed to the discussion of the content of that theology—that Christian interpretation of the "unity of life in God."

Unity and the life of the mind. In part one I suggested that Christian thinking about law is made possible when, among other things, we reject artificial roles suggested by the profession and our law school training, and overcome the spiritual sloth that pretends that there is no eternal beauty, truth, or goodness relevant to our law practice. A commitment to unity helps us to resist a role-centered mindset and treat the deadly sin of *acedia,* the spiritual sloth that I have spoken so much of already.

When we have a vision of a life that is integrated, we begin to notice that

[27]Douglas S. Schuurman, *Vocation* (Grand Rapids: Eerdmans, 2004), p. 52.

it is whole. We seek out inconsistencies and eradicate them. We seek what is good, what is true, and what is beautiful because we know that we were created to seek such things. In short, we care. And once we are rid of our spiritual apathy, a whole world opens to us. We desire to be theologically informed as a partial means to knowing the truth and beauty at the heart of our calling, and we are driven to the local church, the historic church, and our brothers and sisters in the profession to solve problems, develop handles for tricky issues, and make sense of the legal world in the context of our faith.

One of the implications of a commitment to unity for law practice and study is that we ought to begin to notice the *connections* between the stuff of our diverse callings and activities. Our legal work and study has something to do with our devotional practices. Our calling as a parent speaks to our relationships with associates in the firm or our colleagues in the classroom. Our service in the church brings helpful tools to the study of law or the board room. Even our golf game reflects our character and builds virtue. The larger kingdom of God means something in my neighborhood, and the saints of the past have something to say to my client today. If we are moral "one-worlders" then these connections are grounded in reality.

> PROFESSIONALISM AND CHARACTER
>
> **You cannot resolve the tensions in our professional ideal by seeking the ideal, but only by seeking what is right. Your seeking what is right is informed by principle, but it is achieved by character.**
>
> JACK L. SAMMONS JR., *LAWYER PROFESSIONALISM*

Furthermore, if it is true, as I have claimed, that beliefs drive conduct, then it will transform our law practice or studies if we spend some time adjusting our beliefs about lawyers and their world. When we spend time in prayer and reflection about our callings, God's ministry through us is strengthened.

Conclusion

Our first commitment at the heart of integrity is a broad one that warns against compartmentalization and dualistic thinking about our ministry. I've argued here that the first commitment to integrity entails a bold awareness of the harmful instrumentalism in law school, a recovery of vocational thinking across all areas of life, and a changed mind about who we are as lawyers. I'll suggest practical responses implied by these connections after I address the second and third characteristics of integrity, community and truth, in chapters seven and eight.

For Further Thought

1. In what sense is your law practice/legal education/judicial role really "kingdom work"? Make a list, thinking carefully about what you mean by *kingdom.*
2. Is it possible that your calling as a spouse, parent, or child informs and either strengthens or weakens your work in the law? Reflect on whether this is so in your own experience. How can this concept be helpful in your law practice or study? In your relationships?
3. Have you bought into the modern division between facts and values that tells us that there are no true or false values, only choices? How is this harmful to your law practice or study?

7

Community and Trinitarian Lawyering

In a January 2006 survey conducted by the Barna Group, respondents were asked whether "spiritual maturity" required "involvement in a community of faith." A paltry 18 percent of adults "firmly embraced" the concept. Even among those adults with a "biblical worldview" (those who hold to seven key Christian beliefs), a mere one-third thought a community of believers was necessary to spiritual growth. Can there really be such thing as a Lone Ranger Christian? The premise of this chapter will apparently disappoint most readers: There is no such thing as a solitary Christian.[1] The second essential of the life of Christian integrity is a commitment to life in community.

We are called to work out our callings in *koinonia* fellowship in the body of Christ. We share in the give and take of mutually beneficial spiritual gifts, confess our sins to one another, and are accountable to one another in love. Our community also involves recognition of the historic "communion of saints," to which we belong and which protects us against the prejudices of idiosyncratic dogma and the prejudices of our own age. Most important, however, we are in community with God, and we acknowledge that we are able to fellowship with one another only in, through, and from our fellowshiping,

[1]Well, *normally* there is no such thing as a solitary Christian. I overstate slightly. Given the tradition of the desert fathers and Christian hermits, it is indeed possible to follow Christ alone, at least temporarily. On the other hand, the hermits and desert fathers came mainly from communities of like-minded ascetics seeking to devote themselves to prayer and contemplation. I believe it to be clear that long-term solitude is neither the norm nor healthy for Christians. My colleague Craig Stern suggests that while the eremitic life may be out of balance, this couldn't have been true of the likes of Simeon Stylites, who for thirty-six years lived on top of pillar, where balance is at a premium!

communing God, who is himself a holy community. "Communion and communication are inherent in his very being."[2]

The Holy Trinity and Community

We live in community because our God is both one and community.[3] As Professor Paul Stevens puts it, both our "being and our doing"—that is, our identity and our vocation—come from the Trinity. The people of God participate "in the 'in-going' ministry of God (relationally among God the Father, God the Son, and God the Holy Spirit), and simultaneously . . . in the 'out-going' (sending) ministry of God."[4] This trinitarian foundation for participation in God's ministry highlights the importance of community:

> Being *laos* [the people of God] means that members of the people of God have communion with God and with one another without being merged with God or one another. . . . In the same way, the people of God is animated and energized by Christ but it is not lost in Christ. We are in Christ; Christ is in us, but we are not Christ. The church is the body of Christ but not Christ. Further, the members of the body are in communion with one another, but are not unified (in the sense of mutual absorption). We are "in" one another but we are not each other.[5]

We are more complete because we are united, as part of a diverse community, with one another, redeemed and joined in and through Christ our head, called and sent by the Father, and empowered by the Holy Spirit.

The implications for wholeness—for integrity—are enormous. First, the sole foundation for our calling as people bearing the image of God is the relational in-going and out-going ministry of community with others and with God.[6] The normal Christian walk is not akin to a solitary hike in the woods;

---

[2]Robert Letham, *The Holy Trinity: In Scripture, History, Theology, and Worship* (Phillipsburg, N.J.: P & R Publishing, 2004), p. 428.

[3]The best source on this subject as it relates to ministry in ordinary work is R. Paul Stevens, *The Other Six Days: Vocation, Work and Ministry in Biblical Perspective* (Grand Rapids: Eerdmans, 1999), pp. 56-65. The discussion in this section relies on that important work primarily and upon Colin Gunton, *The One, the Three, and the Many* (Cambridge: Cambridge University Press, 1993). Errors and unwarranted applications are my own. An excellent historical and comparative analysis is found in Letham's *Holy Trinity.*

[4]Stevens, *Other Six Days,* p. 57.

[5]Ibid., p. 61.

[6]See ibid., p. 63, and sources cited therein.

it is a team sport. God does indeed call us to practice regular solitude, and some may be called to extended periods of silence and withdrawal from human contact. But even many of the Christian hermits lived within the context of communities called *lauras*.[7]

Second, while the roles within community are diverse, no role is subordinated to another. Again, all ordinary work has the potential to be sacred ministry if done in faith before God (see chap. 4). Loving our neighbors is a high calling that can be accomplished in a rich variety of ways. Therefore, the phrase "only a lay person" should never be uttered regarding life outside the administration of the sacraments.[8] We are the people of God, together, out of which arise some who are called to equip the others for continuing in-giving and out-going ministry.[9] Ministry is God's; his ministry through us does not begin when we latch onto the programs of the church, it begins "when we join God."[10]

Characteristics of Community

Unity through diversity. The eternal ministry of the Trinity itself suggests the basic characteristics of our life in community. First, the Christian life is composed of continual giving and receiving, both in and among the body of Christ and outside of it. This empowering reciprocity was called *perichoresis* by the early church fathers and implies unity in diversity.[11] This idea, in the words of theologian Colin Gunton, preserves both the "one and the many in dynamic interrelations."[12]

Multifaceted ministry. Second, the rich diversity of gifts within the body reflect the fullness of God's in-going and out-going ministry. As Stevens reminds us, there was ministry within the Godhead before creation and before the Fall. Therefore, God's full ministry is more than just redemptive:

---

[7]See Kenneth Scott LaTourette, *A History of Christianity* (San Francisco: HarperSanFrancisco, 1953), 1:225-28.

[8]Stevens, *Other Six Days,* p. 57. Stevens says this phrase should never be found on our lips. But perhaps he overstates the case.

[9]Ibid., p. 57.

[10]Ibid.

[11]See Gunton, *One, the Three, and the Many,* pp. 163-65; and Stevens, *Other Six Days,* pp. 59-65.

[12]Gunton, *One, the Three, and the Many,* p. 164.

> God's ministry is creative and unitive (Jn. 17:21-23) and not only curative and redemptive, thus constituting a broader definition of service and relationship than is normally ascribed to the term "ministry." Like their God the people of God have ministry that is both creative (making) and restorative (mending); ministry both unitive (connecting) and curative (correcting)—thus challenging the common evangelical preoccupation with the Great Commission (Mt. 28:18-20) as the exclusive definition of ministry, as important as that mandate is.[13]

We should expect, therefore, a wide variety of reciprocating ministry within the body, serving within and outside the local church.

The community of the Christian past. Third, God's ministry is eternal. As such, his ministry in and through the saints of the early church can guide us today. Moreover, the communion of saints which the Nicene Creed speaks of, is a community that transcends time. Our fellowship within this community—through traditions, images, and the written words of these brothers and sisters—is no less important than, though different in kind from, our fellowship within the visible church of today. C. S. Lewis's admonition to read "old books" to combat the prejudices of our own age is appropriate again in this context.

In addition, the reality of this vast community challenges our own tendency to think we can be sufficiently equipped by simply reading our own Bibles with the guidance of the Holy Spirit. This is not to belittle the centrality of that important element in the walk of faith, but there is more. In the first place, we receive Christian truth as part of a "handing down," embedded in human tradition.[14] So to escape from tradition as an element of our understanding of Christian doctrine is just plain impossible. That does not mean that any one tradition must hold sway, simply that human tradition is the means by which God has chosen to mediate his revelation in Christ.[15] The very translations of the Scriptures that most of us must rely on, the creeds that form our early instruction, and even the selection of the canon itself are all mediated through other human beings. Stephen Holmes admonishes that we should celebrate our

---

[13]Stevens, *Other Six Days,* p. 57. Note too that the Great Commission anticipates and even requires fully trinitarian ministry: "Teaching them to obey everything I have commanded you." Stevens's complaint is perhaps with evangelicals' preoccupation with *a too narrowly construed version* of the Great Commission.

[14]Stephen R. Holmes, *Listening to the Past: The Place of Tradition in Theology* (Grand Rapids: Baker Academic, 2002), p. 13.

[15]Ibid.

"embeddedness" in the Christian tradition rather than try to escape from it.[16]

Discerning the truth is a difficult process, and we generally recognize that we must rely on a variety of aids in seeking answers to most of our questions, be they theological or practical. To refuse aid would be prideful at best, flatly rejecting the community God has given us: "To refuse to learn from the tradition . . . is to succumb to the pride that says 'because you are not a hand, I don't need you.' "[17] Precisely because we know that the Spirit has been at work in the church for two thousand years, we had better be reluctant, without serious explanation, to think that we have discovered "fresh" truths that others have missed or twisted over the centuries, particularly if there is broad agreement across historical ages and theological perspectives.[18] In short, we have plenty to learn from Christian community across the ages.

David Wells has written that theology has three "essential aspects." First, the "confessional" aspect is the core confession of the church in history that truth comes from the Word of God, and that to live under its authority, as the rule for daily life and practice, is the heart of Christianity.[19] Central to the second aspect, "reflection," is a comprehensive approach to the whole of God's revelation, thoughtfully making connections within and between the various parts of Scripture, understanding the Bible as a whole book. We also reflect on our own understanding in historical context, "seeking to gather the spiritual riches of the past" in order to gain "ballast" for our perspective on the present.[20] Both of these aspects of theology are impossible without reliance on riches of the Christian past and the cooperation of the present body. The bottom line is that in order to do theology, we must live in community.

Wells's third aspect of theology implicates community as well. He says that we must cultivate virtues based on our confession and refection, living lives of moral wisdom based on God's truth.[21] Surely the cultivation of these virtues must be done primarily within the community of the saints. Scripture teaches love of neighbor, service to others, and the complementary operation of the Spirit's gifts. In fact, the doctrine of vocation is nothing if not a claim

---

[16]Ibid.
[17]Ibid., p. 34.
[18]Ibid., p. 161.
[19]David F. Wells, *No Place for Truth* (Grand Rapids: Eerdmans, 1993), pp. 98-99.
[20]Ibid., pp. 99-100.
[21]Ibid., p. 100.

that God moves in history through what he has called us to do: "God has chosen to work through human beings, who, in their different capacities and according to their different talents, serve each other. This is the doctrine of vocation."[22]

The indispensability of others.

So God created humankind in his image,
in the image of God he created them;
male and female he created them. (Genesis 1:27).

Our true "being" is in communion with other creatures. Gunton suggests that Genesis is the message, both positive and negative, of what it means to be human. Positively, Genesis tells us that "humankind is social kind."[23] Adam can find no fellowship among the animals and is completed by fellowship with another human. On the negative side, "the Fall leads to ever more disastrous breaches of communion, culminating in murder, the most serious sin against the image of God."[24] Babel symbolizes that the break in communion with God leads to division of humankind, through the breakdown of their means of communion, language. It is no accident, notes Gunton, that "one of the first actions of the Holy Spirit, the giver of communion, is symbolically to reverse Babel by restoring communication and so communion between the divided nations of the earth."[25]

We are who we are in relationship to God, to others, and to his creation. This means something for the study and practice of law: we are "embedded" in a long tradition, both legal and religious—we practice law as advocates, counselors, or drafters for others, and our work has consequences in our culture and the broader creation.

The antimodern nature of community. Finally, we should see that community stands against modernity and objectivism, and this antithesis has special application for law. The prevailing instrumentalist and objectivist approach to law in the legal academy and profession is typical of modernity, and it flows from a typically modern view of the human person as an "object" to be manipulated. Instrumentalism in law is but a symptom of the modern attitude to-

---

[22]Veith, *God at Work,* p. 14.
[23]Gunton, *One, the Three, and the Many,* p. 216.
[24]Ibid.
[25]Ibid.

ward the world. Creation, including other human beings, exists for me to use to realize my individual desires. Gunton provides the insight that "we shall not understand our place in the world unless we face up to the way in which we are internally related to the rest of the world."[26] Our lives in the legal profession will certainly be transformed by an understanding of who we are in relation to our Creator, our neighbor, and the rest of creation.

In sum, the commitment to live and work in relational community is central to the life of integrity because of the nature of our triune God. We'll finish out this chapter with a brief discussion of the ways a commitment to community should help us overcome the barriers to following Christ in the law. But first I'll suggest practical ways to pursue community in the life of the law.

Lawyers and Community

Koinonia fellowship implies that there are particular ways that Christian lawyers must seek community as part of their lives in the law within the body of Christ.

Communities of lawyers. First, we lawyers should seek fellowship in communities of Christian lawyers. Most lawyers work in small firms or as solo practitioners, though there has lately been a trend toward larger firms. Even in firms, however, legal work is detail work, done alone—research, drafting, rewriting. Group activities tend to be performance oriented, isolating the lawyer rather than drawing him into any sustaining community.[27] Compounding these problems is the common take-charge personality of lawyers that often alienates them in nonlegal settings. We need to pursue relationships with colleagues in the law who share our commitment to the broader body of Christ.

In addition, the moral struggles that lawyers face are not usually a matter of community discussion. Bar associations will sometimes host discussions, generally in the context of continuing legal education courses or impersonal panel discussions. Informal, safe communities where lawyers may process moral and religious struggles are rare. Lawyers are on their own, for the most part, in figuring out what it means to be a Christian lawyer. The autonomous individualism of American culture rears its head again.

---

[26]Ibid., p. 15.

[27]I owe these insights to Sam Casey, executive director of the Christian Legal Society, who has dedicated his career to thinking about community and Christian lawyers.

Professor Rob Vischer has suggested that community is central to one's identity as a Christian lawyer. Noting the problem that "American lawyers today are left to explore the moral ramifications of legal practice on their own," he asks, "What if religious communities of lawyers helped shape the professional identities of religious lawyers?"[28]

Vischer suggests that communities of Christian lawyers must both respond to the current ethical rules and practices that frame the moral life of lawyers and set "a broader, affirmative vision of what it means" to be a Christian lawyer. Communities of lawyers, for example, might even guide the conduct of members through informal consultation with one another on legal issues, by promulgating rules of ethics to supplement those of their jurisdiction, or even forming a panel that would issue advisory opinions for members of the community.[29] But there is a broader point too: the gathering together in Christian community and engaging others in that community is itself a virtuous end:

> Catholic lawyers practice virtue by the very fact that they engage, as a community, in the inquiry into what it means to be a Catholic lawyer. . . . By coming together to talk, as a community, about the ends of their faith and chosen profession, Catholic lawyers have already embarked on the path of virtue.[30]

Vischer notes "the centrality of the individual lawyer" to a Christian law practice. Life, and hence law practice, is defined relationally—in relationship to God and to others. This focus battles the objectivism discussed earlier, as relationships with other lawyers and with clients are not means to an end but ends in themselves.[31]

There are also more tangible benefits to being in such relationships, the foremost of which is accountability. In addition, corporate prayer, wise counsel, and encouragement are more powerful in groups like these. I'll discuss

---

[28]Robert K. Vischer, "Catholic Social Thought and the Ethical Formation of Lawyers: A Call for Community," *Journal of Catholic Social Thought* 1 (2004): 417. Most of Professor Vischer's article addresses the question of what it means to be a Catholic lawyer, but his suggestions and premises apply to the broad community of Christian lawyers.

[29]Ibid. We'll return to these ideas in chap. 11.

[30]Ibid., p. 440. Again, Vischer is speaking to Catholic lawyers, but his prescriptions are broadly valuable to the entire community of faith.

[31]Robert K. Vischer, "Catholic Social Thought and the Ethical Formation of Lawyers: A Call for Community," *Journal of Catholic Social Thought* 1 (2004): 425, paraphrasing Thomas L. Shaffer, *American Lawyers and Their Communities* (Notre Dame, Ind.: University of Notre Dame Press, 1991), p. 198.

suggestions for meeting in community in more detail in part three.

The historic community of the saints. Second, we must also engage the rich heritage of those who have sought truth in the law, guided by the Spirit, throughout history. Our community includes the great cloud of witnesses, who testify to God's truth through their works—written and recorded—while cheering us on. Legal ethics, for example, seeks to impart the wisdom of the past from those who sought to do right in similar circumstances, so we consult such wisdom in our daily legal work. Yet in our search for theological truth, for wisdom on Christian vocation, for guidance in our daily work before God in the law, we often ignore the thinking of the great saints of the church, who have much to say about law and the lawyer's work.

The local congregation as community. Third, in order to function healthily within the community, we need the perspective of those who are not lawyers but who can train, consult, encourage, and teach us what it means to be lawyers and Christians in the context of God's kingdom. Theologians, pastors, philosophers, manual laborers, homemakers, doctors, and executives who live by faith can teach us much about integrating our faith and practice. In addition, the body of Christ will be strengthened as we understand and interact with the varied ministries of God in our midst.

Indeed, one of the great classics of the faith was written by a man with whom lawyers might think they have little in common. He was born Nicholas Herman in the early seventeenth century and was a kitchen helper for most of his life. He washed dishes, carried water, and did mundane chores until his death. Yet collections of his prayers and meditations reveal a mind wholly focused on God. Brother Lawrence's practices and prayers, published under the title *Practice of the Presence of God,* have led millions to a deeper understanding of what it means to set our thoughts on things above and to pursue God in pure, yet practical meditation. We have plenty to learn from others in the body who do not share our calling to law.

My friend Patrick Quirk envisions a Christian community that is the local parish fully operational as a practical community. Lawyers, doctors, plumbers, architects, accountants, nurses, electricians, teachers, and homemakers using their gifts in community, reciprocally in the in-going and out-going ministry of the body. This is not some great vision of networking, but recognition by Professor Quirk that law practice is more than technical advice and medicine is more than prescription writing. This vision sees the diversity of all workers available as a unit within the body of Christ to meet the needs within and outside that body. What if whole people could be loved by those who were called and trained to meet their needs? What if a legal problem caused by an emotional problem exacerbated by financial trouble could be addressed within the community of saints known as the local church working as a team? What if the price of the services reflected the love of Christ, and the perspectives that the professionals professed brought glory to God?

Hurdling the Stumbling Blocks

A life lived in community ought to be able to bring down barriers to serving Christ in the law.

Community and the ordinary religion. In law school, Christian community makes all the difference in the world. A law school education in the company of fellow travelers in the Way is a joyful, albeit challenging, experience that one looks back on with fond memories. Law school alone, on the other hand, is like the trudge up Mount Doom without Sam Gamgee. I know students who have told me that they would never have made it through law school without their Christian Legal Society group. Small groups in the midst of law school provide perspective on the law, accountability, and reminders that the emperor is naked.

In addition, law school is the best time, both in terms of time and interest (students: trust me here; lawyers: you know what I mean) to dig into Hoffman, Tocqueville, Berman, papal encyclicals, Aquinas, Hooker and the rest of the usual suspects. In law school we are in scholarship mode and are in the midst of a general education. Spending some time in study on the side, while very costly, is much easier now than when you have a booming law practice with clients regularly calling and a spouse and children that need your attention and care. Supplemental studies such as these may be pursued in the context of accountability and may be even more profitable if done in the context of the local church with theologians, pastors, and others more knowledgeable to help us through the material. (We'll discuss some practical ideas for these groups in chapter nine.)

Many law students have the idea that the local congregation is unimportant during the law school years. This is simply one of the many little lies that flow from the big lie: *I'll never be any busier than I am now in law school.* Law school is a stressful, busy time, but so is law practice and life. We need to get used to it, setting our priorities during our formal education so that we have habits that are worth keeping after graduation. Our interaction with church leaders is a great resource for us and a big help to them (see chap. 3). Interact with leaders—give them the benefit of your thoughts regarding calling and scholarship. Law students must intentionally pursue belonging to a local congregation or parish. Anonymous attendance is not the point either: students should be involved in the in-going (singing in the choir, teaching Sunday school, assisting in the youth program) and out-going (visitation of the sick, working at the shelter or food pantry, volunteering with Christian Legal Aid) ministries of the local church.

> A RARE PRIVILEGE
>
> **You may be fortunate enough to attend a church that speaks on [vocation]. But whether or not you or your coworker do, the chance to interact with a group of peers who know each other's world, share each other's values, and will help each other to apply biblical principles to workplace issues is a rare privilege.**
>
> DOUG SHERMAN AND WILLIAM HENDRICKS, *YOUR WORK MATTERS TO GOD*

Community, the local church, and vocation. If we in the body of Christ can begin to help each other address the ways that our "Sunday community" has something to do with our lives on Monday through Saturday, I am convinced it would change the world.

Wooddale Church in Minneapolis, like several other churches across the country, has partnered with a ministry called His Church at Work (HCAW) to help parishioners see the vast implications of Christian vocation and ordinary work. Recently, in preparation for a sermon series devoted to exclusively to these issues, Leith Anderson, the senior pastor, sent out questionnaires about the typical struggles and desires of his congregation regarding ordinary work. He found that most of his congregation desired to integrate their faith and their ordinary jobs, but they were not confident in their ability to do so.

This sort of give-and-take between pastor and congregation is a major step in overcoming our second stumbling block. Anderson heard the issues and then instructed his flock from the pulpit. The Wooddale model goes further, however. They have a website devoted exclusively to work-related issues, Wooddale at Work. The website contains resource lists, discussion forums, small group listings and, most important, a clear articulation that this local church knows that ordinary work means something in the Christian walk. When I spoke with one of the pastors in charge of Wooddale's WorkLife Ministry, he told me, "We don't call people *out of their lives* to 'do ministry.' We want to train you *in your life*—you have a ministry right where you are doing the stuff you are supposed to be doing." This is vocational thinking—right here in the American church![32]

One other feature of the His Church at Work model on which Wooddale relies for much of the technical component of WorkLife Ministry, is the daily e-mail "WorkLife Lesson." The daily e-mail contains a short devotional on some aspect of the ordinary life on the job, some questions for discussion, and a prayer. Church members and visitors to the website may subscribe to the free service. One of the Wooddale members, a young father, told his pastor that he was too busy to spend a weekend at a conference on work-related issues or to read a lot about integrating faith and work, but when his e-mail came, he stopped for a minute, spent some time in prayer, and considered the topic at hand. In this way, he feels connected to the body in his quest to live vocationally.

This local-church-driven ministry addresses the need for the recovery of vocational thinking in the context of the local body, a community that can actually do something about it.

Even in congregations not as attuned to vocational issues, we ought to seek opportunities to educate our pastors about what lawyers and other professionals need. What sort of doctrinal instruction might be helpful? What assistance might the church offer us in doing what we do? And how might we offer to aid the body in thinking about service to and love of neighbor as full-time Christian work?

Finally, until you try it, you won't know what a blessing you gain from intentionally seeking out conversations on calling, work, and the church from others within the body of Christ who are not lawyers. Doctors, architects, teachers, plumbers, homemakers, and farmers, among others, can teach us—yes, lawyers—our business. Pastors, particularly, will have spiritual insights from Scripture that we may not have on our own or guidance to resources that are foreign to us. And because we often live in the clouds, forgetting that there

---

[32]See Wooddale's work-related ministry at <www.wooddaleatwork.org>; see also <www.his churchatwork.org>.

are human beings outside our practice areas, it is helpful to fellowship with those that are not likely to be our clients or our colleagues. Perhaps it would not be such a bad idea for the criminal defense lawyer to pray with the CEO, or for the corporate counsel to have lunch after church with the blue-collar worker in the pew in front of him.

In short, the local church really can be a community in and through which we learn how to love God as lawyers.

Community and the life of the lawyer's mind. It should go without saying that community is a primary catalyst for the faithful thinker. We learn as disciples, with other disciples. We practice what we have heard within the safe boundaries of groups of disciples, all learning together. We bounce questions and issues off of each other (and a teacher), all the while sharpening our analysis and skills. The centrality of the diversity of the body is sometimes missed in this context. How can we hear unless someone preaches? How can we read the Scriptures unless a sister translates or a brother teaches us Greek and Hebrew? Where are the Scriptures without the preservers of Scripture, the copiers, the archaeologists, and the guardians of doctrine? The broadly diverse, chronological different, wonderfully dispersed body of Christ is necessary even for the most elemental introduction to the faith.

If all of this is true, what of the more complex issues of calling, the relationship between church and state, the nature of humans, and the social polity? We pursue these questions in and from community—we build on the work of Paul, Irenaeus, Augustine, Aquinas, and Luther, *even if we don't know that we do,* and we learn how to do that from others here and now.

We need to learn from theologians, philosophers, wage-earners, corporate executives, missionaries, lawyers, and pastors as we seek the truth of Scripture applied to the many ideas, institutions, and people that we touch in our law practices.

Conclusion

In closing I want to raise one final issue related to community. By mid-life, a lawyer should be in a position, due to experience, wisdom, financial status, and maturity, to be able to reflect upon and teach to others the larger and thornier issues of the profession. In short, he or she should have the experiences and resources to invest in community and contribute to the heritage of the faithful lawyer.[33] Where are the faithful lawyers? Where are the Christian men and women who have paid their dues and are ready to teach others to be faithful in the life in the law?

Our commitment to community is an important one, threads of which we have seen running through our commitment to unity and the problems at the heart of our stumbling blocks. As we discuss our third and final commitment at the heart of integrity, we'll see the threads of both unity and community as well.

For Further Thought

1. How might it help you to share your struggles with other Christian lawyers? Plan to have lunch with another lawyer who shares your faith this week.
2. What is the role of the local church in your life? How is God using your law-related gifts and talents to serve other believers?
3. Do you ever feel like a lone ranger in your daily work? Is this usually a good or bad thing? Brainstorm ways that you might enter into Christian community more regularly. How would this influence your work?
4. Are you actively engaged—as a mentor, encourager, or friend—in helping others pursue God in their ordinary work? Develop some ideas on how you can begin to do this more intentionally. Consider talking to your pastor about it.

[33]I owe this observation to my friend and InterVarsity Christian Fellowship staffer Bob Trube.

8

Truth and the Integrated Lawyer

Near the culmination of the most famous trial in history, the judge put a question to the accused: "What is truth?" Getting no answer, but knowing Jesus to be innocent of the charges, Pontius Pilate allowed Jesus to be put to death anyway, in order to save himself politically. What is truth? Consider the deep layers of irony in this question, to this man, from this questioner. The Truth himself stood before Pilate, and the truth was that he was innocent. Yet Pilate ignored what he knew to be true to preserve his own power, at the same time that Christ's accusers twisted the truth in service to their own particular power plays. The Truth himself was executed by people who acted as if there were no such thing as truth beyond raw power.[1]

This scene demonstrates both the breadth and the necessity of our commitment to truth. There is a sense in which allegiance to truth is essentially commitment to the Truth, Jesus Christ. God is Truth, and there is nothing true outside of him. In this sense, all other "truths" are united in the one Truth. Flowing from that, however, there is also a sense in which commitment to truth involves recognition of the existence of reality outside ourselves, and a quest to live in a way that first discovers and then corresponds to that reality. We desire to live, believe, think, and act in a way consonant with reality (or perhaps the eternal law) rather than with a state of affairs that does not exist.[2]

---

[1]Suggested by Herbert W. Titus, *God, Man, and the Law: The Biblical Principles* (Oakbrook, Ill.: Institute of Basic Life Principles, 1994), p. 29.

[2]For a good introduction to theories of truth, see J. P. Moreland and William Lane Craig, "Theories of Truth and Postmodernism," *Philosophical Foundations of a Christian Worldview* (Downers Grove, Ill.: InterVarsity Press, 2003), and for a balanced critique, see

There are true and false propositions about guilt or innocence, human nature, the origin of the universe, and the existence of universal moral law. There are also true and false stories and true or false images.

Allegiance to truth in both of these senses—Truth as a person and truth as corresponding to reality—is central to the life of integrity. Our call by the Caller, and our commitment to him first and foremost is the heart of the faithful walk, and an allegiance to his will in the broadest sense—a standard that defines reality—is absolutely necessary as the rule of the faithful life. The life of integrity flows from this multifaceted commitment to truth. We pursue truth in a person who is Truth, and we seek truth as a standard to which we and our world are subject: the truth of God's will, his plan in human history. Our allegiances matter, and from them flow either the integrated or disintegrated life.

In this chapter we'll explore what these truth commitments might entail. First, I'll argue that discipleship—commitment to the One who is Truth—is central to our pursuit. At the heart of discipleship is a truthful introspection that I will call transparency, or truth in the inner person. Second, we must recognize a comprehensive standard by which reality is measured if we are to have integrity. I'll suggest that the traditional framework of Christian worldview is helpful to lawyers in that pursuit. We'll discuss both discipleship and worldview, and then highlight more specific ways in which they will assist lawyers in overcoming our stumbling blocks.

Discipleship

The life of integrity involves a discipleship relationship with the one "in [whom] all things hold together" (Colossians 1:17). The universe itself would implode without Christ, and we are dependent on him for our every breath, our very being. How much more must we cling to him for the "holding together" of our otherwise disintegrated lives? Christ called himself "the way, and the truth, and the life" (John 14:6). To know him is to know the Father, in him is the means to the Father, and through him is the knowledge and experience of the truth. Allegiance to Christ is the commitment that defines all other commitments.

James K. A. Smith, "Who's Afraid of Postmodernism? A Response to the 'Biola School,'" in *Christianity and the Postmodern Turn,* ed. Myron B. Penner (Grand Rapids: Brazos, 2005).

The foundation for a life committed to truth is obedience to the incarnate Word of God and the written Word, the holy Scriptures, which reveal him. "If you continue in my word, you are truly my disciples; and you will know the truth, and the truth will make you free" (John 8:31-32). Commitment to truth, then, is a way of life; it is a life of discipleship.

A disciple is a student, a learner, a pupil of the master. Therefore, the life of integrity is the life of the student before Christ the Master. What do students do? To begin with, they diligently listen to the teacher. "*If* you continue in my word, you are truly my disciples." After disciples hear, they do—they obey. The man who builds his house upon the rock is one who hears the words of Christ "and *acts on them*" (Matthew 7:24, emphasis added). Conversely, the builder on the sand—the one who ends up with a disintegrated house—is the person who hears but "does not act on them" (Matthew 7:26). Integrity is impossible without obedience to Christ.

A student is also in community with other students. It is no accident that Jesus chose a group of twelve—a full classroom—rather than an individual student. Even when he drew away for advanced teaching, there was at least a seminar—three students. This "classroom" is part of the design of the body.

Finally, students imitate their teacher, doing as he or she does as a way of learning the way. Christian students practice in order to understand the teaching of the Master.

In short, discipleship—obedience to the Master in theory and practice—is a true blending of the devotional life and obedience in the world. In spite of all that I have criticized about pietism and its tendency to elevate devotional practice over the life of the mind or the walk of faith in the midst of ordinary life, the pious life of devotion to Christ is essential to the integrated life and growth. A commitment to the truth involves both *being* and *doing* in the presence of the Truth himself.

I could discuss basic discipleship for pages on end, and many excellent books have been written on the subject. In fact, this book might be seen as simply a meditation on the lawyer disciple. The point, however, is not to fully develop the general content of the life of discipleship, but simply to reiterate the basic truth that discipleship stands as a central commitment; without it integrity in the law is not possible.

There is, however, one struggle in the disciple's life that is often ignored, and which I believe to be a prominent issue for lawyers and law students. That issue is self-deception. In my experience, one of the greatest hindrances to our pursuit of truth in the law is the struggle to be truthful with ourselves.

Transparency. In some ways, personal transparency is the trait that holds the other commitments in place. The easiest way to fall victim to disintegration, in other words, is by failing to tell ourselves the truth about ourselves. As Scripture demonstrates from Genesis through Revelation, the human capacity for self-deception is unlimited. If we are to live in integrity, we build on the foundation of truth by applying it to the inner person. The psalmist captures the essence of the issue and its solution:

> For I know my transgressions;
> and my sin is ever before me.
> Against you, you only, have I sinned
> and done what is evil in your sight,
> so that you may be justified in your words
> and blameless in your judgment.
> Behold, I was brought forth in iniquity,
> and in sin did my mother conceive me.
> Behold, you delight in truth in the inward being,
> and you teach me wisdom in the secret heart. (Psalm 51:3-6 ESV)

Christians who are honest about their own ways and see their own sins are able to confess those sins, exposing them to the light of God's truth and grace.

Screwtape and the dim uneasiness of unconfessed sin. In *The Screwtape Letters,* a "record" of correspondence from Screwtape, a mentor devil, to Wormwood, his nephew and novice tempter, C. S. Lewis illustrates the trouble we have in "knowing our transgressions" and keeping our sins "ever before us." Through his advice to Wormwood, Screwtape reminds us that without regular, explicit repentance in prayer before God, we will find ourselves reluctant to open ourselves to him. Screwtape knows that it is far better (from the senior devil's perspective!) that a Christian have a "vague feeling that he hasn't been doing too well lately" than to contend with the "explicit repentance of fully recognized sin." Screwtape discusses the benefits (to those who tempt us) of this "vague feeling" of guilt:

> This dim uneasiness needs careful handling. If it gets too strong it may wake him up and spoil the whole game. On the other hand, if you suppress it entirely—which, by the way, the Enemy [God] will probably not allow you to do—we lose an element in the situation which can be turned to good account. If such

> a feeling is allowed to live, but not allowed to become irresistible and flower into real repentance, it has one invaluable tendency. It increases the patient's reluctance to think about the Enemy. All humans at nearly all times have some such reluctance; but when thinking of Him involves facing and intensifying a whole vague cloud of half-conscious guilt, this reluctance is increased ten-fold.[3]

On one hand, we ought to recognize the silliness of failing to confess our sins explicitly to God; on the other, we harbor "secret" sin as a human habit. The very impossibility of secret sin before God is laughable: we pretend that if we don't mention it, maybe he won't notice! Yet that is our habit, which the words of the apostle John address: "If we say that we have no sin, we deceive ourselves, and the truth is not in us. If we confess our sins, he is faithful and just and will forgive us our sins and cleanse us from all unrighteousness" (1 John 1:8-9).

Confession is the act of putting it all on the table, exposing all to the light, for God—and for us—to see. He calls it sin; we call it sin. It is exposed to the light for what it is, and it's gone. Yet we often desire to hold onto our sin, keeping it in the dark, off the table, refusing to call it what it is. And that's where our trouble begins. Rather than confessing our sin, we lie, and tell ourselves that it is not there. We replace the explicit confession of recognized sin with the vague uneasiness that "we're haven't been doing too well lately" that Screwtape hopes to encourage.

I recognize this tendency in my life very clearly, and I also see a related application by analogy in the lawyer's work. This temptation to distance oneself from God through "vague guilt" has a profound application in law practice. I've found that we lawyers are very good at deceiving ourselves about various misgivings we have about law, leading to an almost universal feeling that our life in the law "isn't doing too well" before God. As Screwtape suggests, this leads us to withdraw our professional lives from the light of God and makes us vaguely reluctant to think about God or his instruction regarding our legal lives. As Screwtape might summarize it, a lawyer will avoid contemplation of God's presence and purpose in his or her law practice when doing so would mean having to face a vague cloud of half-conscious guilt.

In my experience there are a number of areas in which this half-conscious guilt is bred.

---

[3]C. S. Lewis, *The Screwtape Letters* (New York: Macmillan, 1959), p. 62.

Client representation. Many times a lawyer will represent a client or take a case when he or she is not confident of the rightness—the truth—of taking this sort of case or representing this type of client. Rather than using discernment, biblical admonition, wise counsel, and prayer to decide what is or is not permissible in this area, we jump before we pray and end up pretending with God that we haven't undertaken the representation. This, of course, makes it pretty tough to pray through details of the case or submit our success or failure to him, at least in this representation. Again, it's not necessarily that we should not have taken the case; it is that we failed to put our misgivings about it on the table to be exposed to the light. Most of the time this situation does not arise within our general practice area. Usually, it is spur-of-the-moment requests, cases outside of our area of expertise or ethically "different" cases that cause the problems. The point here is not that we need to turn down more clients but that we need to make sure that we are not pretending before God. We avoid that by telling him and ourselves about our misgivings from the beginning, and then doing the right thing so that the entire representation can be carried on in the light.

Ethical decisions. Sometimes we're afraid to investigate the ethical propriety of an action for fear that we might discover that we're doing the wrong thing. We have an internal don't-ask-don't-tell policy. We forge ahead without checking, and then we spend a lot of time and energy pretending that we are doing the right thing. Of course, since we're pretending, we don't want to get God involved. Again, our conduct is not necessarily unethical; we just prefer to "keep it off the table."

Hiding behind "the system." I believe that there are *thousands* of Christian lawyers who have a "dim uneasiness" before God about their very careers. We've already discussed this in some detail, but it bears repeating here. The "system that's set up" is a justification for anything called for by the client, and they don't contemplate anything deeper than "the system." There is some truth in the need to trust trustworthy systems (see chap. 10), but it is a cop-out as a full justification for one's life work before God. As a result of giving all moral authority to a system, many lawyers feel guilt and unease about their work but have no framework by which to approach God without opening up the can of worms that is their legal career!

Cheating on time and bills. When lawyers exaggerate their time or justify an inflated bill because everybody else is doing it, they, not surprisingly, find themselves reluctant to submit billing concerns to God. A similar justification is the self-deception that one is taking a case "just to pay the bills" for now, until he or she can get to a financial place to be picky about the cases taken.

The bottom line is that we regularly fail to examine law-related activities in the light of the truth, submitting our conduct to God. Ironically, this is often true even when our conduct is morally justified. We are simply afraid or, as Screwtape would say, reluctant to express our misgivings to the Lord. By pretending that we don't have any misgivings or that we need not submit our professional work to the light of truth, we create an ongoing atmosphere of self-deception, which in turn leads to a vague cloud of guilt. This dim uneasiness encourages us to further exclude God from our thinking about law and our law practice. Uncle Screwtape would be pleased.

The solution is to walk in our discipleship commitment in every daily decision in the law. The clients we represent, the biblical basis of our practice area, the nuts and bolts of our arguments, the way we bill, everything should be exposed to the light of truth. The integrated life requires that we commit to telling ourselves the truth about ourselves and our law practices, thereby exposing inner darkness to light.

Truthfulness and tragedy. Stanley Hauerwas ties together the themes of self-deception, vocation, and professional identity in his discussion of Albert Speer's autobiography, *Inside the Third Reich.*[4] Speer, known as "Hitler's Architect," was an administrative genius who was at times the number two man in Nazi Germany. He oversaw the Ministry of Armaments, providing hardware for Hitler's army. He disliked politics and was not even a fan of National Socialism. It appears from his autobiography and other historical accounts that his draw into the evil of Nazism was his professional identity. It was his ambition as an architect that served as the catalyst for the moral blindness to his own complicity in the murder of millions. "His self-deception was correlative to his identity as he clung to the story of being Hitler's apolitical architect."[5]

Hauerwas concludes that neither sincerity nor integrity were lacking: it was reality that was missing. Speer refused to tell himself the truth about who he was

[4]Stanley Hauerwas with David B. Burrell, "Self-Deception and Autobiography: Reflections on Speer's *Inside the Third Reich,*" in *Truthfulness and Tragedy: Further Investigations into Christian Ethics* (Notre Dame, Ind.: University of Notre Dame Press, 1977), p. 82.
[5]Ibid., p. 91.

PIP ON SELF-DECEPTION

All other swindlers upon earth are nothing to the self-swindlers, and with such pretences did I cheat myself. Surely a curious thing. That I should innocently take a bad half-crown of somebody else's manufacture, is reasonable enough; but that I should knowingly reckon the spurious coin of my own make, as good money! An obliging stranger, under pretence of compactly folding up my bank-notes for security's sake, abstracts the notes and gives me nutshells; but what is his sleight of hand to mine, when I fold up my own nutshells and pass them on myself as notes!

CHARLES DICKENS, *GREAT EXPECTATIONS*

and what was happening in the political realm that he administered. Interestingly, Speer uses "the system" in the same way that lawyers do: "there was no moral ground outside the system," so he had no external compass to deliver him from his self-imposed delusion. When a delusion is vocational, suggests Hauerwas, the opportunity for delusion is greater, for men and women of integrity may be more willing to rationalize that a wrong is for the greater good, or more tempted to it because they have much more at stake. We have a need to establish unity—coherence—in our identity. Therefore, we might delude ourselves to keep our "story" straight about who we are.

Our themes come together in the terrible life of Albert Speer. Unable to find personal unity in transcendent norms or in the God of creation, his unifying story became the system he found himself in. Unable to find moral center there, he immersed himself in his work, ignoring feelings of uneasiness as too difficult to address and too inconsistent with the false integrated self he was pretending to be. He avoided reality by closing his eyes to the evil around him.

I hope this doesn't sound familiar, but I'd venture a guess that many lawyers are in the same identity-reality matrix based on "the system." That's our tendency—we're human beings. Hauerwas puts it this way, "To be is to be rooted in self-deception. The moral task involves a constant vigilance: to note those areas where the tendency has taken root."[6] That is an excellent summary of our commitment to the truth, which in many ways holds all of our other commitments together.

[6]Ibid., p. 95.

Truth: Discernable, External, Normative

Inherent in this commitment to truth is a question that we have not yet fully addressed. How do we know the truth about our cases, about the biblical basis for our practice, or about the righteous way to solve an ethical dilemma? The answer has two parts. One is found in the community of believers that we discussed in detail in the previous chapter. Worship, liturgy, accountability, confession, mentoring relationships, discussions, and reliance on the wisdom of the past will get us a long way toward discerning truthful solutions to the problems of our daily law practice and study. But we must operate under some standard that will guide these relationships and check our fallen opinions and inclinations about law and law practice. We must be committed to an external standard—a source of discernable, relevant truth. This is the second sense in which we must be committed to truth on the road to the life of integrity in the law, and it flows directly from our allegiance to Christ and our coherent understanding of reality.

Because Christ is the center of all things and God's plan is the unifying true narrative of history, we know that we, along with all creation, are governed by truth that comes from outside of ourselves and guides our belief and action. We might simply describe this standard as "truth" or God's revelation of himself. But it may be more helpful to call it "worldview," since we need a term that captures our commitment to see and understand ultimate truth, even in our fallen state, and apply it to every area of life. The term *worldview* is helpful in this regard because, as author Nancy Pearcey puts it, a sound worldview "is like a mental map that tells us how to navigate the world effectively. It is the imprint of God's objective truth on our inner life."[7]

Worldview. Worldview, "roughly speaking, refers to a person's interpretation of reality and a basic view of life."[8] It is a "conceptual scheme by which we consciously or unconsciously place or fit everything we believe and by which we interpret and judge reality."[9] David Naugle cautions Christians to beware, however, of the "relativistic and privatized connotations" of the term. He warns that, particularly in the postmodern culture, *worldview* may "slump to

---

[7]Nancy Pearcey, *Total Truth* (Wheaton, Ill.: Crossway, 2004), p. 23.

[8]David K. Naugle, *Worldview: The History of a Concept* (Grand Rapids: Eerdmans, 2002), p. 260.

[9]Ronald H. Nash, *Worldviews in Conflict* (Grand Rapids: Zondervan, 1992), p. 16.

the status of personal story," bearing out its relativist connotations—*my* interpretation of *my* reality. A thoroughgoing Christian worldview, on the other hand, is essentially biblical rather than merely personal:

> [Biblical Christianity] suggests that "worldview" entails God's gracious redemption that delivers the hearts of men and women from idolatry and false views of life engendered by satanic deception and the blindness of sin, and enables them through faith in Jesus Christ to come to a knowledge of God and truth about his creation and all aspects of reality.[10]

The commitment to a true standard then involves seeing reality in light of God's work in history, to the story that explains all stories.

Creation, Fall, redemption. The life of integrity presupposes a coherent understanding of reality, and reality is God, and "everything else depends on Him for its origin and continued existence."[11] The world makes sense only in light of the broad biblical story which is centered in the lordship of Christ, the One in whom "all things hold together" (Colossians 1:17). In the beginning, by means of Christ all things were created, (Colossians 1:16) and through Christ, God was pleased to reconcile us to himself (Colossians 1:20-23). Reality, then, is all that flows from God's creation, the human Fall, the redemption of all creation, and the consummation of the rule of Christ.[12] Dutch law professor and theologian Hermann Dooyeweerd called this creation-Fall-redemption theme a "ground motif" of the Holy Spirit, a fundamental framework for understanding reality in a coherent—and Christian—way.[13] It determines our practical responses to our world, not simply our theories about it. It is the narrative revelation of God himself in the history of the world, the unfolding of the ultimate plan of God and the very purpose of human existence.

As it relates to our task of understanding the lordship of Christ over our

---

[10]Naugle, *Worldview,* p. 260.

[11]Pearcey, *Total Truth,* p. 45.

[12]I realize that this paradigm is not uncritically adopted across all theological lines, but I find it least controversial and most helpful to the worldview task at hand. The most common alternative worldview framework in this context is the "two kingdom" model. In many ways the two are not completely incompatible. See for example Russell D. Moore, *The Kingdom of Christ: The New Evangelical Perspective* (Wheaton, Ill.: Crossway, 2004).

[13]I owe this summary of the inscrutable Dooyeweerd to Naugle, *Worldview,* pp. 16-31. This is one of the best theological/philosophical treatments of worldview as well. On worldview generally, see also Nash's *Worldviews in Conflict* and J. P. Moreland and William Lane Craig, *Philosophical Foundations of a Christian Worldview.*

lives in the legal profession, the creation-Fall-redemption ground motif implies some significant starting points.

Creation. First and foremost, we are creatures, entirely dependent on our Creator. God made it all, and there is nothing good outside of his creative work.

Second, God's creative activity is ongoing. "Creation does not preclude development within the world; it includes it. Thus God's plan involves and utilizes the best of human skill and knowledge in the genetic refinement of the creation."[14] Therefore, in a real sense we are the means by which God continues his creative work in the world. Luther also ties the continuing creative work of God to the faithful work of God's people as they love others:

> Creation, the work of God, is carried out through the person who, being faithful to his vocation, is a coworker against the devil. . . . Vocation and the man who fulfills it are used as tools and means for God's continuing creation. . . . God continues his creative work on earth where man's vocation lies.[15]

Likewise, Pope John Paul II speaks of our collaboration with God in his continuing creational activity:

> The word of God's revelation is profoundly marked by the fundamental truth that man, created in the image of God, shares by his work in the activity of the Creator and that, within the limits of his own human capabilities, man in a sense continues to develop that activity and perfects it as he advances further and further in the discovery of the resources and values contained in the whole of creation. . . .
>
> Awareness that man's work is a participation in God's activity ought to permeate, as the council teaches, even "the most ordinary everyday activities."[16]

Third, the doctrine of God's good creation refutes any modern gnostic tendency to view the physical world as evil and to be avoided. God looked upon what he had made and pronounced it "very good."[17] We are creatures, subjects of the good Creator. This understanding makes a difference in everyday life.

Particularly striking for the Christian lawyer is Albert Wolters's claim that

---

[14]Millard J. Erickson, *Christian Theology,* 2nd ed. (Grand Rapids: Baker, 1998), p. 411. On the theological implications of the doctrine of creation, generally, see ibid., pp. 400-411.

[15]Martin Luther, quoted in Gustav Wingren, *Luther on Vocation* (Eugene, Ore.: Wipf & Stock, 2004), pp. 130-31.

[16]John Paul II, *Laborem Exercens* par. 25.

[17]On this see, Albert M. Wolters, *Creation Regained* (Grand Rapids: Eerdmans, 1985), pp. 48-51.

the goodness of creation demonstrates the "goodness" of law as it relates to everything instituted by God. The creational is "fundamentally constituted" or "normed" by order of God's wisdom in the world—essentially his "law." It follows then that "subjection to law is not a restriction upon God's creatures, particularly men and women, but rather it makes possible their free and healthy functioning." "Humanism considers law to be the *contradiction* to freedom; the Bible considers law to be the *condition* of freedom."[18] It is interesting to note here how the creation motif takes us back to the very basics of law itself and the views of Blackstone, Coke, and Aquinas.

Fall. Like creation, the Fall is all-encompassing. The Fall corrupted the creation itself, including human beings. Whatever humans touch is touched by the Fall, so human institutions of all kinds are tainted. Thus, work itself, ordained by God as a blessing, has become toil. Work sometimes abuses the worker and is often itself used to abuse others. It is a source of physical pain, mental frustration, and spiritual confusion. Sin changes work in the same way it changes everything else. Likewise, justice, as attempted by human beings, is tainted by the Fall. Corruption, mistake, and abuse lurk within the system itself, which seeks to fight against these possibilities. We are fallen creatures, living in a fallen creation.

However, we must not confuse the Fall with creation itself. As Wolters puts it, "sin neither abolishes nor becomes identified with creation."[19] On this point Wolters develops the concepts of *structure* and *direction* to build a two-part frame to display the relationship between creation and Fall: Structure "refers to the order of creation, to the constant creational constitution of any thing, what makes it the thing or entity that it is. Structure is anchored in the law of creation." Direction, on the other hand, "designates the order of sin and redemption, the distortion or perversion of creation through the Fall on the one hand and the redemption and restoration of creation in Christ on the other. Anything in creation can be directed toward or away from God—that is, directed either in obedience or disobedience to his law."[20] Because this "double direction" can be applied not only to human beings but also to cultural phenomena and social institutions, such as legal systems, governments, and law practices, Wolters's structure-

[18]Ibid., p. 50.
[19]Ibid., p. 57.
[20]Ibid., p. 59.

and-direction frame will serve us well later in applying these principles to our lives in the law.

Of course the Fall is not the end of the story.

Redemption. Christ is the centerpiece of God's plan of redemption. He redeemed the world. Even creation itself is being made new, and we look forward to the eternal new heavens and new earth. We, likewise, have been redeemed, are being redeemed, and will be redeemed. In the same sense, because of Christ, work and other human institutions can be partially redeemed, even in a fallen world. Not only that: legal institutions, law practices, jurisprudence, governments, and courts are all fallen structures on which Christ's redemption may operate, even here and now. God is redeeming law. And we are involved in God's creative and redemptive work. We should beware, however, of thinking too highly of our role, whether by believing ourselves to be redeemers or by expecting redemption to be consummated fully here and now by our work. Our tendency in the church is usually to isolationism or purely political activism (see chap. 6). Neither is the model for God's continuing work. Yes, political institutions must be engaged with the gospel, but so must all institutions and persons. Our work is a broad one that involves indirect action through our vocations.[21] Our goal is not, in Eric Voegelin's phrase, to "immanentize the eschaton" but to love our neighbors in every area of life. On the other hand, much of our work today remains stagnant because we believe that restoration happens only in the world to come or in the souls of human beings. Despite the ongoing creational work of God through his people and the kingdom work toward redemption, the tension remains: his work is done but remains to be complete; the work of the kingdom of God is already-and-not-yet.[22] This is the starting point for our discussion of redemption: redemption means that the original goodness of the created order will be restored, and this restoration will involve all creation, not just some parts of it.[23]

This battle for redemption continues to rage. As C. S. Lewis put it, "There is no neutral ground in the universe: every square inch, every split second is

---

[21]On the dangers of both the church's "identification with" and "total separation from" the political order, see Lesslie Newbigin, *Foolishness to the Greeks: The Gospel and Western Culture* (Grand Rapids: Eerdmans, 1986), pp. 95-123.

[22]See ibid.; Allen Mitsuo Wakabayashi, *Kingdom Come* (Downers Grove, Ill.: InterVarsity Press, 2003).

[23]Wolters, *Creation Regained,* p. 69.

claimed by God and counterclaimed by Satan."[24] The stuff of this battle is not in the heavens, though it is indeed a spiritual battle. Creation itself is the territory in dispute. Legal institutions, courts, families, corporations, human souls, science, technology, and sexuality are being disputed. The "direction" (to return to Wolters's framework) of these creational institutions, people, and entities may be toward the true King, in the process of redemption, or toward the powers that oppose him—continuing in the disobedience begun at the Fall. Our cultural task is a redemptive one, working to direct people, institutions and entities toward the King:

> We have a redemptive task wherever our vocation places us in his world. No invisible dividing line within creation limits the applicability of such basic biblical concepts as reconciliation, redemption, salvation, sanctification, renewal, the kingdom of God, and so on. In the name of Christ, distortion must be opposed *everywhere*—in the kitchen and the bedroom, in city councils and corporate boardrooms, on the stage and in the air, in the classroom and in the workshop.[25]

Our struggle for integrity in the law is a reflection of God's ongoing drama at the center of the universe, with Christ as its focus. We struggle as partners in his ongoing creative work against the Fall in the power and work of Christ's redemption. As Luther would say, we are God's coworkers "against the devil" in all that we do. This is what we mean when we discuss the lordship of Christ: he is at work over every square inch of creation, redeeming the fallen world, and if we are willing, we can take part in his creative, redemptive work in that world. To live in integrity, we must at least recognize the reality of the ongoing creative-redemptive kingdom work in culture and in law as part of the grand scheme of the Creator.

In sum, the integrated life requires a commitment (1) to become a disciple of Christ and his teachings, and (2) to see, understand, and interpret reality through that relationship because we know that all things hold together only in Christ. We must tell ourselves the truth about ourselves, confessing our sin to God. We need to expose our own inner darkness to the light. This commitment to truth is an obligation of all Christians; doctor or plumber or postal worker, we all must expose our inner darkness to the light by confession to ex-

[24]C. S. Lewis, "Christianity and Culture," in *Christian Reflections,* ed. Walter Hooper (Grand Rapids: Eerdmans, 1967), p. 33.
[25]Wolters, *Creation Regained,* p. 73.

perience forgiveness. Not only is this a matter of devotional piety, but it is also the only way that the person of integrity remains integrated. We must remain in him, the true vine.

In addition, we need to understand our legal work through the mental map of Christian worldview. We must discern structure and direction in the law and the human institutions we work with. We need to understand our daily practice or study in light of the eternal truth of Scripture and the work of Christ in his creation. This too is the duty of all Christians, yet the depth and complexity of this task varies with the calling. Just as a composer has a duty before God to understand music, its uses and its nature, to search the Scriptures and the teachings of the church on the calling of the life of the musician, so we too have a duty to seek a biblical understanding of law—and particularly our daily work in the practice of law.

Hurdling Stumbling Blocks

So how will this commitment help us address the fundamental problems of legal education, the local church, and the legal mind?

Discipleship and law school. Hurdling the ordinary religion of the American law school is a task that goes well beyond those three intense years of legal catechesis. Yet the commitment to the disciple's life serves us best if made prior to our matriculation, for it is in law school that our lifelong legal habits are bred.

While I was a law student, I thought that I was the busiest that I'd ever be. What could be more time-consuming and stressful than this life of constant reading and going to class, trying to maintain sanity in other areas of life? I was wrong, of course. Real life is more time-consuming and stressful than school, by just about

LAW SCHOOL HABITS

The means for deepening one's walk with Christ . . . must be viewed as "nonnegotiable." My experience in working with numerous students—at both the pre-law and law school levels—convinces me that one of the most pernicious notions is the assumption that legal education, because of its unique stresses and pressures, is a hiatus from a disciplined and active spiritual life. Quite the contrary, because law school often sets the tenor for subsequent patterns in the profession, it is especially important for law students to honor God by making Him first in their lives.

CHARLES J. EMMERICH, "KNOWING GOD IN THE LION'S DEN: THE CHRISTIAN IN LAW SCHOOL," *CLS QUARTERLY*

any standard. Client demands, supervising partners, personalities, work schedules and—for me, worst of all—other people's real money on the line, all ratchet up the stress and time commitments in the lawyer's life. In addition, most of us did not have families while in law school, and this added commitment increases the time and stress inherent in real life. Law school is simply training ground. Yes, it is training ground in the law, but God uses it in the fullest sense as training ground for *life* in the law.

Because our daily habits and schedule will drastically change after law school, a commitment to discipleship in law school serves to assist our transition into "real life." The habits that one develops as a student will form the foundation for one's habit as a lawyer, both in and out of the law office. Again, I hesitate to speak mainly to law students here, but they are at a crucial stage in developing the habits that will serve them for good or ill in their professional lives. If I am correct about the characteristics of the disciple that I've set out, then the disciple's life in law school should involve at a minimum, three central factors.

Study. Students must be students of the law and of the Scriptures. One without the other in the law student's life will not do. We cannot be an effective disciple if we do not work to discern the structure and direction of law and its components. In addition, our other callings do not stop while we are in law school. We must study and meditate on God's Word in order that he will bring his light to bear on our families, our leisure, and various other callings.

Devotion. Students may not neglect private and corporate devotional time with the Master. Prayer is a critical element in learning from Christ and discerning his ways and purposes. Without praise, adoration, and confession, we will dry up, unattached to the true vine. Because God calls us to community, our praise, confession, and prayer should not be in the prayer closet only, but should flow from a vibrant community of believers who together adore and worship the King.

Relationships. Disciples learn in community, and law students need mentors, those in the profession and those in school, to sharpen them. When I was a law student, I had lunch with a group of like-minded colleagues almost every day, and we sat and evaluated the day's courses together. Though not all were believers, most of them were, and the consequence was that I was kept mindful of the truth and its application to my studies. We need mentors, peers, and disciples in our lives to encourage us toward true religion in the midst of the ordinary religion of the law school classroom.

Permeating these disciplines, in addition, must be a posture of frank transparency. Our prayer life must include our honest questions about our calling and the things that the law practice may ask of us. Our discussions with mentor lawyers should include the difficult questions of the Christian walk in light of law practice. We must confess our secret sins and doubts to God and to our colleagues about whether we can be called by God in the law. It is never too late to start, but law school is the best time to begin these practices.

Worldview and the ordinary religion. In addition to building disciplines into the lawyer's life, a commitment to truth orients us toward the truth and away from the pragmatism and naked instrumentalism of the legal academy. A Christian worldview reminds us that we have a framework for evaluating all of law, taking every thought captive to Christ Jesus. As law students think about their coursework and class discussions, and lawyers contemplate their cases and clients, there is hope that God's restorative work is ongoing and that we can participate in it. In addition, when we pursue law through the creation-Fall-redemption grid, we have criteria under which to pursue truth in our studies. We have a framework for going deeper than a simple awareness of the false presuppositions behind our law school subjects. Our awareness and boldness is now supported with substance, so that we can do more than react against false ideas: we can work to recognize and develop truth in what we see and hear.

This has two important consequences for the lawyer or law student seeking to follow Christ. First, *we don't throw out Anglo-American jurisprudence.* Well, of course we don't, but sometimes we act as if we are ready to revolt, throwing the baby out with the bathwater. Our role in God's redemptive plan involves discerning the good creational structure in the law and legal institutions, not simply criticizing the effects of the Fall on law and the American legal system. In chapter twelve, I'll develop this idea in a bit more detail, but it is worth mentioning here that the development of the common law system relied heavily on the creational goodness of law (flowing from the will of the Maker), the effects of the Fall on human beings, and our responsibility in that light. Our task is to discern both the creational structure *and* the direction of the law and legal institutions. We have the task to cooperate in God's progressive reform of his creation. In this, we avoid both violent overthrow and a return to an imagined retro-Eden.[26]

[26]On revolution versus reformation, see ibid., pp. 89-94.

The second consequence of having a substantive worldview is that *we know that law is not "bad," requiring something "good" to combat it in law practice.* So much of what is written today about the lawyer's life implies that our task is to overcome the badness of law practice or the evil of law with the goodness of grace, truth, or virtuous lives. If this is the case, what are we doing in this profession?

Truth, vocation, and the church. Our commitment to truth also provides some needed tools for use in overcoming our second stumbling block—the church's lack of vocation-centered discipleship (see chap. 3). If it is true, as Wolters says, that "we have a redemptive task wherever our vocation places us in his world," then vocational thinking is necessary to discerning structure and direction. If we are placed in a family by God's hand as a father, then we have fatherly responsibilities to seek the good structure of the family and participate with God in his work in our family by doing what he has called fathers to do. Likewise, as lawyers, we are placed in the midst of a legal system that reflects God's good purposes in society as well as the corruption of sin. To say that our task is redemptive is to acknowledge that the systems, practices, people, and institutions we work with in the law are not perfect, but that they can be moved toward submission to God's progressive kingly rule in the world. So our task is to allow God to do that work through us so that the ministry of these institutions, practices, and systems become *more* reconciliatory, healing, loving, just, fair, and merciful, rather than *less* so.

Truth and the life of the lawyer's mind. Finally, a commitment to discipleship and worldview requires that we submit our minds to Christ and seek to serve him, as he commands, with all of our mind. Charles Malik has famously said that "at the heart of the crisis of Western civilization lies the state of the mind and the spirit in the universities." So "it is neither a shame nor a sin to discipline and cultivate our reason to the utmost; it is a necessity, it is a duty, it is an honor to do so."[27] Our failure to think Christianly creates a major hurdle to our service of Christ in the law (see chap. 4). How can we discern the direction toward or away from God's redemptive purposes in the law when we don't know how to think about God's purposes in and around torts, contracts, politics, government, or the many other areas in which we might practice?

What lawyers think about law—its nature, its purpose, its foundation—

---

[27]Charles Malik, *The Two Tasks* (Westchester, Ill.: Cornerstone, 1980), pp. 30, 26.

makes every difference in their practice and scholarship. How a young lawyer defines the relationship with a client determines the boundaries and substance of his or her service. Likewise, our broader assumptions about the nature of humans, of God, of the family, or of the state determine how and why we do what we do on the bench, with our clients, in the classroom, or in the library.

God, in his mercy, has revealed to us all we need for life and practice, including special revelation to his people (the Scriptures) by which we can test all we learn from creation, tradition, history, or conscience. The primary tool, then, for the integration of faith and practice is God's revelation. Paul teaches that we will "test and approve what God's will is," when we are "transformed by the renewing of [our] mind" (Romans 12:1-2 NIV). Rather than conforming to an inconsistent standard—"being squeezed into the world's mold," as J. B. Phillips translates it—we are to conform to God's will. We do that by allowing the Holy Spirit to change the way we think.

A commercial practice divorced from the cultural (dominion) mandate and Christian stewardship seems beside the point, a useless exercise. A litigation practice that loses sight of reconciliation and biblical jurisdiction will tend toward hired-gun zealotry. A criminal law practice lacking due regard for jurisdiction or just desert can lead to frustration and cynicism—from either the defense or prosecution perspective.

In short, if we are to live in integrity, we must think truthfully—theologically—about our daily work.

Conclusion

In the last three chapters I've attempted to define integrity as a set of commitments that will tend toward integration of the lawyer, despite his or her various roles and obligations. I've also tried to summarize a number of ways that these commitments—to the unity of life in God, to community, and to truth—might address some of the fundamental stumbling blocks to serving Christ in the law. Along the way, we've seen some repetition and overlap in the potential practical application of these solutions, centering on theology, accountability, the local church, intentionality, and worship. As I close part two in chapter nine, I'll tie up these themes by suggesting practical applications of the life of integrity with all of its commitments.

For Further Thought

1. Can you discern redeeming value in your law practice? To answer, you might begin by thinking broadly about your service to your clients:
   - What are you helping them do?
   - How are they or the things they administer better or more reflective of God's ministry in the world because of your counsel?
   - How has God used your practice to minister to others—bringing reconciliation, financial or spiritual wholeness, restoration, recovery, encouragement, stewardship, creativity, fairness, mercy—to those around you or around those you serve?
2. What is your response when you see the consequences of the Fall in the legal system? Are you tempted to withdraw? Are you tempted to use political or social power to force reform from the top down?
3. How are you doing at exposing your law practice or study to God's light? Do you have a "vague uneasiness" that you're not doing too well in your life in the law? Set aside some time this week to write down your areas of concern. Discuss them in prayer with God, and then find another student or lawyer to talk to about this subject.

9

Integrity in Practice

Spiritual Disciplines

Let's recap our evaluation of the task of the Christian lawyer to this point. The goal of this book is to encourage Christian lawyers and law students who desire a deeper and more fulfilling life in the legal profession. All of us desire to have confidence that we are doing the *good* works that God has prepared for us to do. Yet there are stumbling blocks along the way, and I have identified three that have provided a grid for our search for a sense of calling in the law. First, the typical law school experience and fundamental academic mission lacks moral depth. The ordinary religion of the law school classroom includes instrumentalist jurisprudence and skepticism, and lacks a historical or moral center. Second, the local church has forgotten the doctrine of vocation, replacing it with empty volunteerism, a new sacred-secular dualism, or the Enlightenment perversion of the Protestant work ethic. Third, though we lawyers are good thinkers, we have failed to engage our minds theologically when it comes to the law, or else we have ignored the truth about our lives and practices. We are hamstrung because we don't apply Scripture to ordinary life and culture, or think theologically about who we are and what we do. We do not help our pastors know about ordinary work, and we are not taught by them. The life of the Christian legal mind is either not engaged or not Christian in any meaningful sense.

I have argued that there is a path to overcoming these barriers, and it lies hidden in the forest of the wholeness of human be-ing, or *integrity.* I have identified three major commitments necessary to this integrated life: commitment to the unity of knowledge, belief, and action; commitment to life in community; and commitment to truth. We have discussed each of these commitments in some detail, outlining ideas of how our pursuit of these allegiances might overcome the ordinary religion of law school, recover a vocational perspective, and strengthen the Christian legal mind.

I have not yet suggested many specific habits that the lawyer of integrity might adopt in pursuit of integrity, though we do have some clues about those habits and practices. At the end of chapter five, I anticipated that five major themes would recur as we discussed the characteristic commitments of integrity: theology, accountability, the local church, intentional living, and worship. And indeed these themes have flavored each topic under consideration and given us ideas for more practical approaches to our life in the law. In this chapter, we'll take the next step, identifying core practices—the core intentional, theological, accountable, worshiping practices—of lawyers acting within and through the body of Christ. In other words, let's conclude this part of our discussion by suggesting regular disciplines in the daily work and conduct of the Christian lawyer. We might call this putting *praxis* to our *theoria*.

Daniel

One of the finest examples of the faithful lawyer in a hostile world is Daniel. Daniel was a top-flight legal counsel who knew the law—in fact, when we first meet him, he is in law school in Babylon. He operated in the halls of power in a society hostile, for the most part, to his faith. Yet he was part of God's set-apart people in that place, though he served and worked with folks who did not share his worldview and commitments. He was indeed intentional, a clear theological thinker, accountable on a number of levels, and fully centered in the worship of God.[1] He fits our criteria.

When we begin to look at Daniel's "law practice," we see that Daniel is a model practitioner of what we might call the classical spiritual disciplines. We call these practices, such as fasting, prayer, and study, "classical" disciplines because they are ancient and because they are central to devotional Christianity.[2] According to philosopher Dallas Willard, a *discipline* is "any activity within our power that we engage in to enable us to do what we cannot do by direct

[1]Thanks to my friend Phil Ashey, a priest in parish ministry who works with lawyers as a Christian Legal Society chaplain, for suggesting Daniel and these qualifications for this role.

[2]Richard Foster, *Celebration of Discipline,* 3rd ed. (New York: HarperCollins, 1998), p. 1.

effort," such as practicing on the driving range or in the music studio.[3] They are *spiritual* disciplines because they help us depend on "the ultimate reality, which is God and Kingdom" rather than on the "merely human or natural."[4] Through these practices, we overcome our old habits of thinking, feeling, and doing, and replace them, through practice, with "kingdom habits."[5] Richard Foster lists twelve spiritual disciplines: four "inward" disciplines (meditation, prayer, fasting, and study), four "outward" disciplines (simplicity, solitude, submission, and service), and four "corporate" disciplines (confession, worship, guidance, and celebration).[6] Willard has a "standard list" of sixteen, eight "disciplines of abstinence" and eight disciplines of "engagement."[7]

Using Daniel's example and the themes we have seen so far in our discussions of integrity, I want to highlight three spiritual disciplines for use in our discussion. These practices will not magically "integrate" us, but they will help us to cooperate in the work of God in our bodies and law practices. While they do not line up exactly with "classical" disciplines, they are my candidates for the lawyer's spiritual disciplines.

These "lawyer's disciplines" are the practical side of integrity, but they are certainly not formulas for the Christian life. Instead, they are vehicles for suggesting the types of practices that will flow from our necessary commitments and, in turn, lead to the inner lives we desire as lawyers. I don't mean to suggest that lawyers need to practice fewer of the spiritual disciplines than other Christians. I simply want to focus on those most central to the lawyer's calling *as a lawyer*. Knowing the lawyer's bent, the way we think and what we need, I selected the practices *most necessary* to lawyer's quest for integrity that we've laid out so far.

We need to recall too that simply managing our behavior so that we feel and act more like Christians in the legal profession is a weak and unworthy goal. Willard has criticized this tendency in the church: "One of the greatest weaknesses in our teaching and leadership today is that we spend too much time trying to get people to do things good people are supposed to do, with-

---

[3]Dallas Willard, *The Divine Conspiracy: Rediscovering Our Hidden Life in God* (New York: HarperCollins, 1998), p. 353.

[4]Ibid.

[5]Ibid., p. 354.

[6]Foster, *Celebration of Discipline.*

[7]Dallas Willard, *Spirit of the Disciplines* (San Francisco: Harper & Row, 1988).

out changing what they really believe."[8] We need to change our minds about God's kingdom and its relationship to our law practices and our legal study and scholarship. The primary goal of the disciplines is to transform our orientation toward God and his work. Only by changing our beliefs will we change our action, but even when our minds our transformed, we need training in right conduct. This is but a suggestion about how we lawyers might allow the Spirit of Christ to train us for holiness and usefulness in his work in the kingdom.

I have identified (borrowing Foster's terminology) one outward discipline, one corporate discipline, and one inward discipline.

Outward Discipline

Daniel knew the Word of God, and he knew how to apply it to his life and work. In Daniel 1, our introduction to him is followed by an account of his determination to obey God's law in the face of a contrary edict by the king (and it won't be the last time). He won't defile himself with the king's food (Daniel 1:8). He follows the dietary laws of God rather than please the Babylonian king. Daniel knew the law and its application because he was first of all a student of the Word. However, he also understood how it applied to real life and his surroundings. In other words, he had a well-developed worldview: Daniel and his companions were "versed in every branch of wisdom, endowed with knowledge and insight, and competent to serve in the king's palace" (Daniel 1:4).

If it is true that a true perception of reality (a Christian worldview) is necessary to integrity, then our practices must lead us to truth about reality. To know truth about reality, we need to know and understand what God has revealed about reality. To understand how to apply God's revelation to the reality that surrounds us in our clients, our children, our spouses, and our churches, we need to understand the times and culture in which we live—we need to "get" our spouses and our children; we need to discern our clients' problems and goals. All of this requires wisdom. And wisdom requires study: "Wisdom is the application of knowledge gained from studying both God's written Word and His revealed truth in creation. If we are going to be wise, spiritual people prepared to meet the crises of our age, we must be a studying, learning

[8]Willard, *Divine Conspiracy,* p 307.

community that values the life of the mind."[9] This study is more than Scripture reading. It is a habit of observation and research into God's revelation of himself, including his creation.

It should already be abundantly clear: the lawyer's calling requires discipleship of the mind through study. This is the lawyer's outward discipline. I propose four practical suggestions.

1. *Get off the couch and do it.* Proverbs 1 tells us that the fear of the Lord is the beginning of wisdom. It is our diligent seeking, by God's power, that feeds our search. Wisdom is an *active* pursuit. Consider the verbs of Proverbs 2:1-4 that precede "fear of the Lord" in verse 5: *accept* my words (v. 1), *treasure up* my commandments (v. 1), *make* your ear attentive (v. 2), *incline* your heart (v. 2), *cry out* for insight (v. 3), *raise your voice* for understanding (v. 3), *seek* it like silver (v. 4), *search* for it as hidden treasure (v. 4). When this is accomplished, "you will understand the fear of the LORD / and find knowledge of God" (v. 5). Seeking truth is an intentional process; it requires action on our part. It does not simply happen; it must be pursued.

J. P. Moreland reminds us that the couch potato is a poor model for the person pursuing the disciple's life of the mind: "We let other people do our living and thinking for us: the pastor studies the Bible for us, the news media does our political thinking for us, and we let our favorite sports team exercise, struggle, and win for us. From watching television to listening to sermons, our primary agenda is to be amused and entertained."[10] This passivity is just one of the seven traits of what Moreland calls the empty self, constituted by "a set of values, motives, and habits of thought, feeling, and behavior that perverts and eliminates the life of the mind and makes maturation in the way of Christ extremely difficult."[11] Part of his solution to the empty self, beyond recognizing the problem and choosing to be different, is a change of routine. He suggests that our routines can be changed to "get out of passive ruts" and replace them with habits that create physical and intellectual energy.[12] In other words, turn off the TV and the Internet!

2. *Study Scripture.* Developing a Christian worldview requires a biblical foundation. Proof-texting will not help us develop the mind of Christ in law,

---

[9]J. P. Moreland, *Love Your God with All Your Mind* (Colorado Springs: NavPress, 1997), p. 39.
[10]Ibid., p. 90.
[11]Ibid., p. 88.
[12]Ibid., p. 95.

politics, and culture, and our subjective feelings about particular passages may lead down dangerous paths. Prayerful and serious study is called for. Again, Daniel had to know and understand God's dietary law before he could take his courageous stand.

There is a difference between devotional reading and reading for study. Most Christians read devotionally, seeking personal application of isolated texts—to experience the words in a personal way. When we read devotionally, we do not look so much for information as for experience or personal application.[13] Devotional reading is good and necessary, but our discipline here is involves study. Seminary courses, personal retreats, or lengthy commitments to work through commentaries are useful tools for serious study.[14] In addition, don't neglect survey courses and general theological instruction in biblical and systematic theology to assist you in placing the particular Scriptures in context of God's plan in history. In short, "experience, other books, and live discussion" are indispensable to fruitful study.[15]

3. *Invite John Jay to your study group.* In keeping with the advice that live discussion and other books are necessary to fruitful study, we need take advantage of the experience and expertise of others in our area of need. First, we should involve the saints with whom we work and live to be a part of our study. We must engage the minds of others struggling with vocation and its meaning in the kingdom, others seeking to practice law to the glory of God, and others engaged in the discipline of study who are ready to edify and sharpen us as we try to comprehend and reflect on what we have read.[16] Basic application of Scripture to our work and callings is often a very difficult task in and of itself. We need teachers, mentors, and friends, including others who understand the law and life in it, to come alongside us.

We live in a day in which it is relatively easy to participate in meaningful discussions with legal experts down the ages. Cicero, Augustine, Aquinas, Blackstone, Kent, and Coke are at our fingertips. If our topic for study is a kingdom perspective on law and politics, we could do worse than to have Irenaeus or Thomas More interacting with us around the table through their

---

[13]See ibid., p. 164; Foster, *Celebration of Discipline,* p. 69.

[14]Foster, *Celebration of Discipline,* pp. 69-70.

[15]Ibid., p. 68.

[16]Not surprisingly, Foster has something to say about this too. Repetition, concentration, comprehension, and reflection are the "four steps" to the discipline of study.

written words. Again, the power of the Spirit has been at work in the lives of God's people for millennia—surely our attention to the great cloud of witnesses in the law is warranted. If their wisdom on the application of Scripture to law and legal institutions has so far stood the test of time, it is surely worth *considering* whether it sheds any light on the problems of the twenty-first-century corporate lawyer, prosecutor, or law student.

There is a sense in which ordinary practitioners have lost track of what it means to be part of a profession. We have no sense of history and no idea of our heritage as professionals or the development of the law we serve. In his fascinating essay "Professional Responsibility," Jude Dougherty argues that this sense of calling is an obligation of professionals: "The recognition of those truths that bear upon the fundamental features of [the professional's] work and of the relation of that work to life as a whole is a part of the speculative and practical wisdom required of the professional."[17] Practice is grounded in theory, says Dougherty, and the "normative principles" almost always come from the experiences of the past. The profession must take advantage of the "experience garnered from the past" in order to "recognize that there are certain laws governing nature and human behavior that remain invariant through generations."[18] Our obligation as lawyers, then, is to know our past and to know the wisdom of our forebears on such subjects as the nature and source of law itself, the goal of punishment, the nature of persons, the role of the judge, the place of ethics, the normative justification for the adversary system and so forth. Apparently, we still have some studying to do. Again, Daniel was versed "in every branch of wisdom." He was counsel to the king; he had to apply himself to understand philosophy, politics, diplomacy, and law according to the Word of God *and* in light of the cultural norms of Babylon. He didn't see the Scriptures as a devotional guide only—they were his source of understanding across all branches of his vast learning.

We must also involve our churches in this activity. One of the main goals of fellowship is to stimulate and encourage one another in our lives of faith—including the life of the mind.

4. *Study the times and maybe even* The Times. To study Scripture, the profession, and the foundations of law is already a tall order, but we also need to

---

[17]Jude P. Dougherty, *Western Creed, Western Identity* (Washington, D.C.: Catholic University of America Press, 2000), p. 186.

[18]Ibid.

know something about the culture we live in. We should be aware of what is happening around us in the world. Again, law is a "culture-making" profession.[19] Lawyers influence the imbedded modes of thought, the dominant institutions and the individuals around us through our vocation. Through work in the law, we ought to be salt and light in a place that is "often tasteless and dark."[20] If that is the case, we must understand the times in order to discern where our vocations fit into God's work around us. In addition, the *law itself* makes culture. The West is the West by virtue of the consequences to ordinary life and thought brought about by such things as the rule of law, the Magna Carta, and trial by jury, to name a few. God called the children of Israel to be set apart, a new and different culture, and the first thing he did to set them apart was to give them law.[21] So even when it comes to popular culture, we need clear thinking—intentional, theologically formed thinking. The influence that law has on culture—and the way that culture can drive law—should make us alert to prevailing modes of thought and discourse. The news media, movies, popular fiction, talk shows, advertising and the like greatly influence the way that we think and even how we think about thought and spirituality.[22] Even lawyers need to pay attention.

It is interesting to note that the very definition of law as a "learned" profession connotes a professional obligation to study, to learn.[23] Study is not easy and is time-consuming. Most law students I speak to tell me that it is unrealistic to expect that they would study anything other than the law for the three years that they are in law school. If that is true, then on graduation they will fail fully to understand their calling. As Dougherty says, "One cannot claim status as an economist without having read Adam Smith."[24] Unfortunately, we believe we can claim status as lawyers without knowledge of moral philosophy or legal history. We somehow claim status as Christian lawyers, alongside Edward Coke, William Blackstone, John Jay, and Thomas More, without having studied the book of Exodus, the *Treatise on Law*, the Sermon on the Mount, or natural law.

---

[19]Gene Edward Veith, *God at Work* (Wheaton, Ill.: Crossway, 2002), p. 67.
[20]Ibid.
[21]Thanks to my colleague Natt Gantt for pointing this out.
[22]On Christian thinking and popular culture, see Kenneth A. Myers, *All God's Children and Blue Suede Shoes: Christians and Popular Culture* (Wheaton, Ill.: Crossway, 1989); and William Romanowski, *Eyes Wide Open* (Grand Rapids: Brazos, 2001).
[23]Dougherty, *Western Creed, Western Identity*, p. 185.
[24]Ibid., p. 186.

At a minimum I suggest that law students—and lawyers who desire to be students of the law through the discipline of study—should be intentional about the pursuit of wisdom on a number of fronts related to their callings. This is not to say that we have time to become experts on law and theology or the biblical basis of contract law. But we need to at least be familiar with basic Christian teaching about our calling. For example, we should pursue basic information regarding

> 2 CORINTHIANS 10:3-5
> **Indeed we live as human beings, but we do not wage war according to human standards; for the weapons of our warfare are not merely human, but they have divine power to destroy strongholds. We destroy arguments and every proud obstacle raised up against the knowledge of God, and we take every thought captive to obey Christ.**

- a historical, biblical approach to our area of practice
- the nature and purpose of human law and its relationship to divine law
- human nature and its relationship to human law
- various Christian views of human government
- biblical approaches to the relationship between the church and state
- an understanding of jurisdiction and authority given to various institutions, including the church, the state, families, and individuals, and how such jurisdictions overlap and interact
- the relationship between the civil laws in the Old Testament and contemporary civil laws

Don't be discouraged by this list! Again, we should begin with pursuit and basic familiarity with the fundamentals. It is a life's work to seek to understand even the smallest doctrine that explains God's full purpose of restoration in the law. We move in baby steps, building on what has gone before and leaving it to others who come after to continue to build. But it is never too late to develop good habits of thought regarding our work. In fact, it is likely that we already have some foundation—most of us have been considering these things now and then since law school and perhaps before. It's simply time to formalize our study goals and become more intentional about our task. Start with Scripture, set goals, get off the couch, and concentrate!

Practitioners should begin with the practical: what might help me understand my daily activities better? How might I apply scriptural truth to my area of practice? As we focus on the practical, we'll become aware of areas in which we must pursue more theological matters.

There is a human tendency, especially among lawyers, to become puffed up through study. We need to avoid this, and we will if we remember our focus for study: Christ working through us as we submit to him. In John 5, Jesus rebuked the Jews for trusting in the Scriptures for eternal life, yet rejecting the One about whom the Scriptures testify. We must avoid this error! The purpose of our study is to train our bodies and minds to cooperate with the work of the kingdom. We seek truth as a means of training in discipleship to Christ. If love of neighbor through the law is not the result of our study, something is not right in our studying or in our law practice.

Note how engagement in study helps address the stumbling blocks we identified in part one. First, for example, law students engaged in this discipline will undoubtedly resist the deleterious academic influence of the law school environment, and lawyers who study will be reversing the influence of the instrumentalist bent in their education and practice experience. Again, it is impossible to counter the instrumentalist foundations of current legal thought without biblical, historical, and theological thinking. Second, study will change our shaky doctrinal orientation toward ordinary work, which is the root of our wrong beliefs about the place of our law practices in the kingdom. As we submit ourselves in study, we will be encouraged to avoid the false disjunctions that lead us to compartmentalize our work from our "religious" life, and set us on a path to right belief about life in the law. Right belief will ultimately lead to changed conduct. Our study of Scripture will also encourage us to think vocationally across our various roles. For example, as we learn our calling as lawyers, we will also be mindful of our callings as fathers, mothers, children, church members, and so forth.

Finally, if it is true we stumble because we do not faithfully think about who we are and what we do, then study is a crucial antidote to that barrier as well. In prayer and study, we must submit our thoughts to God on professional identity and the substance of our practice. Once we learn to study as a spiritual discipline, we will understand how to discern the biblical basis for criminal law, a kingdom approach to mergers and acquisitions, and a consistent apologetic of the things we do every day in the office.

Corporate Discipline

Daniel and his Jewish friends had another valuable asset in addition to their wisdom and knowledge: each other. They did not practice spiritual discipline in isolation, but in community. For example, it is pretty clear that Daniel's resolve not to defile himself with the king's food was part of a group decision in which he took the lead: "Let us be given vegetables to eat and water to drink," he tells the guard in the palace (Daniel 1:12). And the culmination of the story is that Daniel *and his three companions* were the healthiest in the court. They took their stand together. We see this dynamic even more clearly later, when all the wise men, including Daniel and his friends, were to be executed for not knowing the king's dream. Daniel first asks for more time and then immediately informs his "small group" so that they can pray: "Then Daniel went to his home and informed his companions, . . . and told them to seek mercy from the God of heaven concerning this mystery, so that Daniel and his companions with the rest of the wise men of Babylon might not perish" (Daniel 2:17-18).

Again, God's very nature implies life in community; work in the kingdom is most definitely a group concept (see chap. 6). If the lawyer's calling to the life of discipleship will never be fulfilled without others, then interpersonal connections are at the heart of the practical walk of integrity in the law. The classic corporate disciplines, especially fellowship, confession, and guidance, are implicated here.[25] Lawyers are often solitary people who work long hours and have little time for others outside of work. Yet to function in integrity, we must do so within the corporate structure God has provided.

Fellowship means making connections with others in the body of Christ. It means shared activities in which we participate together in pursing the disciple's life. Its goal is the spread of the gospel and the advancement of the kingdom. One picture of such fellowship is found in 1 Corinthians 12, where Paul speaks of the gifts in the members of the body: "To each is given the manifestation of the Spirit for the common good" (1 Corinthians 12:7). We all have different needs that are met by the gifts; we function in unity through a diversity of gifts in a way that is impossible for an individual. In this way, we are pushed, corporately and individually, toward true integrity in our lives in the law.

[25]On the disciplines that make up this section, see Willard, *Spirit of the Disciplines,* pp. 186-89 (fellowship and confession), and Foster, *Celebration of Discipline,* pp. 143-57; 175-89 (confession and guidance).

Given what we have discussed about the nature of the commitments at the heart of integrity, such reciprocal fellowship is indispensable to the lawyer's calling. Here are my practical suggestions for engaging in fellowship.

1. *Be connected to a local church.* The corporate structure of the local church is the base from which we're sent to work out our callings. We must be submitted to a local church, and our connection in that body centers on the give and take of the gifts of the people of God—again, reflecting the in-going and out-going ministry of the triune God—in service to one another and the outside world. Today, it seems we spend too much time evaluating what needs our church meets in our own lives, and too little time just serving in the beautiful ministry that the Spirit intends.

We have already discussed the responsibility of the lawyer to learn from those within the body and to come alongside and expose leaders to the challenges in the professional world. There are so many other roles within the body, however, in which we can serve. Lawyers are often found in local churches as Sunday School teachers, but there is so much more. A growing movement through local church-sponsored legal aid spreads the gospel of Christ through meeting the legal needs of the poor. In addition, lawyers can counsel and advise, form corporations, draft agreements, and serve as peacemakers within the body and local community. In the body, lawyers are taught and equipped for their own ministry in law practice, government, scholarship, or the courts. Daniel was part of a larger team that included his Jewish brothers and pagan lawyers. His connection to the other Jews was a source of strength in difficulty and wisdom in times of decision. We need the local congregation in order fully to succeed in law.

2. *Meet for meat.* When we meet face to face, there is a joy and fullness that is impossible in other ways of communicating. "Although I have much to write to you, I would rather not use paper and ink; instead I hope to come to you and talk with you face to face, so that our joy may be complete," wrote the apostle John (2 John 12). Wouldn't it be better if you and I were simply discussing the content of this book across the table from one another over a cup of coffee, giving and taking ideas and responses, sharing stories and emotions, thoughts and half-formed opinions? Sure it would! We need that kind of connection to our brothers and sisters in Christ on a regular basis. And we need it not just in the corporate worship setting (and we do need that desperately) but also in smaller groups designed to shape the integrated lives we've been discussing.

So our connections must have content, and our meetings should be meaty. If our discussion to this point has any truth to it, then we need to intentionally design our fellowship to include biblically and historically based discussions of ordinary work and vocation. It will be helpful to do this with other lawyers, of course. Who knows better the concerns and struggles of the Christian lawyer than the Christian lawyer? There isn't another group that will understand the practical ethical issues and the detailed struggles that we have in the law. I know one lawyer, who meets regularly with an attorney group in a major city, who says that there are no others anywhere, including at home or at church, with whom he can share the detailed struggles he faces in the daily practice of law. Though his family loves him and he has a great church home, the foundation of experience and empathy is great among brothers and sisters who face similar trials in the law. Here's how one Christian Legal Society board member put it to me:

> My small clutch of Christian attorneys is my constant reminder that this profession is about more than making money, or gratifying one's ego. When we meet for prayer, study, or fellowship, it is a time to look not to us, but to Him. I love the folks at my church, but nobody there can understand what it is like to practice law in a way which integrates Christ. Those in my Christian lawyers' small group do. Without them, I would feel alone in what I do.

This kind of meat obviously aids our search for integrity.

I remember the struggles I sometimes had with our Lawyers' Christian Fellowship meetings in law school. At times, I loved to go, joining in the discussion and gaining insight from others. But often I would skip the meetings, knowing that my time would be more effectively spent elsewhere. The difference was the topic at hand. When we met together and kicked around topics at the intersection of law and faith, the meetings were edifying and interesting, even when arguments broke out, the leader was unprepared, or the food didn't come. On the other hand, if we simply tried to discuss a passage in the abstract, particularly when we began to cross-examine one another, it seemed to be a waste of effort.

Over the years since then, I have noticed a similar tension in student groups selecting topics. Should we do straight devotional study and discussion or attempt to tackle, from a biblical perspective, the issues we are facing in class and might face in law practice? Of course, Bible study can always be practical, and a good leader or group can direct applications to the law quite readily. Whatever the means, however, it is my view that we ought not to squander opportunities to discuss matters related to our secondary callings when we are with other lawyers and law students. To be sure, there will be those who want "a break from all this legal talk." But if we don't address these issues among ourselves, where will we form our responses to God's call in the law?

Yet there is value, too, in cross-disciplinary discussions of work. One of the greatest lessons I learned about clients came from listening to a doctor talking about treating his patients as "whole persons." It came after dinner one evening, where folks were simply chatting informally. Two doctors were sharing the struggles of their work, and in listening to that conversation I gained tremendous insight into my own calling to treat clients as more than just walking legal problems. Consider pursuing others in the body who share your desire to minister through ordinary work, regardless of their connections to the law. In addition, we need encouragement and guidance in pursuing our other callings as well. We shouldn't neglect mother-with-mother or father-with-father fellowship. Although it's beyond the scope of this book, encouragement in these noncareer callings is just as central to Christian integrity as is encouragement in our legal lives.

We should discuss our studies with others as we seek wisely to apply Christian teachings to our work. I would venture that most nonacademics do not have groups in which they can discuss the interaction of theology, culture, and practice in any depth. We also need such groups to confess our sins, our doubts, and our failures. Confession within the body is a rare jewel. James tell us to "confess your sins one to another, . . . that you may be healed" (James 5:16). Yet we would rather mask our sins and hide our various disappointments and failures in order that we won't be judged. If we are going to live with integrity in the legal profession, we'll need to find friends who will hear us and discuss with us our sins, our failures, and our deep needs. Confession, says Dallas Willard, "will nourish our faith in God's provision for our needs through his people, our sense of being loved, and our humility before our brothers and sisters."[26] Through this intimacy, we are encouraged not to sin and given guidance as we work out our callings.

Small groups are excellent means to this goal of fellowship and should in-

---

[26]Willard, *Spirit of the Disciplines,* p. 188.

clude an intentional substantive focus, a time of prayer for one another, and some guidelines regarding attendance, confidentiality, goals, and the like in order to make it a safe environment for confession and sharing. There are a handful of good books on small groups, and most churches are alert to the benefits, so resources should be easy to find. In addition, much of life is lived on the fly, and we need to take advantage of the fellowship we enjoy spontaneously and informally. This requires attention too, however, as we are apt to fritter away opportunities for depth even when we are given a serendipitous moment of true fellowship. When God places us in the company of other believers, there is plenty to do in worship, celebration, and praise. Yet there is more: deep conversation, confession, bearing of burdens and simple encouragement that can be done in a moment if we don't waste it. When Daniel faced trouble, he ran to his friends who could "seek mercy from the God of heaven" on his behalf (Daniel 2:18).

There is no substitute, however, for intentional and regular relationships that flow from more general Christian fellowship. Such relationships include elements of guidance, instruction, confession, and encouragement, and we often describe them as discipleship or mentoring relationships. Some make the distinction between discipleship relationships and mentoring, but for our purposes, it is sufficient to emphasize that we need the guidance and wisdom of one who knows our position in life, has in some sense been there before us, and is therefore able to help navigate those waters.[27] Likewise, we should be pouring our wisdom into those whom God places in our lives as protégés or disciples. Paul, who has clearly discipled Timothy, tells Timothy to continue the chain of these relationships: "What you have heard from me through many witnesses entrust to faithful people who will be able to teach others as well" (2 Timothy 2:2). Both relationship and content are necessary. And, as we do in small groups, we must have a purpose in mind as we move forward. Our time should be spent with those who are faithful, both mentors and protégés. We should meet regularly, pray together and focus on the task, whatever it is. We

[27]My own inclination is that what we call "discipleship" is often simply mentoring. Given the breadth of the Great Commission to make disciples, "teaching them to obey everything I have commanded you," it seems that our relationships are too small and shortsighted to be the "discipleship" that Jesus has in mind. Or perhaps, more likely, we're using the same word to describe something a bit different. See, for example, Bob Biehl, Jerry McGregor, and Glen Urquhart, *Mentoring: How to Find a Mentor and How to Become One* (Laguna Niguel, Calif.: Masterplanning Group, 1994), p. 4.

must build trust with one another through time and contact, so we should expect long-term relationships. This one-on-one fellowship is life-changing, if done in the power of the Holy Spirit.

3. *Recognize the entire web of your legal life as part your kingdom ministry.* If it is true, as I have argued, that the primary focus of ordinary work is to love and serve our neighbors, whole new ways of looking at our ministry in the law are opened up. We connect with a much wider variety of neighbors in law practice than just our colleagues in the firm or the classroom. An entire mission field is open to us: every day we see neighbors to love that we call clients, partners, coworkers, friends, secretaries, paralegals, judges, court clerks and personnel, and opposing counsel. This is our mission field! And our mission is a broad one: to love these people as we love ourselves, to serve them in any place they have a need, and to be available to encourage, heal, reconcile, forgive, confront, exhort, share, hug, admonish, or push them as God's minister of his love. These are the connections that God in his sovereign mercy has provided. Too often, I am so focused on "changing the world" that I neglect the very world that God has put in my office to transform through the love of Christ.

When I was a young lawyer, I was having some trouble replacing a secretary who was moving to another part of the firm, and a partner called me into his office to give me some advice. He closed the discussion by admonishing me to remember that legal secretaries are there only to do my bidding, and that they were nothing—they were there to be used and then discarded. By God's grace I was horrified and did not take it to heart, but it reminded me that my obligations are to human beings in all positions, who have demanding roles to work out, just as I do. Years later, at another law firm, I was chatting with a partner who had been practicing law for many years, much of it with the same secretary. In the course of the conversation, I asked him about his secretary and her work. "I can't do what I do without her," he said. "She serves my clients just as much as I do, or more." Which lawyer's secretary do you suppose will be most likely to serve and love her neighbors effectively? Which lawyer is loving his secretary (neighbor)?

Our obligations and conduct toward our opposing counsel, partners, clients, secretaries, students, and coworkers is worth prayerful consideration. They are the connections that God has provided for us to assist us or test us in his kingdom work. According to a lawyer I know who has been practicing for three decades, this is all just a reflection of who one is. "How you deal with your secretary is the key to life and the key to law practice." Absolutely.

There are a number of ways that the discipline of fellowship helps us hurdle the stumbling blocks to Christian service in the law. For example, law students would be lost without study groups, which are plainly the most significant community for many law students. Students need groups not only to decipher the secret code that is the law school class discussion but also to make sense of the cases, statutes, first principles, and philosophies underlying the curriculum and discussion. These groups serve our commitment to the truth as well. The informal discussions that I had with friends over lunch and after class during my first year of law school were indispensable in helping me develop and apply a Christian worldview to the law.

I should pause and note here, too, that there is a danger in study groups becoming a Christian law student's primary community. A student must not neglect his calling to his family or his church community in order to attach himself to a student community. Commitments may need to be adjusted, and other family members must cooperate in balancing the heavy demands of the vocation of student, wife, and church member. But an unbalanced attachment to a law school community often leads to divorce ("my study partners understand my problems so much more than my spouse does") or alienation from the local body of believers ("I just don't have time for church; besides, I'd be letting my study group down"). Fellowship within the law school context is central to the student's calling, but as we've seen throughout our discussions on vocations, God calls us to fill a number of roles at once.

Lawyers, likewise, need fellowship to work through the substantive issues surrounding law practice. When I first began law practice, there was a group of Christian lawyers at another firm in town that met weekly to read relevant books and discuss them and to share struggles and prayer requests. At my firm, I was simply a green lawyer, but in this group, I was a brother in Christ—one that needed some guidance, to be sure, but a brother rather than an underling. This group gave me a place to vent my struggles, to confidentially share interpersonal struggles in my practice, and to learn the wisdom of lawyers who had been practicing for years, but who had no vested interested in masking their own inadequacies and struggles. It was a refreshing, interesting, challenging group, and I still remember and cherish the lessons that I learned from these men. This group helped to overcome the missing moral center in my legal education, since our discussions so often focused on the reality of moral choices in practice, at home, and in the community. It also helped me in my nascent thinking about vocation and what it means to do law as ministry to the glory of God. Here was a group of practicing lawyers, some young, some older, some in criminal practice, some in family law, some in transactional work, some doing litigation, but all with the common desire to submit their life work in the law unto the Lord as faithful service. One of the men in the group had left the pastoral ministry to go to law school. "The Lord told me that there were already plenty of Christian pastors," he said. "He needed more Christian lawyers. So I went to law school." Connecting with lawyers like that, how could I not begin to think more faithfully?

Life in the local church can itself be a helpful lesson in vocational thinking, even if the doctrine isn't preached from the pulpit. Moreover, if we find a place to use our gifts and talents outside of the workplace—whether in the church, at local shelters or for community groups, we are often encouraged to return to the office with a better idea of what our work can be. Service begets service.

It should be obvious how fellowship with others helps us in our commitment to truth and the recovery or the Christian life of the mind. Simple family discussion would help rid us of some of our poor habits of thought. One of our great needs is proper thinking about roles; meeting with others may provide a key to solving that identity crisis.

Inward Discipline

Daniel is a worshiper. When Daniel receives God's revelation of the dream and its interpretation, he "bless[es] the God of heaven" (Daniel 2:19) and worships him. Daniel's prayer life gets him tossed in the lion's den. (Prayer must have been a pretty regular habit if his enemies knew when and where to find him praying.) His responses to power consistently give glory to God; he fasts, he obeys dietary laws, and "no negligence or corruption could be found in him" (Daniel 6:4). Daniel is a man of virtue, whose wise words and righteous conduct change the fate of his people within this hostile kingdom. Despite all this, he still was privileged to spend a harrowing evening with the lions. It is only after he is pulled out and the Babylonian king sings praises to God, that we hear that Daniel "prospered" in his government law practice (Daniel 6:28).

While we must function within the communities God provides, there is indeed a need for solitary reflection. Study is part of our reflection, yet extended contemplation is a different discipline with different ends and objects. True meditative reflection is necessary to the lawyer's calling.

In his great work *Life Together,* Dietrich Bonhoeffer emphasizes the necessity of the community and solitary paths for the whole life: "One who wants fellowship without solitude plunges into the void of words and feelings, and one who seeks solitude without fellowship perishes in the abyss of vanity, self-infatuation, and despair."[28] In my experience, lawyers tend toward the vain, self-infatuated, despairing side of "solitude without fellowship." Yet what is our solitude? Long, lonely hours reading cases and organizing arguments, drafting contracts, and considering options? Daniel too, to be sure, studied and worked long, lonely hours as well. But he also worshiped in his solitude—he prayed, fasted, and considered his ways. We must make more of our solitude, while leaving it now and again for refreshing community. Solitude in the classical sense meant time in the desert or wilderness, to isolate oneself from humanity. While lawyers could use a dose of that practice now and then, our focus here is on a sabbath-oriented consideration of life and meaning, what Aristotle would have called *leisure.* In a sense, this is the complete human purpose, rooted in the *imago Dei.*

At the close of God's work in creation, he rests (Genesis 2:1-3), though he was not "tired out" by his work. The sabbath rest is an important principle closely connected to our nature as image bearers and ultimately to his saving grace. Sabbath rest is a shadow of our rest in Christ accomplished for eternity on the cross. In addition, our sabbath practice of rest as God rested implies not just the holiness of the sanctified seventh day, but our likeness to and representation of our Creator. He is a worker, so we work too. He rests, so we rest. One theologian sums up the sabbath principle as stated in the Decalogue as "man must copy God in the course of his life."[29]

So how are we to "copy" God in his rest? God's rest on the seventh day is not a picture of his recuperation from the difficulties of creation! It is a picture of his finished work and his contemplation of it. "It [rest] stands for consummation of a work accomplished and the joy and satisfaction attendant upon this."[30] What this may imply is that we are created to stop, consider, and contemplate, especially regarding our work and creation. As we have seen in our

---

[28]Dietrich Bonhoeffer, *Life Together* (San Francisco: HarperCollins, 1954), p. 78.

[29]Gerhardus Vos, *Biblical Theology* (1948; reprint, Carlisle, Penn.: Banner of Truth, 2000), p. 139.

[30]Ibid., p. 140.

discussion of redemption—the restoration of creation by God—we have a task that continues, and at its ultimate end stands ultimate rest. Our cycle of work and rest prefigures that ultimate rest. In fact, that is the significance of the observance of the Lord's Day on Sunday in the new covenant, rather than the sabbath (Saturday) observance continuing from the old covenant. We celebrate the victory of Christ ushering in the new creation, which now colors all that we do. We *begin* with the celebration of that victory, we look back on the completed work of the cross, and our six days of work flow from it and come after it.

In chapter two we discussed the deadly sin of *acedia,* spiritual sloth. I argued that we lawyers leave law school marked by a sluggishness about the pursuit of ultimate goodness, truth, and beauty that medieval scholars called *acedia.* This sloth permeates much of the lawyer's life. We are apathetic toward the real purpose of our work in the kingdom, slothful in our pursuit of Christian mind, and spiritually sluggish about the substantive biblical foundations of our very law practices. It is no coincidence that Aquinas called this *acedia* a sin against the third commandment, "Remember the sabbath day and keep it holy."[31] Our "rest" must be a contemplative, joyful consideration of what it means to be created in the image of God. We are created to work and to rest in contemplation of that work and its meaning in relation to God's work—the creation. Part of the obligation that comes with being created in God's image is to pursue what is good, true, and beautiful, and in order to do that we must rest and consider, we must reflect and ponder, we must stop and meditate on God's work and his will. To consider this ultimate good something not worth doing is a deadly sin.[32]

One way to describe this discipline is "true leisure." Aristotle taught that the very purpose of work was leisure. In fact, for the Greeks there wasn't a word for ordinary work other than "not leisure." This is true in Latin as well.[33] So what is this true leisure that forms the baseline for the understanding of human activity? The Christian understanding of true leisure finds expression in the classic concept of the *via contemplativa,* the contemplative life. But true

---

[31]Some count it the fourth commandment. Thomas counted it the third. So who's counting? *Summa Theologica* 2-2, Q. 35. See also Josef Pieper, *Leisure, The Basis of Culture* (Chicago: St. Augustine's Press, 1998), p. 30 and note accompanying text.

[32]Thomas Aquinas *Summa Theologica* 2-2 Q. 35.

[33]Pieper, *Leisure,* pp. 4-5.

leisure in the sense we seek goes beyond that. For some ideas about what our pursuit of leisure might entail, we will return to German philosopher Josef Pieper's explanation of leisure as the antidote to *acedia.*[34] First, true leisure is nonactivity. It involves quiet and the absence of preoccupation, within and outside ourself. Pieper calls leisure "a form of that stillness that is the necessary preparation for accepting reality; only the person who is still can hear, and whoever is not still, cannot hear."[35] Second, leisure is "the condition of considering things in a celebratory spirit." What does it mean to "consider"? Pastor John Piper puts it this way:

> One of the most remarkable capacities of the human mind is the capacity to direct its attention to something it chooses. We can pause and say to our minds, "Think about this and not that." We can focus our attention on an idea, a picture, a problem, or a hope. It is an amazing power. . . . Humans have the amazing ability to think about thinking and to choose to dwell on an object of thought.
>
> This is a gift from God, part of his image in us. It is an immensely powerful means of becoming what we ought to be.[36]

In that pursuit, we celebrate the goodness of God's creation, the mysteries of the created order, of the beauty of God and his world.

Leisure is not vacation, napping, or even retreating, though each of these things may play a role in our pursuit of leisure. Leisure is a condition of the inner person, embracing what God has created him or her to be. Like Daniel, we can exhibit a worshiping heart as we work out the lawyer's calling. We celebrate our roles in continuing creation work, we reflect on what it means to be human, we stop and consider, we struggle with motherhood or fatherhood, we contemplate the sunset, or wonder why God created gnats. Leisure, in its true sense, is the quiet consideration of what is true, good, and beautiful, and it flows from worship of the One who is good.

Both workaholism and idleness are the enemies of the leisure. We can pursue work itself out of a true heart of worship, as workers created in the image of God. Yet when we use work to fill empty souls, to replace our obligation to set our minds on things that are beautiful, or to avoid reflection on our lives and purpose, then work stands in opposition to our callings in life. True work

---

[34]The following discussion relies on ibid., pp. 30-36.
[35]Ibid., p. 31.
[36]John Piper, *A Godward Life* (Sisters, Ore.: Multnomah, 1997), p. 228.

complements true leisure, but work as a tool for fulfillment or as an end in itself is *acedia* in the same sense that pure idleness is. Spiritual sluggishness can take either form: We might choose to fill our hours with mindless amusement, seeking to distract ourselves from the task of reflection and contemplation, or we might fill our hours with productive task after never-ending task, seeking to numb ourselves to the call to reflect and consider.

American culture is beset with both problems, and, in fact, they feed one another. We are obsessed with work as the means to happiness, and we fill our nonworking hours with mindless distraction or expensive toys. Cultural observer David Brooks notes that there are "two work ethics" layered into the American psyche. The first is the perversion of the Puritan work-ethic we discussed in chapter three, filtered through "the secularizing pen of Benjamin Franklin" and moralists preaching the gospel of work. "According to this ethic, it is through work, and our contribution to society, that we define ourselves. Far from being solely a thing you do, work is a way of justifying one's existence, of fulfilling one's purpose on earth, and of creating one's identity."[37] The other American work ethic, "layered on top of this Puritan sense of calling," is that work is the means to "grabbing the goodies." Brooks calls this the "abundance mentality" that believes that "fanatical work is always worth it, because it can be lavishly rewarded." Rising class status is part of the goal: if your neighbor can "pull himself up to the realm of Lexus drivers," someday you can too.[38] People fill their lives with the pursuit of abundance, waiting to be grabbed like candy in a candy shop. "It takes a force of willpower beyond that of most ordinary people to renounce all this glorious possibility. It's easier to work phenomenally long hours and grasp at all the candies than it is to say no. It takes incredible dedication to renounce opportunity, get off the conveyor, and be content with what one is."[39] This observation is a prophetic word to lawyers. Stop working to grasp the candies and *be content with what you are*—and first, take the time to discover who and what you are! This is true leisure, the last of the lawyer's disciplines.

Here are some practical suggestions on how we might stop and be content.

1. *Seek physical isolation.* In order to pursue true leisure, we should seek both inner and outward solitude, both an attitude of "deep inner silence"[40] and reg-

[37]David Brooks, *On Paradise Drive* (New York: Simon & Schuster, 2004), p. 227.
[38]Ibid., p. 228.
[39]Ibid., p. 229.
[40]Foster, *Celebration of Discipline*, p. 97.

ular physical separation from human contact. Jesus clearly had an inner solitude, and he also made it a point at significant times in his ministry to be alone. He was alone in the desert at the beginning of his ministry, he spent the night alone before he chose the Twelve, he "withdrew" from the crowds and even his closest disciples on a number of occasions, and he sought prayer in lonely places from the beginning of his ministry to the end at Gethsemane.[41] In the short Gospel accounts of Jesus' ministry we see him seeking solitude often. If our Lord had a need of solitude for his ministry, we do as well. Daniel too modeled this in his prayer life.

2. *Stop working so much.* Turn down clients. Hire more lawyers. Have a chat with your boss. You can do it.

3. *Stop pursing distractions and mere amusements.* When we do have "leisure" time, we often squander it in mindless activities that lead to idleness rather than leisure. The obvious culprit is television and the Internet, and we ought to fast from "screens" regularly. Television and the Internet serve a purpose, even providing some of the connection with the world that I spoke of earlier. Yet, for the most part, television and obsessive surfing inhibits our ability to think in ways that we need to think in order to love the Lord with all our minds.[42] Video games are not usually modes of recapturing true leisure. On the other hand, family board games, participatory sports, camping, walking, exercise, and reading will move us in the right direction. As with all the disciplines, our intent is important. We willfully choose or deny ourselves activities based on the exercise of solitude, reflection, contemplation, and leisure.

4. *Use the tools at your disposal.* When approached purposefully, conferences, personal and corporate retreats, and business trips can be opportunities for true leisure. Many of our normal activities may be opportunities for true leisure. What reading do you take with you on the road? What do you do when you are alone in your hotel room? Professional and academic conferences often provide food for thought and encourage more contemplative inner attitudes. Take advantage of that and plan some down time for walking and thinking, sitting and reading, or journaling during the conference. Set up an agenda in advance so you can look forward to your leisure time.

There are all kinds of planned retreats, such as the Emmaus Walk or various

---

[41]See ibid., p. 97, and Willard, *Spirit of the Disciplines,* p. 160.

[42]On the topic of television and habits of thought, see Neil Postman, *Amusing Ourselves to Death* (New York: Penguin, 1985).

kinds of silent retreats sponsored by churches or monasteries. Take advantage of what is offered and submit your time to the Lord. Create your own retreat at a camp or conference center in your area. Most retreat centers allow individuals to use the facilities for a lodging fee without need to participate in programming.

We might also make fruitful use of hobbies and other interests outside the law as means of deeper reflection on life. Go to the opera, attend the symphony or an art exhibition, make use of museums and libraries to stimulate the reflective image of God you bear. Likewise, devotional reading may be a means of entering into solitude. J. P. Moreland says that in devotional reading, we should read "slowly and with attentiveness." "The goal is to deepen and nourish the soul by entering into the passage and allowing it to be assimilated into one's whole personality."[43]

Even aptitude testing and spiritual gift inventories can be used as means to reflect on your life, calling, and purpose. Use every opportunity to slow down, to reflect, and consider your ways.

5. *Consider.* What might we consider during our times of solitude? There are hundreds of possibilities, of course. We should "consider our ways," consider how to "number our days aright" and to think of ourselves as we ought to. In addition, we should set our minds on things above and on what is good, and noble, and true, and right (Philippians 4:8). That should get us started. In addition, we should spend some time evaluating our roles as father, husband, elder, lawyer, son, and Cub Scout leader or as mother, wife, teacher, lawyer, and board member. What are we doing with our time? Is it worth it? Is it God's call on my life, or am I wasting his resources? What should my law practice look like? How is my prayer life? We have much to think about.

6. *Pray.* Finally, prayer is at the heart of leisure. In fact, so are the other disciplines: fasting, meditation, and silence. Practice these disciplines too, but above all don't neglect prayer. Sure, it earned Daniel a trip to the lion's den, but it transformed his world and gave him great prosperity in his law practice, to boot!

Like study and fellowship, the discipline of solitude will help us attack our stumbling blocks on several fronts. First, true leisure is the anti-*acedia,* the de-

---

[43]Moreland, *Love Your God with All Your Mind,* p. 164.

finitive solution to the lack of caring at the heart of instrumentalist jurisprudence. Our intentional pursuit of a worshiping life of contemplation and solitude will lead us to the good, the true, and the beautiful in the law (see chap. 2). The solitude of real leisure will also jump start the dead battery of the lawyer's mind. Thinking correctly is a chief byproduct of solitude under the supervision of Scripture and the Holy Spirit. Finally, as we contemplate our work, our duties before God and our callings in every area of life, we will learn to submit all things to Christ in worship. If we will be still and know that he is God (Psalm 46:10), we will come to see clearly the unity of life in the world under his Lordship. We'll see past the ordinary religion of the law school classroom, escape false sacred-secular dualisms, and engage the mind in new and exciting ways to the glory of God.

Conclusion

The practical application of our commitments to unity, community, and truth are truly vast, but I've tried to identify some basic practices that will help us cooperate with the work of God in transforming us into lawyers of integrity. Our goal is to become the kind of people that do naturally—automatically—what Christian lawyers should do in every circumstance. We seek to become who God wants us to be, and then we will more easily follow what he wants us to do. Rather than managing our conduct so carefully, we should desire to change the way we think about God, about ourselves, about law, about the created world, and about our role in the creation. Our actions will follow.

The suggested disciplines of study, fellowship, and solitary worship (or leisure) will help put lawyers in a position to more easily and naturally follow through on commitments to the noncompartmentalized life, to community, and to truth, both in our inner person and as the standard by which we live. Through this process of integration of the whole person, our law practices and lives will be changed by the power of God, and we will notice areas of weakness, strongholds, and even barriers to service we've erected or that otherwise stand in our path. The road will be cleared for the pursuit of Christ in the legal academy, the courts, and law practices.

In part two I have described and discussed the underlying commitments to integrity, their relationship to the stumbling blocks, and some practices that will help us realize our commitment to unity, community, and truth. Let's move to more specific issues in the lawyer's world and inquire whether our commitments and practices will be any help at all with the professional struggles we face every day.

For Further Thought

1. Evaluate your own practice of the inward, corporate, and outward disciplines. Pick one specific practice that would help build integrity into your life. Write down a plan for building it into your week this week and pray through it.
2. Do you meet with a small group regularly? If you do not, develop a plan of action to create or join a small group. Talk with your pastor about it.
3. Do you know other Christian lawyers (or law students) that might be willing to get together occasionally to talk about life in the law? Give them a call and set up a meeting. Discuss whether there would be any possibility of meeting together—even for a monthly luncheon—to discuss faith and work.
4. Do you have a reading schedule? What is keeping you from reading the books that you want to read? Talk to your family or mentor about ways that you can fit serious study into your schedule.
5. Plan a personal retreat that will last three or four hours. Plan to spend some of your time just thinking about your life and calling. Spend some time in prayer and some time just enjoying the setting (wherever it is). Write down your insights before you close your time. Would it be possible to create mini-retreats like this within your work week—even if they were only an hour long?

PART THREE

INTEGRITY IN PRACTICE

10

Professional Identity, Integrity, and Modernity

Why won't sharks attack lawyers? Professional courtesy.

Where do vampires learn to suck blood? Law school.

What's the difference between a herd of buffalo and a lawyer? The lawyer charges more.

Of course, there's a problem with lawyer jokes. We don't think they're funny, and nobody else thinks they're jokes. (Get it?)

Blood-sucking, money-grubbing, overcharging sharks. This doesn't sound like good-natured ribbing. Many folks who know legal culture and the world of lawyers truly hold these opinions, or they're just barely kidding. Of course, many lawyers willingly step into the persona too. For example, on Central Expressway in Dallas, just north of downtown, there is large building that houses a law office. On top, with the firm's phone number, is a thirty-foot plastic shark for every Dallas driver to admire. And a divorce firm in Georgia has "divorce sharks" as part of its web domain name. Apparently, lawyers look like sharks from both inside and outside the tank. Abraham Lincoln put the issue a bit more subtly:

> There is a vague popular belief that lawyers are necessarily dishonest. I say vague, because when we consider to what extent confidence and honors are reposed in and conferred upon lawyers by the people, it appears improbable that their impression of dishonesty is very distinct and vivid. Yet the impression is common, almost universal.[1]

What is going on here?

---

[1]Abraham Lincoln, *Speeches and Writings 1832-1858* (New York: Library of America, 1989), p. 245.

Role Morality and Professional Identity

First, perceptions may be different from reality. Many laypeople perceive that the lawyer's duty to the client is a blind one, completely devoid of moral considerations, entailing a partisan seeking of any of the client's stated ends by any means within the parameters of the rules of ethics, which means might include shading the truth, intimidating witnesses, and hiding evidence. This is certainly a caricature, but one that fits the expectations of much of the lay public. Of course, despite the caricature, the experience of most people who have hired lawyers or go to church with them blunts the perception. While lawyers may talk too much, think they know everything, or generally take over in group settings, they are a far cry from the bloodsucking leeches portrayed in the jokes. In addition, as the quote from Lincoln implies, *specific* lawyers have too much credibility in the eyes of the public for the public's *general* views about lawyers to hold sway as to individual lawyers in one's local congregation or Rotary Club.

Second, however, the prevailing vision among law professors, students, and lawyers is not too far from the caricature of blind duty to the client. Professor Joseph Allegretti believes that the "standard vision of the lawyer's role," resting on the adversary system, leads to the conclusion that the lawyer is like the "proverbial hired gun of the old west." He doesn't like this "standard vision," but finds it to be the dominant paradigm: "The lawyer is the neutral partisan of his client" and does whatever he can to achieve his client's goals, remaining neutral regarding the moral justification of those goals, at least once the representation is undertaken.[2] Allegretti calls this "The Code." Professor Thomas Shaffer calls this "the principle of suspended conscience."[3]

Some lawyers will tell you that this description of the "standard vision" is itself an overstatement of the adversary system and doesn't take into account the nuance and history that actually informs the lawyer's practices, while others will agree that this vision really is in line with the law school training they received and the practices they observe. The truth is that there is substantial disagreement as to what—and whose—moral considerations are "in play" in a legal representation. But it is true that "the ethic of zeal is a traditional aspira-

---

[2]Joseph Allegretti, *The Lawyer's Calling* (New York: Paulist Press, 1996), p. 9.

[3]Thomas L. Shaffer, *On Being a Christian and a Lawyer* (Provo, Utah: Brigham Young University Press, 1981), p. 7.

tion . . . and zealousness [on the client's behalf] continues today to be '*the* fundamental principle of the law of lawyering' and the dominant standard of lawyerly excellence.' "[4] In any event, Allegretti is certainly close to the mark when he concludes:

> All lawyers are heavily influenced by this dominant paradigm. This is what the law schools teach and what the adversary system presupposes. Some lawyers rebel against it, but no one can escape its force. For most lawyers, it is like the air they breathe: invisible, taken for granted, but indispensable to their daily lives.[5]

This conclusion is also borne out by a recent empirical study of young lawyers,[6] which confirms that most of the respondent young lawyers resolved moral conflict by role-morality; that is, they ignored the moral consequences of their lawyering and focused on only their role as advocates resolving purely legal issues.[7]

No matter how we much we dislike this characterization of the "dominant paradigm," our professional identity and cultural stereotypes are indeed major sources of struggle for Christian lawyers, so we need to deal with it. I suggest that we must deal with it as lawyers of integrity, consistent with our commitments to unity, truth, and community. In this chapter I'll try to sort through some options and then develop a possible integrated response. In doing so, we'll see that this struggle implicates the stumbling blocks we've already discussed, and even more interestingly that it is rooted in the very nature of modernity and the general cultural habits of thought that have infected the church and believers within the profession. The pursuit of a solution to the professional identity problem will therefore require us to address the mode of life and thinking that we call modernity, as well as its natural offspring, postmodernity. In evaluating our response to modern professionalism, we will of necessity solidify our approach to the lawyer's calling and the centrality of integrity.

---

[4]Monroe Freedman and Abbe Smith, *Understanding Lawyer's Ethics* (Newark, N.J.: Lexis-Nexis, 2004), p. 71.

[5]Allegetti, *Lawyer's Calling,* p. 9.

[6]Robert Granfield and Thomas Koenig, "It's Hard to Be a Human Being and Lawyer: Young Attorneys and the Confrontation with ethical Ambiguity in Legal Practice," *West Virginia Law Review* 105 (2003). My thanks to my colleague Natt Gantt for pointing this out to me. See Larry O. Natt Gantt II, "Integration as Integrity: Postmodernism, Psychology, and Religion on the Role of Moral Counseling in the Attorney-Client Relationship," *Regent University Law Review* 16 (2003-2004): 233-34.

[7]Gantt, "Integration as Integrity," p. 234.

I'll frame our discussion around the work of Christian legal ethics scholars who have identified the issues and provided an excellent roadmap for possible solutions. I'll begin by examining Allegretti's "four models"—four possible Christian responses to "the standard vision," which he calls the "Code."[8]

Christian Responses to the Standard Vision

In *The Lawyer's Calling,* Allegretti outlines four standard responses ("varying self-images") adopted by Christian lawyers in response to the Code—the prevailing hired gun view.[9]

Christian lawyer: Oxymoron. The first model is to react to the hired gun and decide that a Christian can't be a lawyer. Because the prevailing paradigm does indeed, at least as articulated, conflict with our commitment to unity—we are not simultaneously two moral beings, one a lawyer, the other a human—many Christians reject any possibility for the service of Christ in the law profession, sometimes even after they have already made it through law school. Allegretti calls this response "Christ Against the Code."

In my view, Christians who respond in this way exhibit an unsatisfactory approach to evaluating the problem under our four commitments. First, it capitulates to the "prevailing view" uncritically and avoids both historical and theological worldview analysis of the adversary system and the lawyer's role. To put the question in terms of our worldview commitment (see chap. 8), those who abandon the law so easily have not evaluated the *creational structure* of the institutions their decision is based on. Is the civil justice system part of the progressive development of God's good created order, which, though it is tainted by the Fall, he is working to restore? And is the adversary system part of civilization that has been built on God's good creation that can be "pushed" toward him, or is it simply an unreformable product of the Fall, moving irretrievably away from God's purposes? If not the latter, then a kingdom-minded approach would be to evaluate how lawyers might be useful in pushing the direction of the system toward restoration—toward obedience to God's created order—his law.

In addition, our commitment to community, particularly involving saints of the past, might also advise against this first model. To early American and

[8]Allegretti, *Lawyer's Calling,* p. 10.
[9]Ibid., pp. 7-23.

English lawyers, the amoral hired gun was not a necessary consequence of the adversary system, as so many have argued. There may be other pictures of the adversary system that we are missing in our modern biases. In fact, the suspended conscience model is at least partly a creature that rose from the murky swamp not too long ago alongside the instrumentalist turn in American jurisprudence. Professor Shaffer notes, for example, that both David Hoffman (1836) and George Sharswood (1876) vehemently denied "the idea that a lawyer may suspend his conscience" in favor of a client's.[10] This alone should at least open us up to the possibilities that the "standard vision" is not irrevocable or unbending, and spur us on to further evaluate it biblically.

The system made me do it. A second unsatisfactory response of Christian lawyers is to hide behind "the system" itself. Allegretti calls this response "Christ in harmony with the Code" because it assumes that the hired-gun persona is in harmony with service to Christ; after all, "that's the system we've got." I have found this to be the most common attitude among Christian students and lawyers (see chap. 8). Allegretti comments that Americans are particularly loyal to "democratic ideals" and, by extension, to the adversary system itself. "It is natural for American lawyers," he says, "who are taught to honor the adversary system above all else, to embrace the Code almost as an expression of divine intent."[11] I have seen this confirmed time and again in my work with Christian students.

This "harmony" model, like the first model, also reflects a lack of theological insight into the role of lawyers and the nature of work as a calling. We cannot love our neighbors in the law if we owe an uncritical allegiance to a system. This is true regardless of whether the system is an inherently moral one. The point is that it is impossible to serve Christ with integrity without a critical biblical evaluation of the system. Here too discerning *direction* as part of our commitment to truth is important. Our inquiry may lead to us to conclude that the Fall has tainted the adversary system such that it is improper to adopt any allegiance to it as one's moral standard. On the other hand, and most likely, discerning direction may lead us to believe that we may rely on "the system" in some ways but not in others.

For example, in some cases, we may be able to rely on the systemic advocacy

---

[10]Shaffer, *On Being a Christian and a Lawyer*, pp. 6-7.
[11]Allegretti, *Lawyer's Calling*, p. 15.

principle that separates a lawyer from his or client. Perhaps, though, a Christian lawyer may represent the otherwise reprehensible American Nazi Party on the ground that its right to freedom of speech is so important that even wrong ideas may not be suppressed by the government.[12] To justify this representation, a Christian lawyer might argue that the end of the representation is inherently—and structurally—good (and morally right). On the other hand, the system may not work to shield the lawyer from complicity in evil when the entire purpose of the representation is to further an evil practice, such as pornography or abortion.[13] In fact, there may be other cases where evil will result—perhaps even the case of the Nazis—where more thorough philosophical and theological inquiry is necessary. The point is that we must evaluate our identity and calling before God, rather than accepting the modern sleight of hand that tells us we are automatically morally separated from out legal work.[14]

In addition, our commitments to community would likely lead us into further biblical criticisms of the system as our sole moral compass, as we seek to discern where and whether our involvement in the system will result in love to our neighbors, whether they be inside or outside the system. Schurmann, for example, points out that the doctrine of vocation can be abused by the powerful "to perpetuate abuse of the weak and subordinated members of society." Our respect for the value of all work as important "can slide into slothful neglect for the Spirit's gifts, avoidance of the opportunities for more needed service elsewhere, and quietist acceptance of a corrupt but changeable status quo."[15] If the system—or even parts of it—is corrupt, but changeable, it is our duty to rise and challenge the corruption.

Disintegration. Third, Allegretti suggests that lawyers often respond by simply compartmentalizing their lives—living as human beings at home, at church, and in most of their relationships, but living the life of the "amoral lawyer" at work. We have a private realm and a work realm. I have already ad-

---

[12]A Jewish lawyer represented the Nazis in 1977 to establish their right to march in a heavily Jewish Chicago neighborhood. Philippa Strum, *When the Nazis Came to Skokie* (Lawrence: University Press of Kansas, 1999).

[13]See Teresa Stanton Collett, "Speak No Evil, Seek No Evil, Do No Evil: Client Selection and Cooperation with Evil," *Fordham Law Review* 66 (1998): 1339. Professor Collett sets out a helpful theological and philosophical approach, bolstered by examples and stories, to making these difficult decisions.

[14]Ibid.

[15]Schuurman, *Vocation*, pp. 77-78.

dressed this dualism at length (see chap. 3), and it is the very essence of the disintegrated life. Again, one reason that Christian lawyers ignore the particular call to a life in the law is that they don't have a kingdom perspective. That is, they don't see that God's restoration of his good creation has already begun, and so they see only other-worldly concerns as important. Law practice is, in this view, simply part of the world that is going to hell in a hand basket anyway: "I'm really a citizen of heaven, and all this will burn. I need to pay attention in church, share the gospel when I can, and give my money to evangelization efforts. After all, I've got to feed my family. It's only a job." This model exhibits, by definition, a lack of integrity: no truth-seeking, no connection to community, no vocational evaluation, and a completely dualistic life. This fails our integrity test with flying colors.

Transforming the standard vision. The lawyer's typical apologetic, for the most part, consists of one of these three unbiblical justifications for the Christian life in the law. These are not very convincing (even to the lawyers making them, in my experience!) and obviously reflect shallow—and faithless—thinking. Allegretti rightly summarizes that they all "undermine the connection between a lawyer's faith-life and work-life."[16]

In response, Allegretti suggests that a fourth response is necessary, one that recognizes that "a lawyer's faith is relevant to his work."[17] This "transforming" response will assert that "Christ is Lord of all, even of the legal profession, and that Christians are called to serve Christ in all of life, even their life as professionals. It rejects the artificial separation of life into private and public spheres, with faith-commitments relevant only to the private."[18] In short, there is no artificial identity, only our true identity with Christ as his co-heirs and servants in the callings to which he has called. Allegretti calls this "Christ Transforming the Code."[19] We might call this simply the integrated lawyer's calling.

In the mainstream academic literature, there has been much talk about the identity crisis, but the trouble has always been that there is no other story, no alternative, no ideal other than the artificial role morality. Even the modern alternatives such as the "lawyer-statesman" suggested by the Yale law dean (see p. 78), are hollow and artificial. In all the talk of identity, most commentators

---

[16]Allegretti, *Lawyer's Calling,* p. 20.
[17]Ibid., p. 21.
[18]Ibid.
[19]Ibid., pp. 20-22.

persist in treating "the lawyer" as something adopted, something put on, apart from the *person*. "Can a lawyer be a good person?" is a common question, as if we were seeking the reconciliation of two distinct entities. In addition, any headway that has been made in the academic literature is often lost on practitioners; it has apparently failed to trickle down to the profession or the general public. Any truly transforming vision will reject the disintegrated lawyer-person approach in favor of an alternative vision that values vocation, love of neighbor, and truth.

There have been a handful of helpful suggestions over the years in the pursuit of an integrated lawyer identity, and I want to explore some of them in light of our discussion thus far.

Moral Conversation and the Transforming Vision

The principle of the lawyer's suspended conscience is based in "role morality." As we've seen here and in our discussions on vocation (chap. 3) and unity (chap. 6), when we adopt a disintegrating approach to life, we are not fully submitted to Christ or fully engaged in his ongoing work in creation—civilization. Vocational thinking helps us to submit to Christ *across all of our roles and callings;* our duties to him infuse every particular role. Role morality, on the other hand, focuses on one's lawyer-ness and the responsibilities that come with it, to the exclusion of all else whenever one is acting as a lawyer. Under this view, one's lawyer-ness is all-encompassing and self-defining. Nothing outside of the profession is helpful for the lawyer's normative guidance.

Professor Shaffer begins his discussion of the lawyer-client relationship by evaluating this "role ethics." He adds an interesting admonition to our considerations so far, by pointing out that even if lawyers take a step further and decide that their morality should govern the clients' actions, they are *still engaging in role ethics;* rather than suspending my conscience, I demand, paternalistically, that the client suspend his or her conscience. "So dominant is this role-associated approach to morals in law practice that moral debates within the profession usually assume that . . . the choice is between doing what the client wants and telling the client what the client wants."[20] He adds that when we so limit our choices, we are "delusional" about roles. In one case, "the

[20]Shaffer, *On Being a Christian and a Lawyer*, p. 6.

delusion is that the lawyer has no conscience;" in the other, "the delusion is that the client has no conscience."[21]

The role-ethics approach is disintegrative, of course, and Shaffer correctly argues that both the lawyer's and the client's conscience must be "in play" in their relationship. His ultimate solution is that we must practice an "ethics of care," which recognizes that lawyers and clients learn morally from one another. To do that, they must recognize that they are not "moral islands" and that authentic interaction and moral conversation is necessary. This is not role playing, it is human relationship, where both client and lawyer reciprocally love their neighbor. Shaffer discusses several important characteristics of lawyering based on moral conversation:

> **THE "SYSTEM" AND THE MORAL LAWYER**
>
> **We suggest that lawyers have a moral responsibility for what they know and for what they do. Their responsibility is complicated by the responsibility (also a moral responsibility) that lawyers have to clients, but lawyers should not hide from the complications of the moral life behind the illusion that the adversary system will yield the just result.**
>
> **The issue is not whether moral soundness in life is easy. It is whether lawyers are disabled from pursuing moral soundness. Certainly, determining the directions indicated by justice and mercy may be difficult.**
>
> THOMAS L. SHAFFER AND ROBERT F. COCHRAN JR., *LAWYERS, CLIENTS, AND MORAL RESPONSIBILITY*

- Clients and lawyers will influence each other, so both will need to be open to change.
- A moral conversation requires time and space suitable for reflection.
- Full information is required from both sides, and there is collaboration on the means and ends of the representation.
- The lawyer treats his or her client as if the client is "a child of God" who has been sent to him or her.
- This moral discourse involves risk, and both parties must be open to change.
- A lawyer must develop real professional skills to be able to foster such a relationship; therefore, lawyers must become morally attentive and law students should be trained in "skills of sincerity, congruence, and acceptance."

[21]Ibid., p. 8.

Shaffer concludes by answering the question "Is it possible to be a Christian and a Lawyer?"

> To the extent that one determines to conduct his practice as moral conversation, his advocacy as moral discourse, his lawyer skill as the virtue of hope, his life as an affirmation that justice is a gift and not a commodity one has from the government, I think it is possible to be a Christian and a lawyer.[22]

Though this is a bit of an oversimplification of Shaffer's work, and does not begin to delve into his further conclusions regarding the problems in the relationship, it is clear that the centerpiece of Shaffer's influential vision of the Christian lawyer's calling is this moral conversation, where both lawyer and client grow and pursue proper ends together. Shaffer, in collaboration with Professor Robert Cochran, has continued to develop this approach to professional identity in their ethics text. They conclude that the lawyer's moral conversation is primarily about "client goodness" rather than client victory, autonomy, or rectitude.[23]

> Lawyers who are concerned with client goodness will be concerned with all of these things [client success, freedom, and rectitude] because they are concerned with the client as a whole person, but they will also be concerned with the person the client is becoming as the client is, inevitably, influenced by the lawyer.[24]

Moral conversation and client goodness is an excellent ideal, and it is a good place to begin our pursuit of professional integrity. It's so attractive and so obviously right—why aren't we all doing it?[25] Why hasn't it become the dominant paradigm? I want to continue our discussion by observing the difficulty we face in pursuit of this integrative vision, and then suggest some practices that may enable us to do so more confidently.

Moral Isolation and Modernity

An instructive place to begin our discussion of the problems of the inte-

---

[22]Ibid., p. 32.

[23]Thomas L. Shaffer and Robert F. Cochran Jr., *Lawyers, Clients, and Moral Responsibility* (New York: West, 1994), pp. 40-54.

[24]Ibid., p. 44.

[25]I have no doubt that there are many hundreds of lawyers practicing this way, and many, many more who aspire to it. Yet it is neither discussed nor pursued by most practitioners and law professors.

grated vision of professionalism is, again, with Shaffer. In addition to the "ethics of role." and the ultimate "ethics of care," he discusses a middle ground, which he also rejects, the "ethics of isolation." The lawyers who practice it assume, as in the ethics of care, that the moral conscience of both the lawyer and client are "in play" in the relationship, but, unlike the ethics of care, their "moral positions are merely asserted and either accepted or rejected." There is no openness to change or true moral give and take. Rather than abandoning either the client's or the lawyer's conscience, this approach places them both on the table, to either take or leave. The moral positions are made known, but there is no conversation. While the ethics of role—the hired-gun paradigm—may be the standard vision for the profession at large, I think the ethics of isolation accurately describes the dominant approach of Christian lawyers in practice. We tell the client what we will or will not do, and the client tells us what he or she will or will not do. Then we take it or leave it.

Ethics of isolation are easy to practice today, because it reflects who we are as moderns. The ethics of isolation highlights the characteristic fragmentation of both the modern world and its continuation into "late modernity" or postmodernism.

Colin Gunton summed up the problem of modernity as a problem of "displacement": The displacement of God "into human subjectivity," and the displacement of others, though disengagement from one another.[26] "The key word is *instrumental*: we use the other as an instrument, as the mere means for realizing our will, and not as in some way integral to our being."[27] In modern thought and culture, human reason and will has replaced God as the unifying center of reality. This leads to fragmentation, because if the world is "unified" only by individuals, there is no shared ground for society. The problem of modernity, then, is the displacement of God as the unifying source of coherence and meaning, the disengagement from our neighbors, and a resulting fragmentation of society.

Postmodernism, with respect to this disengagement and fragmentation, is simply a continuation of modernity.[28] Of course, it is also, in some respects, a re-

---

[26]Colin Gunton, *The One, the Three and the Many: God, Creation and the Culture of Modernity* (Cambridge: Cambridge University Press, 1993), p. 71.
[27]Ibid., p. 14.
[28]Ibid., p. 69.

action against it.[29] But both have disengagement at their core: modernism excludes the other, while postmodernism renders the other irrelevant.[30] As Gunton puts it, there is "no single idea of modernity so much as a family of dogmas and practices, among which is postmodernity."[31] Of course there are important differences between modernity and postmodernity,[32] but their continuity in terms of fundamental disengagement, social instrumentalism, and the displacement of God with the autonomous individual will illuminate our present discussion.

The ethics of isolation neatly illustrates, in the lawyer-client context, the fragmented, disengaged modern world. For example, in the ethics of isolation "the assumption . . . is that the lawyer and client both operate in moral worlds but that their worlds are isolated from one another." Likewise, speaking of the isolation ethic in the classroom, Shaffer says "Student answers in the law school moral conversation tend to be of the form, 'I would/would not do that.' Sometimes answers are of the form, 'I just would/would not do that. I'm sorry about it, but it's the way I am, and I am the way I am because I was raised (in the South) (in parochial schools) (by a good Baptist mother).' "[33] In other words, that's how I am, take it or leave it. Shaffer concludes, "Isolation implies that morals are a private affair; they are asserted, not talked about, which is to suppose that morals are not important, literally not *worth* talking about."[34] The ethics of isolation might well be called the ethics of modernity, for it captures much of modernity's character.

The countercultural task. On one hand, this discussion of the problem of modernity as isolation is a near recapitulation in broad sociological terms of our three stumbling blocks: loss of moral center and the rise of instrumentalism in

---

[29]On the important postmodern critique of modernity from a Christian perspective, see Smith, *Who's Afraid of Postmodernism?* and Crystal L. Downing, *How Postmodernism Serves (My) Faith* (Downers Grove, Ill.: InterVarsity Press, 2006).

[30]Ziauddin Sardar, quoted in Gunton, *The One, the Three and the Many,* p. 69.

[31]Colin Gunton, *The One, the Three and the Many,* p. 12.

[32]There are indeed significant differences, even for our purposes in the law. Modernism, while displacing God with the individual as the unifying force in the universe, still holds to the possibility of objective and universal truth. Postmodernism embraces subjectivism and relativism, albeit in ways made possible by modernity, but in such a way as to reject even modernism's reliance on something as fundamental as propositional truth. On important differences in jurisprudence, see Dennis Patterson, "Postmodern Jurisprudence," *Law and Truth* (New York: Oxford University Press, 1996).

[33]Shaffer, *On Being a Christian and a Lawyer,* p. 17.

[34]Ibid.

legal education, compartmentalization and role morality in thinking about calling, and the loss of a rational basis for the unity of theological truth (see chaps. 2, 3, and 4, respectively). In addition, it reminds us of our commitments: the displacement of God is addressed by our commitment to unity (chap. 6), disengagement from the other is addressed by a commitment to community (chap. 7), and subjectivism is taken on by the commitment to truth (chap. 8).

On the other hand, recognition that the problem of professional identity is wrapped up in the problem of modernity (and postmodernity, if you prefer) demonstrates the complexity of our task: we can't just "try to do better" or read our Bible more faithfully or determine to adopt the "ethics of care." The task of following Christ in the law is morally difficult and requires practice, wisdom, and virtue. It requires that we *be* something in relation to God and other creatures. In this sense, our discussion in this chapter builds on chapter nine's emphasis on the lawyer's disciplines. To overcome the spirit of the modern world, we need to develop habits of thought and conduct that match up with the Spirit of the kingdom. The fact is that we are ourselves modern lawyers, and the call to walk Christianly in law involves a self-conscious, intentional resistance to much of the way of life we are immersed in.

There is some doubt too whether we are equipped for the task. The "dogmas and habits of thought" that make the modern world what it is make it difficult for us to practice the things we think are central to the integrative task. It is good to decide that the ethics of care (or some other transforming vision) is the solution to our identity confusion. But we are immersed in a world where it is difficult to practice such an ethic. The reality is that we cannot simply choose the ethics of care over the ethics of isolation—we don't know *how* to practice the ethics of care!

My colleague Natt Gantt has spent some time exploring important connections between role morality (the "ethics of role" in Shaffer's terms), integrity, and postmodernism (late modernism, if you like), and he suggests that lawyers "neglect" moral conversation with clients because the dominant cultural worldview makes it difficult to "integrate their moral concerns into their legal counseling."[35] He demonstrates that both "social and philosophical obstacles" of modernity make integration difficult.[36]

[35]Gantt, "Integration as Integrity," p. 241.

[36]Ibid., p. 241, citing MacIntyre, *After Virtue*, p. 204.

The social obstacles come, not surprisingly, from fragmentation: "work is divided from leisure, private life from public, and corporate from the personal."[37] This is the root of the compartmentalization that inhibits vocational thinking in the church as well (see chap. 3). If there are some places or times wherein we are not moral beings, then moral understandings that guide our lives, say, on Sundays, cannot speak to us there. Moral integration is simply irrelevant when a lawyer divorces private morality from public life and work. This compartmentalization, moreover, can be exacerbated by the nature of some law practice. With minute specialization and large-scale litigation, both client conversation, moral or otherwise, and big-picture moral reasoning become secondary to the technical aspects of the legal issues. The fragmentation of modernity works against us in a number of ways.

In addition to fragmentation—the social obstacle to the moral conversation—postmodernism (or late modernism) also presents philosophical obstacles, reinforcing the hired-gun vision of law practice and encouraging ways of thought that discourage moral dialogue. These obstacles to moral conversation flow naturally from dominant philosophical characteristics of postmodernism: (1) the relegation of religion to the merely personal and the tendency to moral relativism, (2) the resulting illegitimacy of public discourse on religion and moral integration, and (3) modernity's view of the individual and the individual's view of the self.[38] Because these directly oppose the moral conversation so important to the lawyer's calling, let's look into the consequences of each.

Subjective religion. The first two issues flow from the modern drive to displace God. Postmodernism privatizes religion in a social sense in a similar way to which modernism privatizes it in the political sense. Early modernism displaced God politically by making him irrelevant to any political or cultural task. Religion is fine—in fact, God may be real and powerful—but "your" faith is irrelevant in the public square. Even if there is a cosmic order or an abiding truth at the heart of the universe, we have no confidence in our ability to know and apply it to civil polity. This should bring to mind our discussions regarding Richard Posner's brand of philosophical pragmatism (see pp. 34-35). Late modernism, likewise, displaces religion, but adds the social dimension. Religion has social significance, for it sustains important social groups, but there

---

[37]Gantt, "Integration as Integrity," p. 241, citing MacIntyre, *After Virtue*, p. 204.
[38]Gantt, "Integration as Integrity," pp. 240-62.

is no cosmic significance, no hegemony, no reality about God at work. God is himself a human artifact, a social construct that we use, just as we use others to provide meaning in a world that revolves around me.[39] The catch phrase here is "whatever works for you."

There are consequences of this displacement for the moral conversations we seek in law. There is no longer common moral ground or a common source for a concept of the common good. All that remains is some gut sense of propriety, or even less helpful, a code of professional ethics. As Professor Cochran points out, an appeal to professionalism as a moral ideal is pretty uninspiring to the postmodern world:

> The leaders of the profession call on lawyers to go beyond the incentives of the market and beyond the requirements of the professional rules—to seek justice, to be more honest and tolerant, to be less adversarial and selfish, and to give more of their time and resources to the poor. They call on law professors to instill these values in law students. The moral basis for this call to service is our status as professionals. The word "professionalism" appears almost as a mantra, a word which if repeated often enough will release mystical moral power. But, whatever power it once had, calls to professionalism no longer seem to inspire.[40]

Professionalism is indeed a poor substitute for relevant faith, which has always driven morality. Given the postmodern preference for merely "personal" faith, it is unlikely that even Professor Cochran's suggestion that lawyers seek meaning, each from his or her own religious tradition, will have much traction.[41]

Ironically, subjectivism has produced a good number of twisted moralists. The postmodernist says, If it is *true* for me, it is also *right* for me.[42] Our subjective "truths" have turned into objective rights, all the while believing, to paraphrase Gene Veith, there is no virtue but tolerance, nothing false but to believe in truth, and no sin but to believe in sin. This, of course, has consequences for law and policy too. If there are no moral grounds for truth, then law itself is in danger; it becomes simply a power struggle to see who has the

---

[39]I owe this formulation to my colleague C. Scott Pryor. See also Newbigin's *Foolishness to the Greeks* on the public/private distinction in modernity; and Downing's *How Postmodernism Serves (My) Faith* on the relativistic tendencies in postmodernism.

[40]Robert Cochran, *Professionalism in the Postmodern Age,* quoted in Gantt, "Integration as Integrity," p. 242.

[41]Cochran, *Professionalism in the Postmodern Age,* pp. 318-20.

[42]See Gene Edward Veith, *Postmodern Times* (Wheaton, Ill.: Crossway, 1994), p. 195.

right to exercise sheer will. That, indeed, is the legacy of modernism in the law. The combination of "desires make rights" and "power is the source of law" is deadly to moral vision. Law becomes a place where desires and choices become rights.

Privatized religion. The second philosophical problem of modernism is religion's loss of its place in the public square.[43] As Newbigin puts it, "The dichotomy between the private and public worlds is fundamental to modern Western culture."[44] The axiom "religion is the business of the church and home and has no place in public" is "part of the American way."[45] This phenomenon has been chronicled heavily over the past two decades, so I won't belabor the facts here. My point is that this state of affairs works to discourage even lawyers inclined to moral discourse. It is a matter of "cultural etiquette" to avoid penetrating moral dialogue.[46]

Realistically, though, it is not as if attorneys are actually pressured to avoid moral conversations necessary to a transforming law practice. We have not been kicked out of the public square; we have abandoned it through fear. We have not been forbidden to morally engage our clients; we have failed to attempt it. We have ourselves been transformed by modernism. We have a vague sense in the back of our minds that it may not be all right to have moral conversations in the law office based on religious understandings of the world. We wonder, perhaps even subconsciously, if it might even be sinful to "impose our views" on someone else. We doubt our very ability to know what is true, good and beautiful, even in the law, our own area of expertise and training! Even worse, we are afraid that our postmodern clients might think poorly of us if we do seek to engage in moral conversation with them—*Well,* we tell ourselves, *they are not interested in this discussion anyway.* So we chicken out.

The fragmented self. Professor Gantt's most important observation develops the implications of the third philosophical problem that postmodernism causes lawyers: the postmodern self. The key characteristic of a postmodern view of the human person is "fragmented." Gantt writes that the individual

---

[43]Gantt, "Integration as Integrity," p. 244. See also Richard John Neuhaus, *The Naked Public Square* (Grand Rapids: Eerdmans, 1984).

[44]Newbigin, *Foolishness to the Greeks,* p. 15.

[45]Neuhaus, *Naked Public Square,* p. 20.

[46]Gantt, "Integration as Integrity," p. 244.

self "is not fixed but varies from context to context and is subject to widely varying and often competing social and cultural influences."[47] Veith, likewise, describes postmoderns as "highly oriented toward playing roles."[48] While the doctrine of vocation teaches that we have different roles but our identity is consistent within those roles and centered on the person of Christ, postmodern thought "insists that there is no identity apart from our social roles."[49] We're all just acting, playing language games to manipulate the social circumstance we find ourselves in. There is no "real" identity; no unified person. Given our emphasis on the lawyer's vocation and role, the implications for Christian lawyers are significant:

> If society begins to see the individual as lacking a coherent core self, lawyers are likely to find it easier to see their lawyering roles as unrelated to their other roles in life—roles like parent, spouse, or friend. The temptation would be especially strong when conflicts develop among the roles. . . . Postmodern fragmentation, coupled with this internal drive to avoid cognitive dissonance, could exacerbate role separation. Lawyers facing role conflicts could simply divorce the personal from the professional. Unless they are trained to view their lawyer role with moral overtones, which is unlikely in today's legal culture, lawyers could cut morality from lawyering with the crisp click of the postmodern scissors.[50]

In short, the very air we breathe in the postmodern atmosphere encourages almost every disintegrative habit we've addressed. The very act of integration is challenged head-on by our lack of moral resources for the task.

Professor Gantt points out that personality theories in psychology demonstrate that fragmented role morality can actually have harmful psychological effects and lead to "emotional maladjustment." Because we are created to maintain an integrated self, it should be no surprise that disintegration causes problems. On the other hand, a person must make fairly complex metaphysical evaluations in order to maintain an integrated self yet still be able to justify why changes in role or circumstances justify changes in conduct. In short, we must be able to distinguish among our roles and responsibilities—we are multifaceted—without becoming a different person everywhere we go and in everything we do—we are not fragmented. Any healthy individual has differ-

---

[47]Ibid., p. 245.
[48]Veith, *Postmodern Times,* p. 84.
[49]Ibid., p. 84.
[50]Gantt, "Integration as Integrity," p. 247.

ent facets that change based on social roles, but psychologists distinguish between the "complex self-concept" and the fragmented self-concept.[51] It is only when a person manifests these different self-aspects and, at the same time, maintains an integrated, unified view of him- or herself across those roles, that he or she will exhibit emotional health.[52]

This discussion of the fragmented modern assists our quest for professional integrity. First it demonstrates that philosophical modernism and postmodernism may actually harm the psychological health of individual lawyers seeking to come to grips with the call to law. Second, it reminds us of the difficulty of practicing integrity in the face of the contradictions of our world. It should serve, then, as a call to humility and patience with others, and as a challenge to shun pat answers and simplistic critiques. Third, it also demonstrates the necessity of a "complex self," essentially a vision of the Christian life that understands one's callings and the varied duties they each entail as well as the unity of the human person in relation to God, others, and creation.

> ENLIGHTENMENT AND POSTMODERN CULTURE
>
> **The public world is the world of facts upon which every intelligent person is expected to agree—or to be capable of being persuaded. . . . In contrast to this is the private world where we are free to follow our own preference regarding personal conduct and lifestyle, provided it does not prevent others from having the same freedom. There are no "right" or "wrong" styles of life. . . . This separation of value from fact is reflected in the separation of private from public life that is one of the characteristics of our culture. And . . . the response of the Christian churches—or at least of the Protestant churches—to the challenge of the Enlightenment was to accept the dichotomy and withdraw into the private sector.**
>
> LESSLIE NEWBIGIN, *FOOLISHNESS TO THE GREEKS*

Professionalism and the Three Commitments

How does our threefold commitment to integrity stack up in the face of the modern challenge?

[51]Ibid., p. 253, citing Catherine J. Lutz and Scott R. Ross, "Elaboration Versus Fragmentation: Distinguishing Between Self-Complexity and Self-Concept Differentiation," *Journal of Social and Clinical Psychology* 22 (2003): 538.

[52]Ibid.

First, let's not assume too much power in the modern mindset—though we should not underestimate its influence all around us. We seek a *transforming* vision, and we are participants in the power of One who transforms us by the renewing of our minds, when we resist being conformed to the artificial mold of modernity. We are not slaves to our environment; we are salt and light in it. The power of God is at work in and through us, so we do not despair.

Even the postmodern critique of modernism might encourage us here. It reminds us of our deep situatedness in Enlightenment thinking, our detachment from community, and our arrogance regarding our own objectivity. While much of the postmodern turn merely perpetuates the autonomy and disintegration of modernism, we have plenty to learn from it. We are not slaves to our culture; we are members of an alternative culture—with its own language, architecture, and ritual, from which we "profess" redeeming law practices.

Second, our three central commitments to unity, community, and truth are not simply tossed out the window because we now realize that they may be more difficult to pursue than we thought. Integrity is still the answer, especially to the questions posed by the modern world that is, by definition, disintegrated. Our task then is to develop the distinctions between "role ethics" in the modern sense and vocational thinking across roles in the theological sense. We need, in short, to develop a theologically complex self-concept.

To do that, let's turn to our threefold commitment to integrity.

Unity. First, we should evaluate the way we look at ourselves as lawyers. Have we created a false persona that our spouses and Bible study partners wouldn't recognize if they saw it in action? "Lawyers must see their roles as attorneys as an extension of who they are at home, at church, and in life."[53] Stop and read that again. Do you need to see yourself at the office as an extension of who you are at home and at church? This is a very interesting way to direct one's mind toward integrity. Our professional lives should flow out of our most important communities. Our parish life and family life should inform how we practice law in a very real way.

Second, we should embrace our task as truly countercultural and respond in a broadly countercultural manner. The challenge of modernity is a call not only to resist the fragmented self in professional role ethics but also to resist

[53]Gantt, "Integration as Integrity," p. 255.

its materialism, consumerism, and moral skepticism. We can become better "Christian lawyers" by facing the challenges to faithful living across all of life Christianly. In all of this, we are called to be laborers in and alongside the church in helping it form a biblical response that shuns both false dualism on one hand and triumphalist cultural optimism on the other.

Third, it is not enough—if we are to have a truly transforming vision—to pursue moral conversation and reject false identification with gunslingers, without pursuit of identification with Christ. We started our discussion with some difficult questions of "identity." At the heart of Christian faith is the truth that the believer is united with Christ and identifies with him: "It is no longer I who live, but Christ who lives in me. And the life I now live in the flesh I live by faith in the Son of God, who loved me and gave himself for me" (Galatians 2:20). How does this most fundamental of doctrines relate to our discussion of professional identity?

We've seen from the beginning that to disconnect faith from one's life in the law "defies the unity of the human person and the all-encompassing reach of faith," in the words of professor Rob Vischer.[54] Our life in Christ is indeed all-encompassing, and it is that life from which our ontological unity comes. Being united with Christ means more than one thing; it means everything. All of life is lived as an expression of that unity. We have died with him, are raised with him, suffer with him, serve with him, hope with him, and practice law with him. As the eyes of our hearts are enlightened as we come to know him (Ephesians 1:18), we will understand more and more what it means to be united in the diversity of the Savior. Our relationships can even now reflect that unity, and we will see miracles, reconciliation, healing, confession, mercy, justice, and compassion through our work. Our pursuit of our professional integrity through knowledge of our unity with Christ will do as much as anything else to fight the fragmentation oppressing us from the prevailing culture.

I might suggest some practical approaches, along the lines of the lawyer's disciplines that we discussed in chapter nine, but with an eye toward the problems of professional identity in the modern world:

- Read serious literature and sound theology instead of only contemporary authors.

[54]Robert K. Vischer, "Catholic Social Thought and the Ethical Formation of Lawyers: A Call for Community," *Journal of Catholic Social Thought* 1 (2004): 419.

- Meditate on who you are in Christ according to the Scriptures and study law-related passages in depth.
- Practice devotional exercises recommended by your local congregation.
- Think of ways to involve your family in your legal work—through dinner conversation if nothing else.
- Sit down and consider—actually contemplate—how your character as a ___________ (e.g., father or mother) is reflected in your lawyering. Write some things down to refer to later. Do the same exercise regarding your role in your church.
- When the television is on, engage your brain. It is through this "idiot box" that the modern disease is caught and spread. When in doubt, turn it off.
- Combat the spirit of consumerism that feeds the spirit of the age. Read advertisements critically, and avoid impulse buying. (Can you believe that little piece of advice is in a book about lawyers? I can't either, but there's no extra charge for it.)
- Use your above-average analytical skills to evaluate what you watch, what you read, the fashion trends you see or follow, and the discourse you hear in the media.
- Develop ways to understand your clients as multifaceted human beings.

Community. Since one of the ideals of the transforming vision of law practice is moral engagement, it is not surprising that our commitment to life in community is central to that professional vision, and we are never up to the task alone. First of all, we must remember that we are rooted in a community larger than lawyer-client relationship. As Professor Shaffer put it, "groups of us lawyer Christians go along without mutual, self-conscious awareness of our being the church."[55] Our participation with lawyers of faith and brothers and sisters in Christ is a sure defense against the fragmenting climate of modernity, and our recognition of our place in a larger body that must be salt and light in the world reminds us that we are not responding to a worldview but to a fallen world.

This brings the lawyer's discipline of fellowship again to mind. Moral dialogue between lawyer and client begins with like-minded professionals. Gantt reminds us that "lawyer-to-lawyer discourse is important because it

---

[55]Shaffer, *On Being a Christian and a Lawyer,* p. 220.

promotes the solidarity of the legal community and invigorates lawyers' moral faculties."[56]

We also should remember as we seek to love our client neighbors that they are just as tempted to disengagement as we are. Often we are simply the instrument to the end that is their will. Our task is first to have compassion and empathy and then to engage them—through open and loving conversation—in the task of moral integration. Knowing this, we will also be mindful to check our fear of "offending" one who is not interested in spiritual things and moral dialogue.

Professor Vischer has some excellent suggestions—what he calls "the tools of ethical formation"—for communities of Catholic lawyers to use as vehicles for integration:

- making relevant literature available to members
- facilitating informal consultation among members
- more formal consultation with a panel of Catholic lawyers designated to provide advice on ethics
- an ethics board of Catholic lawyers that would issue advisory opinions on relevant issues
- the promulgation of ethics rules designed to supplement (but generally not to contradict) the jurisdiction's governing body of rules[57]

These are obviously excellent tools for the broader Christian professional community as well, and we might add them to the list of practical suggestions in chapter nine on the discipline of fellowship. Participating in the joy of community helps guide us to professional integrity.

Truth. Vischer also reminds us that the process of ethical formation is much broader than anything that can be captured in ethics rules. He observes that such formation must begin with "the narrative of God's dealing with creation."[58] This observation confirms the central place of our commitment to truth—particularly, worldview—in our quest for professional integrity. That narrative of God's work in creation is the basis of any worldview analysis (see chap. 8).

This narrative, first, reminds us of the centrality of redemption in the law-

---

[56]Gantt, "Integration as Integrity," p. 260.
[57]Vischer, "Catholic Social Thought," p. 432.
[58]Ibid., p. 437.

yer's work. God is at work to redeem fallen creation, including us, our families, our clients, and the institutions we work in. Second, it reminds us of our own sin. An understanding of our own sinfulness is an important component of worldview: "The Christian story should inform (indeed should be the foundation of) the [Christian] lawyer's worldview, encompassing not only her view of the clients who walk through her door, but also her view of herself and the function she serves in the legal system."[59] Indeed, the professionalism struggle is about relationships—but not only about relationships between lawyers and clients. It is also about our relationship to all of the created order, including "the system" itself. In fact, as this discussion of modernism has made clear, our struggle to find integrity in vocation is fought within the context of a centuries-long development of "dogmas and practices" that have led to concrete institutions, governments, and public practices. This confirms what I have already said about law being a cultural calling to discern both structure and direction in law-related institutions and systems. Though I have addressed some of this, it is worth a more detailed evaluation.

Structure and Direction in the Legal System

Shaffer and others have warned that justice is not something that the government gives. This is true, yet human institutions have a role to play as agents to whom God delegates his authority (see Romans 13:4, for example). We have also demonstrated that reliance on "the system" as a moral guide is unwise and dangerous. Yet we cannot simply dismiss any system as inherently evil until we have evaluated its place in civilization—the ongoing creative work of God mediated through human beings—and its direction—whether and how its creational goodness is being restored or thwarted. We all desire to avoid capitulation to "the system," but treating the legal system or its components as evil is itself an abandonment of one's calling as a Christian lawyer. It is simplification every bit as dangerous as the role-based hired-gun ethic. It's great to seek to be in moral dialogue with our clients, but to what end? What place is there in our various systems for the Christian litigant, defendant, or incorporator? We must truthfully evaluate the relative direction of the system in order to operate as lawyers within it.

In this sense I disagree with those who argue that the state is inherently un-

---

[59]Ibid.

trustworthy in its role as minister of justice, or more to the point, that the adversary system itself cannot work. Scripture teaches that we are to give the civil authority its due (Matthew 22:21) and that the civil ruler is appointed by God as an agent—a servant—of God *to do us good*. Its delegated authority is to punish wrongdoers (Romans 13:4) and to praise those who do right (1 Peter 2:14). None of this leads to the conclusion that the civil government is always trustworthy or even speaks to the structure of the adversary system or secretary of state's incorporation practices. Yet the structure of civil government is creationally good, and with the caution that it is made up of sinful human beings who distort that goodness and abuse that power, we need to evaluate its programs and initiatives with some specificity. Indeed, much good work has been done along these lines, from a variety of religious perspectives, and a comprehensive evaluation is beyond the scope of this book.[60] Yet a full Christian analysis of these things is almost a life's work; how can a practicing lawyer make judgments sufficient for ordinary life and work? We look to revelation and the work of the saints in applying it in history, and, by the power of the Holy Spirit in the communities he has given us, work out a faithful response as we continue to evaluate, holding fast to what is good.

In any event, a faithful response is much broader than client-lawyer community; we operate within social and cultural structures rooted in the created order, beginning with the law itself. Moral conversation in itself will not solve the problematic relationships we have to law, governments, and culture. We need an ethics of care *and* an ethics of salt and light. The Holy Spirit, through his people, renews creation from within the very structures themselves: "The kingdom of heaven is like yeast that a woman took and

[60]We will look to the court system and the principles of litigation in the final chapter. There are several excellent general sources on Christian perspectives on government and politics. See Oliver O'Donovan, *The Ways of Judgment* (Grand Rapids: Eerdmans, 2005); J. Budziszewski, *The Revenge of Conscience: Politics and the Fall of Man* (Dallas: Spence, 1999); Oliver O'Donovan and Joan Lockwood O'Donovan, eds., *From Irenaeus to Grotius: A Sourcebook in Christian Political Thought* (Grand Rapids: Eerdmans, 1999); Oliver O'Donovan, *Desire of Nations: Rediscovering the Roots of Political Theology* (Cambridge: Cambridge University Press, 1996); Michael Cromartie, ed., *Caesar's Coin Revisited: Christians and the Limits of Civil Government* (Grand Rapids: Eerdmans, 1996); Herbert W. Titus, *God, Man, and Law: The Biblical Principles* (Oak Brook, Ill.: Institute in Basic Life Principles, 1994); Doug Bandow, *Beyond Good Intentions: A Biblical View of Politics* (Wheaton, Ill.: Crossway, 1988); and Harold J. Berman, *The Interaction of Law and Religion* (Nashville: Abingdon, 1974).

mixed in with three measures of flour until all of it was leavened" (Matthew 13:33).[61] We "mix in" wherever we are placed. Recall that we are involved in *pushing* our institutions—from the adversary system to the criminal justice system, to the department of motor vehicles, to the local opera company—in a Godward direction. Not by political power—direct and revolutionary action—but by being salt and light wherever we find ourselves—indirect and renewing action. We are called to participate within these structures only as God permits and directs. The ethics of *being* salt is superior to the ethics of vigorous *salting!*

The difference in these approaches to participating in God's ongoing creative work, in the words of Albert Wolters, is the difference between reformation and revolution. How are we to confront the adversary system? By progressive renewal, not by violent overthrow.[62] It is a strategy for "historic change":

> In the light of our worldview, it is clear that God calls his people to *historical reformation* in all these areas [that is, on a societal and cultural plane], to a sanctification of creational realities from sin and its effects. What was *formed* in creation has been historically *deformed* by sin and must be *reformed* in Christ.[63]

We are never called to abruptly eradicate every aspect of the established system and replace it with a totally new one.[64] Instead, our calling requires us to understand that no societal order is absolutely corrupt, and to see first what is good within the societal order. This, while not revolutionary, is truly out of the mainstream. We seek to change the world through slow, historical reformation, not revolution. In the law practice it means we pursue moral conversations with our clients, hating what is evil about the system and avoiding it, but holding fast to what is good and participating in the goodness of the system to the glory of God.

There are dangers in this mindset, of course. The first is a cultural optimism that, in the name of seeing the good in the creational order, forgets that everything in creation is tainted by the Fall. Second, in our zeal to work with God in his renewing efforts, we may begin to see legal work as redemptive in itself.

---

[61]I owe this example to Albert M. Wolters, *Creation Regained* (Grand Rapids: Eerdmans, 1985), p. 90.
[62]Ibid., p. 91.
[63]Ibid.
[64]Ibid., p. 92.

"Attributing greater significance to work risks making it demonic as work then becomes an idolatrous activity through which we try to secure and guarantee our significance, to make 'our mark' on history."[65] We should beware of revolutionary means, the graffiti tendency, and turning work into an engine of redemption in and of itself. God is at work, and he will use us if we continue in humble obedience to him.

Conclusion

Any transforming vision of the lawyer's calling recognizes the complex moral relationships between client advocacy, the adversary system, and legitimate differences in conduct from role to role. In addition to sorting out these complex relationships, an integrated vision must take into account the unity of the human person, the role of life in community, and discernment of truth in both relationships and societal institutions.

It is not a simple task, and lawyers who view roles and institutions simplistically will have difficulty in their callings. We must adopt a theologically complex self, by which I mean one that truthfully discerns duties in various callings within various human structures and professional relationships. This involves personal risk, pain, and moral difficulty. It requires a theology of the system itself, a theology of one's practice area, and a moral evaluation of every representation, will, pleading, argument, brief, and phone call.

What do we seek in all of this? Moral engagement. Love of neighbor. This requires virtue, so we also seek humility, patience, wisdom, and temperance. This requires discipline. This is integrity.

We will return to some of this in chapter eleven, where we will discuss habits and virtue under the framework of the lawyer's typical struggles.

For Further Thought

1. Can you define the difference between role morality and vocational thinking as it relates to your own practice?
2. Do you like lawyer jokes? Do you think the legal profession is concerned about its reputation? Suggest some solutions.
3. How well do you engage in moral conversation with your clients? What are

[65]Stanley Hauerwas, quoted in Douglas J. Schuurman, *Vocation* (Grand Rapids: Eerdmans, 2004), p. 84.

your strengths in this area? Weaknesses? If you would like to be better at it, develop a plan that includes reminders in your office.

4. Is individualism a good thing or a bad thing? Think of ways that it serves and ways that it harms your law practice.

11

Lawyers' Vices—Lawyers' Virtues

I had lunch with a high school sophomore some time ago at a Christian camp. He was motivated, intelligent, mature, and a professing Christian. I asked what he thought he might do with his life. "I want to go to college—probably Stanford—then get an MBA, take over an existing business or raise one from the ground up and make a ton of money, then retire at forty-four." Then what? "I want to play golf every day." When I asked him if that was what the Lord desired for his life, he said simply "I don't know; I've never thought about it." I've never thought about it! You may be thinking, *Well, he's just a kid.* True enough. But this young man had been raised in the church. He was attending a Christian leadership camp. And I've talked to many Christian law students in their mid-twenties whose ideas of a successful life are not far from this.

What is a successful life? I find that Christian lawyers' ideas of success, though they widely vary, are not much different from their nonbelieving colleagues at the bar. Make a good living. Get rich. Change the world. Fight for rights. Serve my clients. Feed my family. Retire early. Play golf. Make money to give to my church. Get rich, retire early, and go on mission trips. Some of these goals are excellent (some more excellent than others, to be sure) and may even be exactly the success that God desires for us. But if we've learned anything from our discussion so far, looking at these sorts of goals as our measure of the successful calling is backward.

The call of God is to be a certain kind of person and to follow him in a certain kind of way at certain posts to which he posts us. The particular professional or family or church goals that we have will flow from who we are and what God is doing in and through us. Our premise has been that

that God calls us as integrated persons, across roles and activities. This is an issue of who we are, not what we do. The commitments at the heart of integrity have led us to disciplines that allow us to see and think rightly. Our outward behavior follows. Although we have not spent much time developing the idea of the lawyer of virtue, in those words, the integrated lawyer always becomes a lawyer of virtue. In this chapter I will address the issue of virtue and vice specifically in the context of the vices that we lawyers seem inclined to, whether by training, temperament, or simple force of cultural habit.

A handful of issues repeatedly appear in the lives of Christian lawyers that relate to the character of the Christian as a lawyer. Again, whether it is law school, the typical attorney temperament, or the substance of the law practice, a number of vices (don't you like "issues" better?) surface as if they are simply hazards of the lawyer's calling. Though the symptoms are many, I think the roots are few: money and power. These things are not evil in themselves and may sometimes appropriately be used as gear for our journey in the kingdom. Yet these two areas are a breeding ground for the vices natural to the legal profession, and we ought to address them specifically before closing out this discussion with a meditation on success from the book of Joshua.

As Richard Foster notes, "there is a place in the Christian life and experience" for power and money; "when properly placed and effectively functioning, they have the ability to enhance and bless life." On the other hand, "the demon in money is greed," and the "demon in power is pride."[1] In the Christian tradition these sins have always been ranked one and two: pride then avarice, the top dogs of the seven deadly sins. I believe these to be lawyers' favorites, as well.

Let's start with money.

Money

Peter Kreeft remarks that money has a sort of "umbrella" temptation, because it is the means to many other things besides just green ink on paper.[2] It is our means to stuff, which can be a means to status or pleasure or power. We also

[1]Richard Foster, *The Challenge of the Disciplined Life: Christian Reflections on Money, Sex, and Power* (New York: HarperCollins, 1985), pp. 12-13.

[2]Peter Kreeft, *Back to Virtue* (San Francisco: Ignatius Press, 1992), p. 109.

see money as the means to security—the lie of self-sufficiency closely related to pride. Martin Luther for this reason called *security* the ultimate idol.[3] Kreeft believes the reason that money is such a difficult issue in American society is that our society "encourages competition and economic aggression rather than contentment."[4] What an important insight for lawyers! As one commentator explains it:

> Big firm lawyers are, on the whole, a remarkably insecure and competitive group of people. Many of them have spent almost their entire lives competing to win games that other people have set up for them. First they competed to get into a prestigious college. Then they competed for college grades. Then they competed for LSAT scores. Then they competed to get into a prestigious law school. Then they competed for law school grades. Then they competed to make the law review. Then they competed for clerkships. Then they competed to get hired by a big law firm.
>
> Now that they're in a big law firm, what's going to happen? Are they going to stop competing? Are they going to stop comparing themselves to others? Of course not. They're going to keep competing—competing to bill more hours, to attract more clients, to win more cases, to do more deals. They're playing a game. And money is how the score is kept in that game.[5]

Professor Schiltz is thinking specifically of "big firm" lawyers, but much of this insight applies to lawyers in many different types of practices. Lawyers are competitive, and their training has encouraged their competitive nature. And don't miss his last tidbit: money is just a way to keep score. Money is the means to status, to prestige, to *winning*. And for many of us in the law, *winning* is what our ordinary work is all about.

The problems often begin before law school, with the student's expectations of the "lawyer's life." First, with high expectations of how much "real lawyers" make, it's easier to justify student loans that "won't be so bad" to pay off on a lawyer's salary. During law school, the debt load often creates pressure to perform academically and sometimes creates pressure to take a certain kind of job "just to pay off my loans." In 2000, the average law student graduated

---

[3]Martin Luther, cited by Stanley Hauerwas and William H. Willimon, *Resident Aliens* (Nashville: Abingdon, 1989), p. 131.

[4]Ibid.

[5]Patrick J. Schiltz, "On Being a Happy, Healthy, and Ethical Member of an Unhappy, Unhealthy, and Unethical Profession," *Vanderbilt Law Review* 52 (1999): 871.

with $55,000 in debt;[6] in 2005, this figure was $76,000 for private law school and almost $49,000 for public law school graduates.[7] This is very close to the $80,000 median salary of 2004 law graduates in private practice and dwarfs the median for the public sector ($36,656).[8] Not that these salaries are low, but in relation to the typical debt load, they are much less attractive than private practice. Part of the reason that so few students are able to go to lower paying jobs—even if they want to—is the debt load.[9] Many students articulate a desire to be more creative in their approach to law practice, to serve in a nonprofit organization or start a business. Yet the draw to private practice, particularly to large firms in the major cities, is huge, since it is a much easier start to pay off student loans. Of course, for students interested in big-firm practice only for the salary, life is almost immediately miserable. The training and camaraderie are excellent, but the hours and personal sacrifices necessary to succeed in the environment of major law firms are significant. Those motivated solely by money either burn out or get "sucked in" to the lifestyle and pace within the first three years of practice.

> **It's okay to give God credit, but he can use cash, too.**
>
> R. G. LeTourneau, *R. G. LeTourneau: Mover of Men and Mountains*

Second, new law graduates with their eye on the "prize" of big salaries and lifestyles are more likely to unintentionally commit to such a lifestyle long-term. When very young lawyers assume that their salaries will continue to be large for their whole careers and, at the same time, assume that a lawyer's lifestyle needs to be or ought to be at a certain (usually high) level, they begin to make choices and plans that will lock them into high-paying jobs for their careers. If opportunity knocks with a more satisfying small-town practice, a move to public-service law, an

---

[6]Roger Roots, "The Student Loan Debt Crisis: A Study in Unintended Consequences," *Southwestern University Law Review* [29] (2000): 501.

[7]Leigh Jones, "As Salaries Rise, So Does the Debt," *National Law Journal* (February 1, 2006) <www.law.com/jsp/llf/PubArticleLLF.jsp?id=1139393114101>.

[8]Ibid.

[9]See ibid. For a slight twist on this issue, see Lewis A. Kornhauser and Richard L. Revesz, "Legal Education and Entry into the Legal Profession: The Role of Race, Gender, and Educational Debt," *New York University Law Review* 70 (1995). They argue that it is not educational debt per se that keeps graduates out of lower paying jobs, but the student's lack of commitment to "the non-profit" sector in the first place and other social factors.

invitation to teach, a call to the public sector, or a short-term missions trip, they are often unable to answer due to debt, financial commitments, or financial investments.

We can easily become enslaved to our possessions and lifestyle. Much of the trouble lies in the nature of money itself. It is both a tool for the kingdom of God and a power that seeks to dominate us and inspire worship: "You cannot serve God and wealth [*mammon*]" (Matthew 6:24; Luke 16:13). Christ spoke about money and riches more than any other topic:

> For Christ money is an idolatry we must be converted *from* in order to be converted to *him*. The rejection of the god mammon is a necessary precondition to becoming a disciple of Jesus. And in point of fact, money has many of the characteristics of deity. It gives us security, can induce guilt, gives us freedom, gives us power, and seems to be omnipresent. Most sinister of all, however, is its bid for omnipotence.[10]

Yet in Christ's teaching and the Epistles, money is also discussed as a means of blessing, for example, in the gifts that people gave in the church and to its mission, as demonstrated in the parable of the widow's mite and in the parable of the talents. The most interesting discussion of money and God's people comes from Christ, as recorded in Luke 16:1-8.

The dishonest steward. Jesus tells the parable of a steward who is fired by his master for squandering the master's property. The steward is to provide a final accounting before he leaves his master's employ, so, in order to gain the favor of the master's debtors, he calls them in, one by one, and reduces their debts. They are now, of course, favorably disposed toward him. When the steward then renders the final accounting to his master, his master commends him for his shrewdness. Jesus then comments on his parable.

First, he remarks that "the children of this age are more shrewd in dealing with their own generation than are the children of light" (v. 8). This shrewdness that he exhorts us toward is not a general shrewdness in dealing with our generation, but has something to do with actual mammon: "Make friends for yourselves by means of dishonest wealth so that when it is gone, they may welcome you into the eternal homes" (v. 9). Just as the steward used wealth to gain the favor of those who would later welcome him into their homes, so we are to use wealth ("unrighteous mammon") to gain friends who will have eternal hospitality.

---

[10]Foster, *Challenge of the Disciplined Life*, p. 28.

Second, Jesus says, "Whoever is faithful in a very little is faithful also in much; and whoever is dishonest in a very little is dishonest also in much. If then you have not been faithful with the dishonest wealth, who will entrust to you the true riches?" (Luke 16:10-11). Finally, he closes by reminding us that a servant cannot serve two masters: "You cannot serve both God and wealth" (v. 13).

We are stewards. We are reminded by Christ to be shrewd stewards who look to eternity, even as we handle money—unrighteous mammon. It is a tool that can be used to make "eternal friends." Those eternal friends are not the subject of the parable but are simply a figure representing the rewards that God has for us for faithfulness.[11] God is the one who rewards us eternally. The idea is that we are to use money for eternal purposes. We are worse than the children of "this age" because we focus only on the present in our attitudes about money.

In addition, faithfulness with money is a barometer of character. We will know a lot about a lawyer by the way he or she handles money. Money is apparently a "small thing" compared to the "true riches" that God desires us to manage. But a person's character is evident, whether in handling small things or large: a faithful steward is faithful, regardless of the size of the trust. Of course, some of us are still learning that we are *stewards* for one who is restoring his kingdom rather than *owners* in our own right.

Generosity. Surely one of the great lessons of this parable is that we are to be *generous.* I believe one reason that lawyers have such difficulty being generous with their money is that it is earned, for the most part, by the hour. Every cent can be traced to a particular minute of work. Rather than leveraging money to make more, our time is our currency. This, of course, is no excuse. The children of this age do better than we do at looking to the long-term use of our funds. In most ways, our future would be best served by giving our money away more freely.

Rather than using money as a tool for eternity, our tendency is to use it as a tool for our own ends. We use money to manipulate people and relationships. In addition, we see giving as a means of getting rather than the other way around. We see giving as means of getting more material blessings rather than

---

[11]On this, see Darrell L. Bock, *Luke 9:51—24:53,* Baker Exegetical Commentary on the New Testament (Grand Rapids: Baker, 1996), p. 1334.

serving the purposes of the kingdom and setting up eternal rewards. I have even heard some preachers teach that giving money to their ministry is like "sowing a seed" that will result in more money and financial blessing. This is backward: the reason we receive is to give, not to get more.

R. G. LeTourneau was, in his own words, "a mechanic that God blessed." After some hard times, he began an earth-moving business at age thirty-one. Eventually he began to invent larger and more effective machines, and at the end of his inventing career, he held over three hundred patents. Wikipedia, the online encyclopedia, notes that nearly 70 percent of the earth-moving machines used in World War II were LeTourneau machines. LeTourneau saw God's hand in bringing about his success, and he realized that he was simply a steward of what was given him. He determined to live on 10 percent of his income, and give 90 percent away. "The question is not how much of my money I give to God, but rather how much of his money I keep for myself."[12] That's the question, all right.

Wisdom and unrighteous mammon. Wealth is, at least in some sense, unrighteous, according to Jesus. We might say that its structure is not rooted in God's good creation, and that it will not be restored in the kingdom. Its only good use, therefore, is as a tool for "making friends" or conversion to something eternal. Perhaps this is one thing Jesus had in mind when he said, "How hard it is for those who have wealth to enter the kingdom of God" (Luke 18:24). Wealth is not really a kingdom commodity. But it can be exchanged for kingdom commodities! This exchange, however, requires wisdom—shrewdness in both financial and spiritual matters. Our talent at rationalizing makes this even more difficult. "I'm really not that well off." "I worked hard for this, and I deserve it."[13]

But more troubling than our justifications and rationalizations is our worship of money and what it brings: it's the scorecard in "the game," it shows me I'm better than my neighbor, it proves to my parents that I've done it on my own, it's the means to buy the pleasures to numb my pain and to lose my insecurities. This is idolatry. We attach value to money that is far beyond its worth, and we scramble for it as if it will bring us the ultimate life.[14] What will we do when it is gone? Will we be able to worship the one who is actually wor-

[12]R. G. LeTourneau, *R. G. LeTourneau: Mover of Men and Mountains* (Chicago: Moody Press, 1967), p. 90.

[13]See Hauerwas and Willimon, *Resident Aliens*, p. 131.

[14]See Foster, *Challenge of the Disciplined Life*, pp. 28-29.

thy of our worship, the one who can deliver the good life?

Stewardship. I had a friend in high school who had attended a seminar with his parents that included a session on the difference between an attitude of stewardship and an attitude of ownership. They had learned the principle that all of our possessions are entrusted to us for use at God's direction, and that God is the owner of all that we have. The day after the seminar, my friend was driving the family car and was involved in an accident. He called home to inform his parents, and when his dad answered the phone, my friend said, "Hi, Dad. I just needed to let you know. I wrecked God's car." He wanted to make sure that his dad was thinking stewardship more than ownership.

An attitude of stewardship is the first step to fighting the "demon greed." How can we hoard if it belongs to another? How can we not obey the principal, if we are merely agents?

One of the tragic characters in J. R. R. Tolkien's *Return of the King* is Denethor, the Steward of Gondor. Gondor is a nation-state waiting the return of its true king. In the meantime, it is ruled by a line of wise and powerful stewards from which Denethor comes. He knows the return of the king is imminent, yet he is so obsessed with the evil around him (the coming onslaught of the enemy) and his own sins, even his great wisdom fails him. He is blinded to his only real duty: to be faithful with what has been entrusted to him. Ironically, it is his knowledge that the true "owner" may be returning that finally heightens his paranoia and, eventually, brings his destruction. In the end, at the only time it really mattered, he decided that his kingdom was his own to do as he pleased. He forgot he was a steward of the kingdom.

I am threatened when God reminds me—usually by prodding me to give something away—that my possessions and money are from him, for him, and owned by him. I hold on more tightly when I get my security from things rather than from God himself, the owner of all things. He owns the "cattle on a thousand hills," and indeed "the whole earth" is his: "The earth is the Lord's and all that is in it, the world, and those who live in it" (Psalm 24:1). To supplement the old saying, we need to simply "let go, and let God . . . use his stuff."

Christian lawyers live as stewards in a number of ways. We generally do well as stewards of our client's funds that must be held in trust, and we usually guard client secrets with care. But how will we fare when God demands an accounting of our stewardship of mammon?

Integrity. It's interesting that the pursuit of money and possessions in many ways is the direct antithesis of the pursuit of integrity. Let's wrap up our financial discussion by observing how money can threaten our very commitment to integrity:

- Unity. "No one can serve two masters; for a slave will either hate the one and love the other, or be devoted to the one and despise the other. You cannot serve God and wealth [*mammon*]" (Matthew 6:24). If we are slaves to our stuff and our money, we are by definition disintegrated, trying to serve two masters that demand complete allegiance across all of our callings.
- Community. James ties our desire for things to broken community:

  > Those conflicts and disputes among you, where do they come from? Do they not come from your cravings that are at war within you? You want something and do not have it; so you commit murder. And you covet something and cannot obtain it; so you engage in disputes and conflicts. You do not have, because you do not ask. You ask and do not receive, because you ask wrongly, in order to spend what you get on your pleasures. (James 4:1-3)

- Truth. Stanley Hauerwas and Will Willimon point out the connection between possessions and lying in the early church in the account of Ananias and Sapphira (Acts 5). Recall that Ananias and Sapphira sold a piece of property and kept some of the proceeds, and took the rest to Peter, implying that they were giving all to the church. " 'Ananias,' Peter asked, 'why has Satan filled your heart to lie to the Holy Spirit and to keep back part of the proceeds of the land? . . . You did not lie to us, but to God.' Now when Ananias heard these words, he fell down and died" (vv. 3-5). His wife, Sapphira, came in three hours later, not knowing what had happened, and kept up the lie. She fell down dead too. Hauerwas and Willimon explain:

  > The first real crisis in the church . . . was a crisis over possessions. . . .
  >
  > Is it not interesting how Luke links money to self-deceit? Peter accuses Ananias and Sapphira, not of greed, but of lying. There is something quite natural about the lies of Ananias and Sapphira, for we all know the way we rationalize and excuse our own covetousness, acquisitiveness, and greed. . . .
  >
  > Our lies are the correlate of our materialism, for both our materialism and our self-deceit are our attempts to deal with our insecurity, our finitude by taking matters into our hands.[15]

[15]Hauerwas and Willimon, *Resident Aliens*, pp. 130-31.

Holding fast to our integrity, developing aggressive generosity, pursuing wisdom, and developing an attitude of stewardship will go a long way toward combating the hold that money has on our hearts. But if we continue to think of the successful law practice (or life) in financial terms, we will be constantly on the verge of a return to the worship of false gods. There is indeed no outward sign of success, no material scoreboard for kingdom points.

Power

There is power in the knowledge of God. Power can liberate the oppressed. Creative power can edify and enlighten. There is power in authorities who nurture, discipline, direct, and shepherd. There is power that can cultivate economic growth, foster interpersonal communications, inspire workers, and build relationships. Power, in perspective and in the proper hands, can create, encourage, and build.[16] Yet the love of power is the root of pride, and pride in turn leads to an improper desire for power. This relationship between power and pride is the stuff of legend and provides some telling insights into the lawyer's struggles.

Knowledge and pride. One of the great stories to examine the relationship between power and pride is the Faust legend, in which a scholar sells his soul to the devil in return for earthly power. Christopher Marlowe's version of the legend, his play *Doctor Faustus,* expressly links the relationship between power and pride to knowledge that brings conceit, a clear lesson for lawyers.

We are introduced to the learned doctor in his study, surrounded by his books. The first words we hear from him are spoken aloud as he talks to himself about what he will "profess." Indeed, Faustus is a "professional" who professes theology, law, medicine, and philosophy, among other pursuits. Yet his learning gets the best of him. He excels at theological disputation (he is a doctor of theology), but his arrogant "cunning" in such matters—ingenious argumentation, really—leads to his downfall. He laments each of his areas of learning. He ticks down the list: philosophy is unsatisfying, medicine not miraculous enough, law is fit for "a mercenary drudge" and is "too servile and illiberal," so he settles for divinity. But as he considers divinity further, he dismisses it. He reads "the wages of sin is death" and then "if we say we have no

[16]On the topic of creative power and the power of ministry, see chaps. 11 and 12 in Foster, *Challenge of the Disciplined Life.*

sin, we deceive ourselves and the truth is not in us." He concludes from these verses that divinity is fatalistic, so he pursues the black arts of magic:

> O what a world of profit and delight
> Of power, of honor, of omnipotence
> Is promised to the studious artisan! . . .
> A sound magician is a demi-god!
> Here tire my brains to get a deity![17]

His desire to be like a god leads to his profession, which, of course, in turn leads to a pact with the devil to sell his soul in exchange for the power he desires. His vast learning and "logic" have led him astray.

There is certainly a link between knowledge and pride. Paul tells the Corinthian church that knowledge "puffs up" (1 Corinthians 8:1) and the preacher of Ecclesiastes concludes that "those who increase knowledge increase sorrow" (Ecclesiastes 1:18). And we have all experienced the "know-it-all" who arrogantly lords his or her knowledge over all who will listen. So lawyers are certainly vulnerable to "puffing up" in this area—we are some of the most educated, well-read men and women in America.

Knowledge and love. On the other hand, Paul's point in 1 Corinthians 8 is not that knowledge is harmful in itself. He notes elsewhere his pleasure that the Roman church is filled with knowledge and goodness, and on numerous occasions Paul prays that believers will be filled with knowledge. His point is not that knowledge itself puffs up, but that knowledge without love can be harmful: "Knowledge puffs up, but love builds up" (v. 3). Knowledge without love—that is, knowledge that is applied without regard for its consequences in community—makes one arrogant. He is speaking directly to the issue of food offered to idols, that those who possess knowledge will *know* that "no idol in the world really exists" (v. 4). With that knowledge, they will be able to eat without sin. Nonetheless, Paul cautions that they should not make their fellow Christians stumble, so that "by your knowledge those weak believers for whom Christ died are destroyed" (v. 11). We sin by using our knowledge without proper regard for others.

This is characteristic of pride: it excludes neighbor, while looking out for self.[18]

---

[17]Christopher Marlowe *Doctor Faustus* 1.1.51-53, 59-60.
[18]Kreeft, *Back to Virtue,* p. 98.

Twisted learning. If we look closely at Faustus too, we will see that it is not his knowledge per se that leads him to the devil, it is incomplete knowledge and arrogant sophistries that cause him to twist the truth. More specifically, his reading of the first half of Romans 6:23 ("For the wages of sin is death") without the second half ("but the gift of God is eternal life") and 1 John 1:8 without verse 9 ("if we confess our sins, he is faithful and just") leads him to search for power through the dark arts. It's not so much knowledge itself but his "ingenious" interpretations—the scholar's game of clever reading—that lead him to sell his soul.

> **Through the standard pedagogical technique [of law school], students are taught to ignore the binding quality of law. The indeterminacies of rules and their applications to fact situations are played up, along with the flexibility of purpose and policy analysis. Law is all about making arguments, is the message, and there is *always* some argument to be made. After three years of exposure to this, graduates departing law school understandably think that legal rules are simply tools lawyers utilize on behalf of whichever side they represent. They have learned, to repeat Llewellyn's fitting phrase, to "manipulate the machinery of law."**
>
> BRIAN Z. TAMANAHA, *LAW AS A MEANS TO AN END: THREAT TO THE RULE OF LAW*

Of course, this doesn't make us feel any better about ourselves, for no one plays technical word games with the truth like a lawyer does. We create lawyers by teaching them to argue both sides of an issue and to argue contradictory facts in the alternative. The more creative and ingenious the argument, the better. Of course, Jesus had a thing or two to say to the lawyers of his day who used word games to turn knowledge into a trap for their neighbors. He was crystal clear too that the problem was pride:

> The scribes and the Pharisees sit in Moses' seat; therefore, do whatever they teach you and follow it; but do not do as they do, for they do not practice what they teach. They tie heavy burdens, hard to bear, and lay them on the shoulders of others; but they themselves are unwilling to lift a finger to move them. . . . They love to have the place of honor at banquets and the best seats in the synagogues, and to be greeted with respect in the marketplaces, and to have people call them rabbi. . . . The greatest among you will be your servant. All who exalt themselves will be humbled, and all who humble themselves will be exalted. (Matthew 23:2-4, 6-7, 11-12)

This rebuke connecting religious legalism and pride is a shockingly relevant warning to those of us at the bar. It is the lawyers who tie burdens on the people's backs and do not lift a finger to help them.

Andrew Murray puts the issue squarely before us:

> Humility, the place of entire dependence upon God, is from the very nature of things the first duty and highest virtue of His creatures.
>
> And so pride—the loss of humility—is the root of every sin and evil. . . . In heaven and on earth, pride or self-exaltation is the very gateway to hell.[19]

Humility is entire dependence on God; pride is dependence on self. So why wouldn't we simply depend on God in humility? Because we desire power.

Better to reign in hell. *Paradise Lost* opens with Satan and his generals lying in a lake of fire in hell, having just been defeated and chased from heaven. Here, in utter defeat, in a place of misery and torment, Satan utters his famous words:

> Here we may reign secure, and in my choice
> To reign is worth ambition though in Hell:
> Better to reign in Hell, than serve in Heav'n.[20]

Pride is the original sin. Eve ate the forbidden fruit in response to the great temptation: "You will not die; for God knows that when you eat of it your eyes will be opened, and you will be like God, knowing good and evil" (Genesis 3:4-5). When Eve "saw that the tree was good for food, and that it was a delight to the eyes, and that the tree was to be desired to make one wise, she took of its fruit and ate" (Genesis 3:6). Kreeft explains:

> Pride is the greatest sin. It comes not from the world or the flesh but from the Devil. It comes from Hell. It was the Devil's original sin, perhaps the only sin possible for a pure spirit. . . .
>
> Pride was also Adam's (our) original sin, the desire to be like God, over the Law rather than under it.[21]

It is the first and greatest sin because it is the violation of the first and greatest commandment, "You shall have no other gods before me." Pride puts itself before God.

---

[19]Andrew Murray, *Humility: The Journey Toward Holiness* (Minneapolis: Bethany House, 2001), p. 11.

[20]John Milton *Paradise Lost* 1.261-63.

[21]Kreeft, *Back to Virtue,* p. 97.

Who's number one? Surely pride, the greatest of all the deadly sins, is the professional sin of lawyers. "There can be only one Number One," says Kreeft. "Pride is essentially competitive."[22] So too are lawyers. Of all the characteristics in all the literature on the trouble with the profession—whether it be money, dissatisfaction with work, too many hours worked, depression, drug addiction, or the like—vying for the top lawyer attribute is *competitive.* Of course, neither competition nor love of it is sin. But pride fuels competition, and an unchecked spirit of competition will most certainly lead to pride.

Professional Hazards

Life in the law seems a minefield of power and pride. We are competitive know-it-alls who have been encouraged in these ways by our training and practice, and yet who operate in relationships in which our knowledge—our expertise—gives us power over others. I'd like to identify a few possible landmines in the field so that we might better avoid them.

Client counseling. We saw in chapter ten that the pursuit of an ethics of care—the habit of engaging clients in moral dialogue and relationship—is a big step on the way to integrity in the realm of lawyer identity. Yet in this pursuit, pride is a barrier in a way that will make such a relationship impossible. Recall that moral isolation is the common posture of the Christian lawyer in client counseling. It takes on the appearance of moral concern, yet it is interested only in articulating moral stances, without the openness to change or the expectation that the other—lawyer or client—will grow.

When the lawyer assumes that the lawyer's conscience governs and what he or she will or will not do is determined by moral fiat, the result is a paternalistic relationship that assumes that the client is unable to grow and that the lawyer is correct on all counts. This is pride. As Shaffer puts it, "Moral isolation is an arrogant idea as well as an untruthful idea."[23] When a lawyer makes moral judgments without relationship, those judgments are often careless. Without concern for the complex life circumstances of the client, proper moral reasoning may be impossible. In addition, moral judgments are usually made without "a hint of doubt about the principles or the experience on which they rest."[24]

---

[22]Kreeft, *Back to Virtue,* p. 98.

[23]Shaffer, *On Being a Christian and a Lawyer,* p. 19.

[24]Ibid.

Humility demands more than that.

Codes of ethics and Christian lawyers. When I practiced law, I paid attention to the ethical rules only when I was involved in a case involving disqualification for conflict of interest. I had very little concern for how the rules might apply to what I did with clients or in litigation. This was not because I was an unethical lawyer. I was scrupulously careful about client secrets, conflicts of interest, inter-firm relationships, financial matters, and the like. The problem wasn't that I was dishonest but that I had way too much confidence in my own honesty! I knew I would never steal from a client or cheat a client on a fee or go back on my oral agreement or mislead opposing counsel. I believed my own high standards as a Christian were well above the rules of ethics—those rules were for those who wanted to do the bare minimum. I had a higher standard. Of course, this was utter foolishness, and I was a very fortunate young lawyer never to have been trapped in my arrogance by the many pitfalls of the ethics rules.

My case was a case of pride, pure and simple, and I've heard it repeated by many Christian law students: "Ethics codes are just the bare minimum; our service to Christ requires a higher standard." This is a recipe for disaster if it results in ignorance of the rules of ethics in the governing jurisdiction. Codes of legal ethics are the wisdom of those who have gone before, helping us define the standard. Without the rules of ethics, we don't even know what the issues are. Indeed, sometimes the rules do not go far enough, and sometimes the rules allow more than an honest lawyer can do. But that is no excuse for not understanding what the profession considers to be righteous conduct. "[We are] taking precaution that no one should discredit us in our administration of this generous gift; for we have regard for what is honorable, not only in the sight of the Lord, but also in the sight of men" (2 Corinthians 8:20-21 NASB). Ethics rules tell us what others believe to be righteous conduct in the law. To ignore them is foolish pride.

Law school idealism and the road to cynicism. I think that most students go to law school with the goal to "do good." Not all, to be sure, but most students who enter American law schools have some idea that they will enter the legal profession to help people, the government, businesses, the country, the poor, or their particular political or religious cause. There is, at least in the beginning, a sense that law can be *service*. Service is a sure-fire solution to pride. Somehow, however, it seems that service-oriented idealism is out the window well before the third year of law school; it is replaced by a spirit of cynicism that any lawyer can spot.

Cynicism is a particularly nasty cousin of pride; it tends to question the goodness and sincerity of others, with an unbecoming condescension along for the ride. Cynicism, therefore, has every consequence of pride: it rejects community by refusing effort in that direction, it thwarts truth by believing the worst, and it tends toward bifurcation and compartmentalization in the Christian, since it is likely incompatible, in its bitter forms, with faith in Christ.

I have a lawyer friend who identifies cynicism with "inside knowledge." We lawyers are cynical because we've seen what people are like. We've heard what they say in depositions, we've looked at the documents, we know that the story is always a little bit different from the truth. More than that, we know that everybody has a secret. No wonder we have a tendency to question the sincerity and goodness of human beings! But my friend is a Christian, and he insists that we are not permitted to give way to cynicism. It's the simple reality of original sin, and it shouldn't surprise any believer. And more than that, we should recognize that there are plenty of hypocrisies, plenty of dark secrets, and a false façade or two right here in my own wicked heart. There's no need to be cynical. We face the reality of sin and grace every day.

Status or money as power. We are confused about trappings. If we work in a nice mahogany-paneled law office, make a six-figure salary, see our names in the newspaper, or receive regular community or bar recognition, we forget who we are. Bernard of Clairvaux remarked, "It is no great thing to be humble when you are brought low; but to be humble when you are praised is a great and rare achievement." We ought to be aware of the temptation to pride in situations where we have money, status, or accolades, but sometimes we just need to be told to get over ourselves. A solid Christian community (and a blunt spouse) is very helpful in this regard.

Pride and integrity. Like the love of money, pride destroys integrity by eroding its essentials:

- *Unity.* Pride asks us to serve two masters: ourselves and God, which is impossible. We must choose. C. S. Lewis's heavenly guide in *The Great Divorce* sums it up perfectly: "There are only two kinds of people, in the end: Those who say to God, 'Thy will be done' and those to whom God says, in the end, '*thy* will be done.' "[25]
- *Community.* Pride excludes neighbor by its essential competitiveness and

[25]C. S. Lewis, *The Great Divorce* (San Francisco: HarperSanFrancisco, 2001), p. 75.

the desire to look out for ourselves alone. Pride is the great destroyer of community.

- *Truth.* Pride is the first and the ultimate lie. Satan exalted himself above God, and Adam and Eve believed that they knew better than their marvelous Creator. The lie that underlies all other lies is that we know better than God. Our story, our plan, and our desires are somehow superior to his story, his plan, and his desires.

So how do we address this great hazard of the legal profession and this deadliest of sins? In the words, again, of Bernard, when he was asked to name the four cardinal virtues, "Humility, humility, humility, humility."

The One Model

One of G. K. Chesterton's narrators remarks, "It is always the humble man who talks too much; the proud man watches himself too closely."[26] In a sense, this is the challenge of humility: get your eyes off yourself. It is all-encompassing: "the place of entire dependence on God." It is an attitude, a way of life, a posture toward the world and our neighbors. It is the un-discipline. We don't "do" it, we either are humble or we are not. "To be genuine, humility must abide in us and become our very nature. . . . [H]umility is not a posture we assume for a time—when we think of Him or pray to Him—but the very spirit of our life."[27]

> **Superiority and inferiority complexes are both based on pride because both cause our minds to be on ourselves. . . . Humility is not debasing ourselves; it is getting our focus off of ourselves altogether. Belittling ourselves is not humility, but a hidden form of pride. We are still the center of our own attention.**
>
> JAMIE LASH, "BECOMING A PERSON GOD CAN USE: DEVELOPING A SERVANT'S HEART"

There is but one model for a life of humility, one place to go, and that is to our great example and Savior:

> Do nothing from selfish ambition or conceit, but in humility regard others as better than yourselves. Let each of you look not to your own interests, but to the interests of others. Let the same mind be in you that was in Christ Jesus,

[26]G. K. Chesterton, *The Man Who Was Thursday* (New York: Modern Library, 2001), p. 14.
[27]Murray, *Humility*, p. 53.

who, though he was in the form of God,
did not regard equality with God
as something to be exploited,
but emptied himself,
taking the form of a slave,
being born in human likeness.
And being found in human from,
he humbled himself
and became obedient to the point of death—
even death on a cross. (Philippians 2:3-8)

The simple first step is to regard others as better than yourself. This is difficult, but necessary. Consider other people, dwell on their gifts and their talents that you don't have, and think over their accomplishments. Think the best, and regard them as better.

Second, there is no greater antidote to pride than to care for and serve others. Do you know what your secretary is going through? Do you understand your client's real concerns, or just his or her legal issues? Look. We must open our eyes and work to find out what those around us are interested in. Then we'll forget about ourselves. Law professors can be an arrogant lot. But I know a few who are some of the most humble people I know. As I have thought about their attitudes and humility, it occurred to me that their aim is to love and serve their students with their great knowledge and skill, not to make themselves look good, or to become famous, or to lord it over their students. This *servant's* heart is the source of their humility.

To have the mind of Christ is possible by the power of the Holy Spirit (1 Corinthians 2). By his power, we can take the attitude that Christ took as the suffering servant who came to bear the sins of the world.

We need to give up our "rights." Whatever we think we are entitled to is nothing compared to the deity of Christ, which he did not "exploit" as he came to serve. We need to empty ourselves of our self-importance and adopt a life of servanthood. Return to the idealism of your first year in law school. How were you determined to serve, and how might you accomplish it today?

Finally, we need to be obedient. There is nothing more to the successful life in the law than this. If we do what God asks, we will have success.

The illusion of power. One final thought that ought to make it easier for us to think of others as better than ourselves: We have nothing in reality to gain by pride or power. Our example, Christ, did not consider equality with God something to be grasped—yet he was and is God! We continue to grasp at our position, our status, our power, only to find that it is not much to begin with. Christ really gave up his position in heaven to be a servant, obedient to death. We are giving up only illusory visions of grandeur!

Doctor Faustus discovered this too late. As we see him progress from the prideful, brilliant Renaissance man in act one, we begin to notice something about his choices in the use of his newfound diabolical power, bought with his very soul: They're silly. He has the power to do all that he desires, and he spends his time on parlor tricks and slapstick shenanigans, like conjuring Helen of Troy for a group of scholars with whom he had disputed about women of beauty. We, like Faustus, are willing to risk all to gain the power we desire, only to discover that we are small and petty people who don't really know what do with it once we have it. I hate to pick on professors again, but the old joke about power struggles in universities says it all: The reason that faculty politics are so nasty is that the stakes are so small.

Having examined the pitfalls of a handful of false visions of success, I'll close by setting a vision for true success.

Success: Six Ideas from Joshua

For Christian lawyers, success in law practice likely is not the same thing that our law school classmates or colleagues at the bar pursue. Or is it? Perhaps we can wrap up our discussion of vices with a brief look at some principles of success found in Scripture. It is often our view of success—our real belief, not what we say we believe—that derails us on the issues we have been discussing in this chapter. If we really want to succeed, we must pursue something other than success itself. I suggest that success comes only through obedience. We must pursue faithfulness rather than success.

God makes this clear to Joshua as he prepares to lead the children of Israel across the Jordan into the Promised Land. The land had been promised to Abraham four hundred years earlier, yet the sins of the people in the land were not yet complete, and the people of Israel were not yet ready. After years of slavery, their disobedience in the wilderness cost them another thirty-eight years of waiting. Finally, it was time to move. The Lord spoke to Joshua and told him to cross the Jordan, that he had given them the land, and that he would be with them. He adds:

> Only be strong and very courageous, being careful to act in accordance with all the law that my servant Moses commanded you; do not turn from it to the right hand or to the left, so that you may be successful wherever you go. This book of the law shall not depart out of your mouth; you shall meditate on it day and night, so that you may be careful to act in accordance with all that is written in it. For then you shall make your way prosperous, and then you shall be successful. (Joshua 1:7-8)

The book of Joshua is a blueprint for the Christian life. Some commentators call the book, in addition to a historical journal of God's working in his people, an Old Testament picture of the New Testament Spirit-filled life.[28] This sounds about right. In these words and narrative of the entering of God's Promised Land, God provides a story of the successful life of integrity. Like any story, the book of Joshua is too rich to be distilled into principles, but I'd like to highlight some of the valuable lessons we learn along the way about the successful life in the law.

> **I do not pray for success;**
> **I ask for faithfulness.**
>
> Mother Teresa

The most obvious thing from God's directive to Joshua is that he will be prosperous and successful if—and there is a clear predicate—if he *thinks* (meditates), *speaks* (not depart from your mouth), and *acts* (do according to it) according to the law of God. Obedience to God is the only way to success.

First things first: Remember who you are. After God miraculously brings the people over the Jordan—into hostile territory, by the way—he commands them to stop. Stop thinking about conquest, stop thinking about setting up shop, just stop and remember. In Joshua 4, God commands the people to set up memorial stones in Gilgal so that when their children ask them about the stones, they can tell them what God had done.

As the kings of the surrounding city-states hear of the miracle of the Jordan, they are afraid. It is time to strike, right? No. God was not finished with reminding the people of his work in their lives and their relationship to him. On the eve of one of the greatest military campaigns in ancient history, God commanded Joshua to disable his army: All the men were to be circumcised.

---

[28]See, for example, J. Vernon McGee, *Thru the Bible,* vol. 2 (Nashville: Thomas Nelson, 1983).

Due to their disobedience, they had not been circumcised in the wilderness, and it was time to mark them as participants in the covenant with their God. Not only that, but the people were to celebrate Passover for only the third time, to remember who they were as God's delivered people, and who their Deliverer is. With the celebration too they looked forward, albeit unknowingly, to ultimate deliverance from eternal bondage.

Before getting to the business of conquest and possession, God set the priorities: you are to know who you are in light of who I am.

Who you are is more important than what you do, whether in law, at home, or in church. Indeed those things can only flow out of who you are. And our identity is wrapped up in our deliverer and his story from creation to redemption and restoration (see chap. 10). If we get this part wrong, our priorities in law practice will be wrong.

What do you do that reminds you of who you are in light of who your Deliverer is? Are you seeking to know his Word, as he commanded Joshua? Do you participate in the sacraments with your brothers and sisters before him? Are you engaged in the disciplines that remind you of your smallness—and your dignity—in the love of Christ? As we do these things, surely we will see our pride for what it is. Certainly our blindness as to the role of money will turn to sight. Surely our pursuit of success through status and pleasing the world will stop.

Is God on your side? After the army recovered and the people were ready for battle, Joshua looked up one day and saw a man in the camp with a drawn sword. He confronts him: "Are you one of us, or one of our adversaries?" The answer is a classic: "Neither; but as commander of the army of the LORD, I have now come" (Joshua 5:12-14).

God is not on your side in your law practice. He is not "for" your financial success or your election to the school board. The answer to whether he is for us or against us is simply, no. He is here and he is in charge: "But as commander of the army of the LORD, I have now come." Joshua falls on his face and takes off his shoes.

Where are we lawyers on this issue? Are we doing stuff "for God"? Are we asking him to help us do what we want? God has work to do in our families, with our clients, in our offices, with the court personnel, with kids on the sports team we coach, or in the Sunday school class we teach. It is his work, and he is in charge. Are we face down with our shoes off, or are we urging God to follow our lead? If we make sure we know whose agenda we are about every day, the pride, the temptation to power trips, the financial expectations will all diminish. That's one reason that morning devotions are such a standard recommendation: if we start with an exercise in submission to the One who is the commander of our life, we will be able to see the battles and struggles of the day in the light of his plans and get ours lined up accordingly. We ought to make it a habit to figuratively take off our shoes every day as we enter our offices or classrooms, because the commander is there, and he has work to do.

We must fight, but . . . In the Christian life we need to work. Works won't save us, but we were created *for* good *works* (Ephesians 2:10). God gave the people of Israel possession of the land that he promised them, and he won the battles for them. But they drew their swords, died, stood courageously, and did all the things that warriors do. He fought, but they fought too. And when they fought, he won the battles in his way. In fact, most of the time the victories were not standard military affairs, and each fight was an occasion for God to demonstrate his control and sufficiency in every situation. So they fought, but they had to fight his way. He was in charge of victory. There is no formula for success here or in the conquest of the Promised Land. Thankfully, we do not wage war with weapons, and that violent conquest was a unique and limited call of God to a special people at a special time. Our warfare is spiritual, fought with the divine power, not human weapons, against arguments, thoughts, and obstacles to true knowledge (2 Corinthians 10:3-6). But the story is the same: there is not one way to win every battle to take thoughts captive, to defeat arguments, or to overcome pride and sin in our own lives.

At Jericho, God's people marched around the city silently once a day for six days, with the priests and the ark of the covenant, not the warriors, leading the way. On the seventh day, they circled the city seven times and on the seventh blew the trumpets and gave a shout. Thus the great walled city of Jericho was defeated. They never fought against another walled city in this manner again, despite their success. Ai, for example, was conquered by a fake retreat, and the southern cities were conquered as God threw hail stones from the sky to kill their soldiers, and he caused the sun to stand still at Joshua's request. These exploits, likewise, are not repeated. Yet when the Israelites tried to defeat Ai with their own methods (and with sin in their camp), they were routed. There is no formula but this: we accomplish the task God has before us in the way he desires it to be done. And it's likely a different method every time.

Do we treat our clients as fungible means to the working out of our legal expertise, or as unique, valuable, eternal human beings who God has sent to us for his purposes? It's easy to fall into habits that ignore the uniqueness of the clients and lawyers we see every day. We need to see God's image in them and his hand at work. Success requires our obedience, every day, in every circumstance. Are we open to the change that moral conversation will require? Our victory over the struggles we face in the law is in God's hands; we must simply struggle in the way he desires. This is the difficulty of course; how to know his desires? Our discussion so far should provide some guidance. But there is not much more than an allegiance to his Word, his people, and his practices.

Community (again!). Community has been at the heart of so much we have discussed in our search for professional integrity in the lawyer's life. But it bears repeating: even the seemingly ordinary struggles are played out on the stage set by providence with the company of players God gives us.

The bulk of nine full chapters of Joshua (Joshua 13—21) is dedicated to the division of the land. As God told the Israelites many times, he had given them cities that they did not build, with vineyards they did not plant, in a land flowing with milk and honey. The land was apportioned in community—the first community in God's work—families. As he began in the garden of Eden with a task for Adam's family, he continues his work with his people through the family. The land was apportioned by tribes and subdivided according to clans. God carries out his work through community.

While family was the first unit, established and ordained by God, the primary community God works through—using families here too—is the church, the body of Christ. Success will not come except as part of his body, in whatever we do. There is no such thing as an individual Christian (see chap. 7). We need not belabor the point regarding the centrality of professional community, Christian community, and family. But let me suggest that Professor Gantt's insight is key: who we are as lawyers must be an extension of who we are at home and at church, and not the other way around.

Providence. One of the most striking passages in all of Joshua comes near the end of the book, when the Lord, speaking through Joshua, recaps the fact and the lessons of the conquest. In Joshua 24:2-13, the personal pronoun for God is used approximately nineteen times to indicate God's action on behalf of his people:

> Thus says the LORD, the God of Israel: Long ago your ancestors . . . lived beyond the Euphrates and served other gods. Then *I took* your father Abraham . . . and led him . . . and made his offspring many. *I gave* him Isaac. . . . Then *I sent* Moses and Aaron, and *I plagued* Egypt with what *I did* in its midst; and afterwards *I brought* you out. . . . Then *I brought* you to the land of the Amorites, who lived on the other side of the Jordan; they fought with you, and *I handed them over* to you, and you took possession of the their land, and *I destroyed* them before you. . . . When you went over the Jordan and came to Jericho, the citizens of Jericho fought against you, and also the Amorites, the Perizzites, the Canaanites, the Hittites, the Girgashites, the Hivites, and the Jebusites; and *I handed them over* to you. *I sent* the hornet ahead of you, which drove out before you the two kings of the Amorites; it was not by your sword or by your bow. *I gave you* a land on which you had not labored and towns that you had not built, and you live in them; you eat the fruit of the vineyard and oliveyards that you did not plant. (Joshua 24:1-5, 8, 11-13, emphasis added)

There is no doubt who the actor is and who the recipients are. God did it all. It was his plan, beginning with the call of Abraham all the way through the conquest. The centerpiece of the passage, I think, is the second half of verse 8: "they fought with you, and I handed them over to you, and you took possession of their land, and I destroyed them before you." God brought his people to where they were to be, won the victory that he placed in their lap, and then finished the work by destroying the enemy. In between, however, is one of the few active verbs for Israel in the entire chapter: "you took possession."

God calls us by placing us where we need to be. Did you choose your parents? Your children? Your country? No. But you are called by God to honor *that* father and mother, to raise *those* particular children, and to submit to *this* governing authority. How do you know? You know you are called because you have been placed in those positions by God's providence. Your job is to take possession of what God has accomplished by obeying him in every position he has given you.

Remember and choose.

> Now therefore revere the LORD, and serve him in sincerity and in faithfulness; put away the gods that your ancestors served beyond the River and in Egypt, and serve the LORD.
>
> Now if you are unwilling to serve the LORD, choose this day whom you will serve, whether the gods your ancestors served in the region beyond the River or

> the gods of the Amorites in whose land you are living; but as for me and my household, we will serve the LORD. (Joshua 24:14-15)

This is the call to faithfulness: Choose this day whom you will serve, whether the gods that the legal culture serves—success, money, ego, status, stuff, prestige, golf, sex—or the Lord.

The Outward Signs of Success

The real trick in this life is that there are not really any external indicators of success. A person with money may or may not be truly successful. The closest thing to an external indicator is godly contentment, but that is an internal condition that cannot be reliably spotted. Our best course, of course, is to be faithful and leave the externals to God. And they take many forms.

Consider Joshua, who lived out his life after his military victories in peace and security, working with his hands. His externals look pretty good. So do Daniel's, in the end, but he spent a night with lions on the way to his successful law practice. And there are others who warn us that success is a matter of faithfulness, not comfort. John the Baptist, for example, was successful in his mission. He was faithful. He was set apart. He was praised by Christ as the greatest born of women. And he was beheaded in a dungeon, still a little confused about whether his mission had been successful. What of Paul? Executed, most likely, for his great success in spreading the good news.

What are we to make of these men?

Examples.

Let's move now to a discussion of tools for theological integration as we finish exploring how to apply our commitments to law practice and study.

For Further Thought

1. Evaluate your own use of money for eternal benefits. How are you doing? If you are a law student, what expectations do you have about wealth? Are your desires and expectations pleasing to God?
2. Do you see evidence from your own experience that money is a power that desires our allegiance? How have you successfully avoided that allegiance (so far), or what plan do you have for resisting?
3. Can you imagine living on 10 percent of your income and tithing 90 percent? Could you do it if you made a certain salary? Would you be willing to

commit to give away everything you earned in one year in excess of a set amount—say $80,000, $100,000, $200,000? Why or why not?

4. Why are many lawyers, law students, and law professors arrogant? What can you do about your own tendency to pride?
5. Have you held fast to the idealism with which you entered law school? Why or why not? What would be the benefits of regaining it?
6. What is your definition of success? Is it biblical? What is your plan for pursuing it?

12

Law and Truth

I had been practicing law for about six years, mostly in commercial litigation, when I first interviewed for a law faculty position. I was sitting across the table from the dean of the law school where I wanted to work, doing my best to sound scholarly. They needed someone to teach corporations, and I was giving my opinion as to why it would be only a bit of a stretch for me. I had formed some corporations and had been involved with a board or two in my short time of practice. "What do you think is the biblical basis for a corporation?" the dean asked. I can't really remember what words I used in brainstorming the possibilities, but the upshot, to one reading between the lines, was, "I haven't the foggiest idea."

I had been working with corporations for six years, had studied them in class in law school, and had represented them in court. Yet I had never considered whether this human entity was consistent with a Christian view of civilization. This would not have been much of a failing had I been engaged in making violins or composing concertos, for example, but for one who helped people create these entities, this demonstrated a serious lack of integrity. I had failed to engage my mind faithfully with regard to the very substance of my calling. And I know it's not just me.

If what we've discussed so far is correct, we need some tools to help us think Christianly about the nature of law and its content in the postmodern world. Again, to fully develop and apply the biblical, historical, theological, spiritual and ecclesiological implications of even one small area of law is often the work of a lifetime of study, and practice. But to move in that direction is our calling. We build on what others have done, leaving a heritage others can build on. So I want to close out our discussion of the lawyer's calling by providing some ideas for further digging. The ideas set out here will hardly be worthy of the term *framework* or *sketch;* they are more akin to a brainstorm. We'll take some time to look at principles central to developing more intentional approaches to particular practice areas, then move on to suggestions for digging.

Our task is tied closely to our commitment to truth, of course, and it is largely dependent on worldview. The creation-Fall-redemption ground motif and an integrated method of applying general and special revelation will be our guides even when not expressly acknowledged in our search.[1]

As we have seen throughout our discussion, truth and our response to that truth ("belief") will drive our conduct. In the context of developing proper perspectives on the substance of what we do every day, there is a cluster of principles (perhaps doctrines) that are central to our task: (1) the nature of God and his relationship to his creation, (2) the nature of creation, including the nature of the human person and its relationship to the created order, and (3) the nature of law, its source, and its relationship to the human person. We will take for granted in our discussion that human law should be grounded in divine character and that our law practice and study is subject to God's kingship, worked out in cooperation with his plan for his creation. Our goal is discovery: to discover what God thinks about our law practice or studies and how to agree and cooperate in his work in and through them.

Discovery

When I first started teaching at a Christian law school, I had some catching up to do. As my story about corporations demonstrates, I was not too far down the road in Christian thinking about some areas of law. How to go about educating myself in the specifics of Christian thinking about law? The best option would have been to build a better foundation with a more rigorous education. For me, this was just a bit impractical, so I started building on the foundation I already had. My experience, however, might serve as a note of encouragement to students: a broad, liberal education is helpful to the law and a beneficial aid in seeking truth in the professions. A good dose of philosophy and logic, art and music, history and theory, some serious (orthodox) theology, literature, political science, economics, and business will cut down on the learning curve later in life.

---

[1]On creation-Fall-redemption see chap. 8.

And the learning curve for me was steep. So I gathered some recommendations, and began to read, learn, and talk to teachers. I began to read my casebooks, of course; this provided the specifics on which I hoped to gain a biblical-theological perspective. In addition, I started a program of reading systematic theology in order to familiarize myself with the broad theological themes I would eventually bump into. I also started to dig into the writings of scholars on various Christian approaches to law, legal history, and political theory. I read selections from Augustine, Aquinas, Calvin, and Luther, and bits of what others had written in application of their thinking. I turned to my faculty colleagues for help in explaining things to me; I asked for recommendations, explanations, and encouragement on every level. And every day I spent hours talking to others more knowledgeable than me about the stuff I wanted to learn. And I prayed. I asked God to reveal applications and insights from the Scripture, to show me where to dig, to empower me by his Spirit, and to not let me be humiliated in front of my students. In addition, I continued to serve in my church, care for my children, love my wife, and submit myself to God's discipline and direction. Eventually, even for me, it began to get easier. I started to figure out where to dig, where I needed help, and where I didn't. And now, fourteen years later, I am still learning.

I tell this story about my own digging, not so that readers might follow it as a formula, but to encourage in broad outline one way to seek truth in law. It is a life's process and involves a devotional walk with God, the discipline of study, and the participation in Christian community. Every Christian lawyer may participate in this sort of life, whatever outward form it takes. For me, the end was teaching law, so my journey was likely broader in scope than a practitioner's might be to begin with. In addition, due to the urgency of my task, it was perhaps more intensive than many readers will wish to pursue. God will provide wisdom as you seek to honor him in your studies and practice.

The process of thinking and learning is never done in a vacuum and is never accomplished with "just me and my Bible." The substantive application of the lawyer's calling is our response to Paul's admonition, "what you have heard from me through many witnesses entrust to faithful people who will be able to teach others as well" (2 Timothy 2:2). Again, life in community is key.

Learn, Trust, Teach Others

One of my colleagues practiced law for fifteen years before deciding that he needed even more education in order to understand his calling from a deeper biblical-theological-historical perspective. He also had hoped someday to teach law from a Christian perspective, and he "wanted to be able to do it responsibly." So he decided to pursue theological education, and after seminary he returned to practice. Eventually he joined a law school faculty, where he teaches commercial law courses from a biblical-theological-historical—that is, Christian—perspective.

My friend's story demonstrates several important points about our pursuit of truth in law. First, it confirms that we are all called to be theologians in some sense. While we are not all called to seminary, we are all called to serious Christian thinking that requires the direction of others. Second, it reminds us of the importance of community: this colleague, Professor Scott Pryor, is one of a handful of colleagues who helps teach me in my scholarly thinking. He is part of the community in which I learn, engage in dialogue, and exchange ideas. His education has directly benefited me and many of my colleagues. Finally, Scott's story demonstrates the principle of discipleship that Paul had in mind with Timothy. Scott's goal was and is to teach others to engage in the theological digging that he longed for in his own practice. In fact, he has published several models of integration in the area of contract law with the goal that Christian teachers, students, and practitioners might be encouraged and assisted on their own road. To make the circle of community and faithful discipleship complete, I'll base much of our discussion in the next pages on his paradigm for theologically informed historical development of the foundations of law.[2]

A Paradigm for Integrated Thinking

Professor Pryor's paradigm is designed for biblical-theological integration in the law school classroom and in scholarly writing, but it is perfectly adaptable to the practitioner or law student who desires to move toward a deeper understanding of his or her calling. Likewise, while the target of the model was originally the narrow legal doctrine of "contractual impossibility," its general approach will assist anyone seeking truth across a wide array of practice and

[2]C. Scott Pryor, "Mission Possible: A Paradigm for Analysis of Contractual Impossibility at Regent University," *St. John's Law Review* 74 (2000). See also C. Scott Pryor, "Consideration in the Common Law of Contracts: A Biblical-Theological Critique," *Regent University Law Review* 18 (2005-2006): 1.

subject areas. Good grief, if it can work to help a lawyer think biblically about "contractual impossibility," it ought to be able to help with just about any legal problem short of the Employee Retirement Income Security Act.

The skeleton of the paradigm consists of three perspectives from which we criticize, analyze, and apply elements of law: revelation, community, and self.[3] In short, a lawyer seeks to discover norms "in the Scriptures and in dialogue with the Scriptures" as part of an historical tradition and a present community, and in light of who the lawyer is and what he or she is authorized to do.[4] We work out norms (through general and special revelation) in light of community (historical and present) existentially (in the context of our dignity as a human and in the context of calling, role, or office).

This paradigm is not a formula for application to our work. Yet it will be helpful in making sure that we do not lose sight of important issues as we faithfully evaluate our work, our role, and the law itself. We will expand this three-dimensional paradigm in order to describe in more detail what a lawyer or law student might do in order to work it out.

Revelation (normative). *General and special revelation.* The Scriptures instruct us on all matters relating to our relationship with God. They carry the authority of God, and as such they are our primary resources, even for discerning direction in our law practice or study. God also reveals himself to us through his creation, his work in history, experience, and conscience.[5] These nonbiblical sources of norms are called "general revelation" because they are available to all people generally.[6] Special revelation is God's words addressed to specific people, such as the Bible or his direct address to Moses at Mount Sinai.[7]

So the Bible is the clearest statement of God's will on any matter, including the law, and is the standard against which all other truth claims are measured.[8] In addition, however, as Pryor explains:

---

[3]Pryor, "Mission Possible," pp. 694-98. Pryor calls these the normative, historical/situational, and existential perspectives.
[4]Ibid., p. 705.
[5]See Wayne Grudem, *Systematic Theology* (Grand Rapids: Zondervan, 1994), p. 122. See also Pryor, "Consideration in the Common Law of Contracts," p. 10.
[6]See Grudem, *Systematic Theology*, p. 122.
[7]See ibid., pp. 122-23.
[8]Pryor, "Consideration in the Common Law of Contracts," p. 10.

> We may also have confidence that we can discover God's norms for the law of contracts from sources other than the Bible. Non-biblical sources of divine norms are frequently labeled as general revelation. God did not abandon the world after the Fall. God the King continues His covenantal rule over His creation. Correctly interpreted, general revelation in the forms of the testimony of the human conscience, the results of trial and error throughout history, and the empirical sciences, such as economics, can also reveal the mind of God on the law of contracts.[9]

Dialogue with the text. Pryor suggests that a dialogic model—a give-and-take dialogue between text and reader—is an interpretive stance that will help lawyers avoid both "uncritical objectivism" and "blatant subjectivism" in biblical interpretation.[10] Objectivism, which Pryor identifies as the tendency of modern evangelicalism, consists of fooling ourselves into thinking that we can empty ourselves of all preconceived notions and come to any biblical text as a blank slate. The reality is that "we can never escape ourselves, or divest ourselves or our convictions, or turn ourselves off."[11] On the other hand, we know that the text itself has meaning independent of the reader. Pryor suggests that the reader come to the text with questions and look to it for answers. The answers, in turn, "shape the interpreter whose subsequent questions cannot help but take into account the results of the first series of inquiries."[12] There is still the danger that we will distort the meaning through our own "dirty lens" unless we are careful to continue to allow Scripture to shape our efforts and perspectives, even before we come to a particular text. In addition, this dialogue is unlike the moral conversation we seek to enter into with our clients: we must be open to change, but the Scripture is not—we are in dialogue with the infallible Word that speaks with authority into our lives and practice. Yet we interpret Scripture with Scripture, always careful to maintain some level of mistrust of our own perspectives. Moreover, as we participate in this dialogue, we must rely on the Holy Spirit to "awaken our understanding of the significance of God's revelation."[13]

It should be apparent that this discussion of the normative perspective (revelation) includes the existential *I* in relationship to the Scriptures themselves. The dialogic model implicates both the existential and the normative perspec-

---

[9]Ibid.
[10]Pryor "Mission Possible," pp. 699-700.
[11]Gordon J. Spykman, *Reformational Theology,* quoted by ibid., p. 699 n. 24.
[12]D. A. Carson, quoted by Pryor, "Mission Possible," p. 700.
[13]Pryor, "Mission Possible," p. 702.

tives: as I search the Scripture, I am aware of my limitations and role, and also my ability as one created in God's image, to discern spiritual truth from God's revelation in his Word and around me.

The big picture. We must start somewhere in our critique of our practice area or legal doctrine in light of God's standard. How do we know where to begin? We must have some knowledge of the big picture to be able to bring to bear the *revelation-community-self* paradigm on any particular issue. It is simply a practical question of where to start an evaluation. If we're thinking about tort and personal injury law, should we consider our three-part paradigm in light of the atonement, creation and the cultural mandate, or another principle or doctrine?

In order to make decisions about where to begin to approach an issue, we need some general biblical knowledge under our belts. We can learn to think biblically through three means of biblical analysis: exegesis, biblical theology, and systematic theology.[14]

Exegetical theology. Exegesis "seeks to fix the meaning of individual statements and passages." The reader studies word by word or phrase by phrase to "discover exactly what God seeks to impart in his Word."[15]

Biblical theology. Biblical theology is "that branch of theological inquiry concerned with tracing themes throughout the diverse sections of the Bible . . . and then with seeking the unifying themes that draw the Bible together."[16] Biblical theology is the history of God's redemptive plan across the various epochs recorded in Scripture.[17]

Systematic theology. Systematic theology constructs doctrine and dogma by topic, extracted from the whole of Scripture and organized into a logical system.

If we will frame our study across these available strands of biblical analysis, we'll begin to see and relate doctrinal norms to our practice and study. It may be helpful to see the normative perspective as corresponding to our commitment to truth (see chap. 8). God has normed his creation by his law. We are all subject to this law, and it forms the basis of all that we do or think, in the law or otherwise. When we bring a revelation-based perspective to our think-

---

[14]Ibid., p. 720.

[15]*Wycliffe Dictionary of Theology* (Peabody, Mass.: Hendrickson, 2000), pp. 204-5.

[16]Grant Osbourne, quoted in Pryor, "Mission Possible," p. 721.

[17]See Derke Bergsma, *Redemption: The Triumph of God's Great Plan* (Lansing, Ill.: Redeemer Books, 1989).

ing about law, we safeguard our commitment to truth. The integrated lawyer is grounded in serious and regular interaction with God's Word.

Community (historical/situational). The second point in our tripartite paradigm for biblical-theological integration is the community perspective. We must bring God's authoritative Word to bear as normative on any legal issue, practice area, or course of study. But the lawyer's dialogue with revelation does not occur in a historical vacuum.[18] We've discussed the individualistic ("just me and my Bible") tendencies among Protestant evangelicals already, but it bears repeating: we must recognize our place in the history of biblical interpretation, realize that the Holy Spirit has been at work in the church for two thousand years, and admit that we are subject to the disease of individualism so contagious in our culture.

> The practice of Christian interpretive dialogue has continued from the close of the apostolic era up to today. It is surely a serious omission for one engaged in dialogue with the Scriptures today to ignore the results of the previous 1900 years of questions and answers. The previous dialogue sets the boundaries of orthodoxy for the [lawyer seeking to work out his or her calling].[19]

Professor Pryor suggests that lawyers and students seeking to understand norms in light of historical community should be familiar with the early ecumenical creeds (the Apostles' Creed, the Nicene Creed, and the Athanasian Creed) and the interpretive work of ("at least") the first four ecumenical councils (Nicea, Constantinople, Ephesus I, and Chalcedon).

In addition, the lawyer will seek to collect what past students of the law and theology have written or said on a particular issue. "Whereas the normative perspective focuses on Scripture, the historical focuses on human culture."[20] Any historical narrative that we develop will also have normative value, as well, since law develops historically in a very real sense. This is also one of the great benefits of Christian integration in the law: knowing our roots gives us confidence in our continuation of the Christian traditions infused into Anglo-American common law, and a better understanding the developing norms of the American legal system.

Obviously, the historical perspective is based on our second characteristic

---

[18]Pryor, "Mission Possible," p. 702.
[19]Ibid., p. 703.
[20]Ibid., p. 723.

commitment: the commitment to community. Recall, first, that the task of Christian discipleship in the law is one that we undertake in Christian community (see chap. 7). Our commitment to life in community means, among other things, that even in the nitty-gritty of applying scriptural norms to our law practices, we will continue to be in community within the body of Christ.

However, the historic perspective also requires that we consider those in the legal community around us who do not share our views regarding truth, goodness, and the lawyer's calling. We should engage the ideas of the broader legal profession, in addition to our regular fellowship within the body with like-minded professionals. We need to be able to engage the postmodern legal mind in a way that accepts its challenge and enters into its perspective. The situational/community perspective implicates our lawyer's disciplines once again, which reminds us to be engaged with the surrounding culture and to study the trends and habits of our times. Here are some of Pryor's suggestions:

- Consider the felt needs of the times and lawyers in your community. What are they thinking about the law and their lives?
- What responses do you see from the broader profession, including judges, professors, and lawyers? Critique and analyze these as well.
- Make use of and pay attention to all forms of analysis: economics, science, social science, public opinion polls, psychology, philosophy, logic, and language and literary studies. We need to know our times and our neighbors.

Practicing lawyers and law students are pretty good at engaging the larger culture and staying abreast of developments within the legal community: the challenge is to integrate faithful and truthful service with our daily tasks in the law office.

Self (existential). Finally, the existential perspective considers what it means to be human beings created in the image of God and what we are authorized (or called) to do based on our office or our role. We consider our place in the universe and in the situation in light of our humanness and the dignity that comes with being created in the image of God. This perspective corresponds in many ways to our first commitment, unity (see chap. 6). We recognize our limits based on role and calling, yet we understand our duties in that regard and the privilege that accompanies God's image in us. Much of our discussion of the first two perspectives assumed this existential perspective: What are we called to do as scholars but investigate and engage other scholarly communities? How are we to read a text except by bringing ourselves into dialogue with it?

For lawyers, the existential perspective is implicated in the adversary system, where one's role in that process requires careful consideration. In addition, our relationships with clients or opposing parties and even the criminal justice system will remind us that we deal with human beings created in God's image, which brings with it certain consequences that cannot be ignored in the law or in our practices.

Again, this paradigm is not a formula. It is a tool to keep us focused on the whole task rather than just one piece of it. As Pryor put it to me, "we cannot take just one thing and make it everything—bringing multiple perspectives to an issue keeps us centered." If our tendency is to proof-text, tradition and community will keep us in line; if we chase after modern fads, revealed norms will bring us back to reality; if we have desire to apply Scripture in ways inappropriate to office or role, the existential perspective reminds us of context. This is no guarantee that we'll get everything right, of course! But it will give us the proper *perspective* from which to build. For those interested in building further, I have set out examples of partial application of the paradigm on three important legal themes in the appendix.

All of this is simply to encourage the act of truthful integration that goes hand in hand with the transparent life, the lawyer's disciplines, and the rejection of false dualism. None of our work need start from scratch. We can build on the work of others thinking in the area even today (in this sense the appendix can be both an example of how to "do" integration and a resource to apply to certain practice areas). In addition, not everyone is called to write down every thought and conclusion. In fact, for most practitioners and students, the process of integration will involve reading and evaluating what others have written in order to take one more step toward a Christian understanding of work.

To close our discussion I'd like to suggest some normative and historical ideas that might come in handy in the same way. These are simply suggestions, broken down by topic, to encourage the process of theological thinking that I have argued is no longer prominent in the legal profession.

Normative and Historical Resources

I have argued from the start that our true beliefs are reflected in every aspect of our lives; if they aren't, something is wrong. On one hand, we might not really believe the things that we say we believe. On the other, we might be pretending that we are not who we are. Either way, we are disintegrated. The solution is to admit hypocrisy and live truthfully or to change our minds about reality. Like all human beings, we are religious—we all have fundamental presuppositions about reality that drive what we do.

Historical perspectives. *General legal history.* The law, likewise, reflects fundamental "doctrines" about reality.[21] It is religious. We should not be surprised, then, when we are able to trace the historical development of the law in relationship with developments in the institutional church and shifts in the fundamental (religious) presuppositions in the surrounding culture.

The field of legal history is vast and specialized, and I claim no expertise in it. Yet, as the Pryor Paradigm presupposes and our commitment to community confirms, we are all obliged to mine theological and legal truth in the company of our forebears. I suggest three areas where investigation will be most productive.

First, lawyers ought to know enough about church history and legal history to understand something of the historical relationship between the two, if only just the fact of the relationship itself. The development of the Anglo-American legal system is a reflection of the influence of the Christian faith on Western civilization.[22] To be sure, the common law system and its consequences were influenced by the Enlightenment and other modern phenomena. But it should be our goal as Western lawyers to understand and evaluate our heritage. For example, with regard to the rule of law itself:

> To draw the connections between the Christian faith and the rule of law cultivated in the common law tradition is not to suggest that the Christian faith is the only possible basis for the rule of law. . . . Nor is it to deny the influence of notions from outside Christianity. . . . [T]he Christian religion provides an especially rich soil for the growth of the rule of law, and . . . the flourishing of the rule of law in the common law tradition owes much to the Christian faith.[23]

Second, American lawyers should understand the founding of the United States and the theological-legal-political theories that resulted in our unique polity and the legal system in which we operate:

---

[21]See, for example, Craig A. Stern, "Crime, Moral Luck, and the Sermon on the Mount" *Catholic University Law Review,* 48 (1999): 801-42.

[22]On this point, see Harold L. Berman, *Law and Revolution: The Formation of the Western Legal Tradition* (Cambridge, Mass.: Harvard University Press, 1983).

[23]Craig A. Stern, "The Common Law and the Religious Foundations of the Rule of Law Before Casey," *University of San Francisco Law Review* 38 (2004): 499.

> Apart from Christian conceptions of a Creator Who asks to be worshiped in spirit and truth, and a Christian conception of the inner forum of inalienable conscience, George Mason's *Virginia Declaration of Rights,* Jefferson's *Bill for Establishing Religious Freedom,* and Madison's *Memorial and Remonstrance* would lose all cogency and sense. These documents owe their derivation to a Jewish and Christian worldview, and do not spring from any other.[24]

Because the United States is such a mixture of the biblical and the classical, filtered through the Enlightenment, knowledge of our political roots will help us make sense of the legal system we operate in daily.

Natural law. We ought to understand the role of natural law as a historical (and perhaps normative) perspective that informs the work, whether we know it or not, of the Christian lawyer.[25] Though we've discussed this in some detail in chapter two, it bears discussing the importance of natural-law thinking to the lawyer's task. For example, natural law—or general revelation—provides a useful bridge to discussions of norms with those who do not share a Christian worldview. In addition, we need to be reminded that law is not simply a human artifact but reflects the created order.

Natural law may be a bridge to our rationalist modern neighbors as it was to the Aristotelians of Aquinas's day. Of course, our world is a far cry from the world of Aquinas, whose project was to synthesize the faith with truthful pagan presuppositions in order to demonstrate the truth of the faith and its utility in the world. As one contemporary Thomist puts it: "The single greatest obstacle to profiting from Aquinas's treatise on law lies in the notion that each of us is autonomous, a law unto himself, and that it is possible to have a shared sense of the good or to form a society on that basis."[26] It appears that we live in a world where the obstacles to profiting from this great work are nearly insurmountable.

In addition, even some Christians are uninterested in the natural law and its implications. Natural law scholar J. Budziszewski notes:

> Now it may be asked why a Christian should be interested in the natural law at all. If one already has the Bible what use is it? At best it would merely repeat in

---

[24]Michael Novak, "The Faith of the Founding," *First Things* 132 (2003): 32.

[25]In the Roman Catholic legal tradition, much of the historical—as it relates to teachings of tradition—may be normative as well.

[26]Ralph McInerny, introduction to Thomas Aquinas, *Treatise on Law* (Washington, D.C.: Regnery Gateway, 1956), p. xviii.

> cursive a small part of what God had already written in great block letters. . . . It may [even] seem as though the Bible is the only source of moral knowledge.[27]

His answer is that the Bible teaches otherwise. God has revealed himself through general revelation (that is, to all humans, not just particular people). General revelation includes the testimony of creation itself, the fact that we are made in the image of God, our physical and emotional design, the law of conscience (written on the heart), and the law of consequences.[28] Budziszewski believes that the "new kind of pagan," in contrast to those in the world of Aquinas, is harder to reach because the classical culture that taught of the good, the true, and the beautiful does not "press into" the broad culture in the way that it did in the twelfth century. Budziszewski therefore suggests that our focus should be on the law of conscience as a means of apologetics informed by special revelation—the Scriptures: "The main use of general revelation, including the natural law, is apologetics: giving a reason for the hope that lies within us."[29]

This is the great and worthwhile project of the integrated lawyer: to give a defense of hope in a fragmented, confused world.

I have a colleague who believes that in the broader culture it is indeed possible to have a shared sense of the good and move toward real community on that basis. He has undertaken a contemporary continuation of this medieval challenge by appealing to "moral realism," which he has defined, in a play on the American Law Institute's Restatement series, as the "Restatement of the Obvious":

> Topic One: Principles of moral realism
> Section 101. There is an objective reality.
> Section 102. Human beings can know something about it.
> Section 103. There are some things that everybody ought to do.
> Section 104. The Gap. [Human] law is not the same as morality or religion.
> (1) There is a law that is the same as morality and religion
> (2) There is a [human] law that is not the same as either
> (3) There is a legitimate question about the gap
> Section 105. Christians know these things because God has revealed them not

[27]J. Budziszewski, *Written on the Heart: The Case for Natural Law* (Downers Grove, Ill.: InterVarsity Press, 1997), p. 180.
[28]Ibid., pp. 180-81.
[29]Ibid., p. 184.

> only by the illumination of the Holy Spirit, but also in creation, conscience, and the Bible.[30]

This is an important and worthwhile project that I think we all participate in. It is, in a sense, a step beyond the call to integrity, a next—and necessary step—toward the neighbors who do not share our worldviews. This is the challenge of service to and engagement of the world. Moreover, it is a demonstration of the reality of moral truth—truth that is as "real" and discernable as gravity. Natural law thinking, in this sense, is a remedy to the "fact-value" and "public-private" dualisms we have addressed.

Practice Perspectives

To bring a bit more practical edge to our discussion of the perspectives through which we ought to evaluate our work in the law, let's consider applications of the integration paradigm for advocates, and counselors.

Advocates: Litigation and conflict. Litigation deserves its own discussion, and it is appropriate that we attempt to apply our conversation on integrity by addressing it.[31] It is the source of much of the poor reputation of lawyers, the culprit for much of the unhappiness of lawyers, and the beginning of many of the moral conflicts that we have seen in chapters ten and eleven.

The human cost. Lawyers who try lawsuits often become callous to the toll that they take on the human beings involved. Litigation is almost always physically and emotionally grueling for individual participants. With the exception of large corporations, whose representatives drive the decisions and participate in the process, I have never seen a client that was not emotionally affected by involvement in litigation. Professors Shaffer and Cochran discuss a breach of trust suit filed by one brother against another, in the course of which the defendant committed suicide after days of withering cross-examination.[32] Litigation exacts a high toll on the parties, even in seemingly mundane disputes.

Alternative Dispute Resolution (ADR) programs have arisen in response to

---

[30]Thomas C. Folsom, "The Restatement of the Obvious: Or, What's Right Got to Do with It? Reflections on a Business Ethic for Our Times," *Regent University Law Review* 16 (2003-2004): 347-49.

[31]The best place to begin in thinking about the subject of conflict personally and professionally is the classic by Ken Sande, *The Peacemaker,* 3rd ed. (Grand Rapids: Baker, 2004).

[32]Thomas L. Shaffer and Robert F. Cochran Jr., *Lawyers, Clients, and Moral Responsibility* (New York: West, 1994), pp. 5-6.

> **The primary benefit of resolving disputes through the church is that it preserves our witness for Christ. This process prevents a public quarrel that would dishonor Christ, and it encourages biblical solutions and genuine reflection. These results bring praise to God by showing the power of the gospel: God really has delivered us from our sins, and he is actively working in us to conform us to the likeness of his Son. For these reasons, alone, we should make every effort to resolve our differences outside of a courtroom.**
>
> KEN SANDE, *THE PEACEMAKER*

the need for lawyers and clients to have options at their disposal to resolve disputes outside the stressful and costly mechanism of litigation. ADR is a blessed and hopeful development. Cochran, among others, has argued that a lawyer may be committing malpractice if he or she fails to mention to a client that there are alternative means of resolving disputes. He has gone so far as to suggest that the rules of ethics ought to *require* that a lawyer disclose ADR options before proceeding with litigation, so that the client may make an informed choice.[33]

Mediation. Mediation is perhaps the best remedy to the problems inherent in the adversary system and in the litigation process itself. A lawyer-mediator has freedom to seek the healing and restoring ends of litigation through a means that diminishes the financial and emotional toll of most lawsuits. A party has freedom to learn and share with an opponent without great risk. Yet mediation and other alternative means of resolving disputes are often overlooked by pastors and Christian lawyers, and even by Christian law students considering career options. It is such an obvious means of facilitating healing and reconciliation in relationships that this ought not be so.

Ken Sande calls alternative dispute resolution methods, such as arbitration and mediation, "assisted peacemaking."[34] This is ministry in the law worth pursuing. We in the church should be the first in line to embrace mediation; yet for the most part, it continues to take a back set to standard adversarial methods.

The local church. The most overlooked alternative to litigation among Chris-

[33] Robert F. Cochran Jr., "Professional Rules and ADR: Control of Alternative Dispute Resolution Under the ABA Ethics 2000 Commission Proposal and Other Professional Responsibility Standards," *Fordham Urban Law Journal* 28 (2001): 895.

[34] Sande, *Peacemaker*, p. 26.

tians is the local church. This is odd, because Scripture clearly teaches that the local church is the place for believers to resolve their disputes with one another, and it sets down some fairly clear procedures and goals. One passage that speaks to the matter is 1 Corinthians 6:1-8. Paul asks the believers why they dare to take a grievance against another Christian "to court before the unrighteous" rather than "taking it before the saints" (v. 1).

Peace among Christians and proper means of reconciliation are so essential to our witness for Christ that God commands us to take unresolved disputes to the church rather than to the civil courts. Many pastors have neglected to teach regularly on this passage, so most Christians are completely unaware of this command or believe that it no longer applies. Worse yet, many churches deliberately ignore this passage and do nothing to help their members settle their legal disputes in a biblical manner.[35]

Paul suggests that it would be better to be wronged than to have lawsuits among believers tried "before the unrighteous."

The Christian in court. The Christian lawyer who represents Christians must be aware of scriptural alternatives that are absolutely necessary to resolving conflict. In addition, if the lawyer is involved in a true moral conversation, operating under the ethic of care, then he or she will certainly discuss with clients who profess to be Christians possible limits to the use of the civil courts suggested by 1 Corinthians 6.

The dispute resolution procedures that Jesus preached are not given as options but as norms. First, we are to go to a person that has offended us in order to regain that relationship and bring reconciliation. Next, if the offending party will not listen, we should take two others with us as witnesses, again in order to win over our brother or sister. If that fails to resolve the dispute, then we tell it to the church so that the church may speak to the issue (Matthew 18:15-17). Some see an important relationship between this passage and the 1 Corinthians 6 passage about lawsuits among believers. Christian lawyers who desire to love their neighbors need to understand what it means to help their Christian clients live in obedience to Christ. More importantly, we need to decide whether Christ's teaching should shape our advice to clients or not. Let's take a closer look at the 1 Corinthians passage to guide our thinking.

[35]Sande, *Peacemaker*, p. 54, citing 1 Corinthians 6.

1 Corinthians 6. Ken Sande notes that there are three views on the 1 Corinthians 6 passage. The first is that "this passage forbids lawsuits against Christians and non-Christians."[36] This was likely the medieval view as well:

> Let us plainly conclude, therefore, that it is not the part of Christians to dispute at law before any judge about any matter, whether of property of person or to seek their own rights, since for a Christian man there can be no greater justice, nothing more equitable, than to suffer and put up with wrongs.[37]

Sande finds this view difficult to support, since the language of the text uses "brother" ("member of the church" NRSV) and Paul earlier admonishes the church not to judge nonbelievers (1 Corinthians 5:12).

The second view, according to Sande, is that the passage "forbids any and all lawsuits between people who profess to be Christians."[38] This view is not consistent with the passage itself nor with the rest of Scripture, which suggests procedures on how to deal with those who profess to be Christians but who will not listen to the church.

The third view deserves careful consideration. Sande suggests that the most reasonable view of the passage is "that it forbids Christians to sue persons who are members in good standing of a Christian church that is faithful to Scripture." The point is that the local church is the primary means of resolving disputes among brothers and sisters; if a person has been removed from the fellowship of believers, however, then "that person has been removed from the protection of the church." Under this view, the procedures taught by Christ in Matthew 18 assume primary importance. Resolve conflict person-to-person or within a small group of witnesses, or within the larger community of the local church. "If your opponent (or you) refuses to listen to the church, and if the church obeys Scripture and removes such a person from the fellowship, the dispute can then be resolved legitimately through the civil courts if necessary."[39]

Mathew Henry takes a similar view: "Note, Christians should never engage in law-suits till all other remedies have been tried in vain. Prudent Christians

---

[36]Ibid., p. 280.

[37]John Colet, *Commentary on First Corinthians* (Binghamton, N.Y.: Medieval & Renaissance Texts & Studies, 1985), pp. 127, 121.

[38]Sande, *Peacemaker,* p. 280.

[39]Ibid., p. 281.

should prevent, if possible, their dispute, and no courts of judicature decide them, especially in matters of no great importance."[40]

This process does not resolve all the difficulties since it does not address the offended party's attitude or motivations or speak to the problem of conflicts between members of different congregations. Sande makes helpful suggestions on both issues. First, if the offending party's church does not follow Scripture in the matter, he suggests that the offended party ask the leaders of his or her church to meet with the leaders of the opponent's church to help resolve the issue through discussion or arbitration. If the other church won't listen, the offended party's church might declare the other church unfaithful to Scripture as to this conflict and permit the offended party to pursue civil remedies. The first option, of course, would be to consider simply dropping the matter and suffering loss.[41]

Sande suggests a final check on the Christian seeking to go to court. "In addition to exhausting your church remedies, you must be sure that the rights you are seeking to enforce are biblically legitimate."[42] This excellent advice requires theological collaboration on the part of lawyer and client in evaluating the Christian client's claim. It is a true measure of whether a lawyer is truly interested in pursuing an ethic of care. In addition, motives are an important element in litigation decisions. Sande suggests that the final condition that must be met before the bringing of a lawsuit involves its purpose:

> Therefore, do not file a lawsuit unless you are confident that it will somehow (1) advance God's kingdom (e.g., by promoting justice or providing a positive Christian witness to those who observe the action); (2) benefit your opponent (e.g., by invoking the power of the state to force him or her to bear the consequences of wrong behavior, which may help the opponent to behave more responsibly in the future; see Rom. 13:1-7); and (3) enhance your ability to know and serve Christ (e.g., by preserving rights and resources needed to minister to others or provide for those who depend on you).[43]

Now comes the hard part: are you willing to counsel Christian clients along these lines, not forcing them to see it this way but entering into the moral con-

---

[40]Matthew Henry, *Commentary on the Whole Bible* (Peabody, Mass.: Hendrickson, 1991), p. 2254.
[41]Sande, *Peacemaker*, p. 281.
[42]Ibid., p. 282.
[43]Ibid., p. 283.

versation that includes potential duties to God? If we are serious about loving our neighbor and walking in integrity, we'll most certainly have to answer that question.

Restitution and reconciliation. Advocates need to think about the purpose of litigation. In one sense, litigation is the means for justice in the rawest sense: just desert. A wrongdoer is punished according to his or her deeds. This is a biblical and appropriate use of litigation. But what of restoration, restitution, or reconciliation? Perhaps the best place to start is in the Exodus case laws, immediately following the Ten Commandments (Exodus 20:1-17; 21:18-36; 22:1-6, 22-25). These are the major passages regarding the civil law and tort theory, and they should be instructive for discerning God's goals and methods in the law of personal injuries.

All of this must be read and evaluated, of course, in a broader theological context concerning the jurisdiction of the state, theories of punishment, Christ's atonement, and the role of the civil ruler. In addition, biblical and systematic theology will help resolve the difficulties of the relationship between the Mosaic tort laws and the American system. In other words, it will be helpful to know why it is unwise (or wise) to transplant these laws as the basis for our tort law.

> CLASSROOM HYPOTHETICAL
>
> **Paul comes into your law office one morning and tells you he needs to sue someone for violating a written agreement. In the course of telling you the factual background, he says, "I would have thought better of Donald. We've gone to church together all these years."**
>
> **Does this raise any issues for you as his lawyer? How would you advise him regarding lawsuits between believers?**

The Exodus laws and general propositions will be helpful in evaluating strict liability and fault-based regimes, perhaps suggesting one as superior to the other in certain circumstances.[44] Likewise, these laws' approach to human and divine roles in causation and resulting human responsibility will be helpful as well. The question whether compensation is a biblical goal for a tort system is another central question on which the Scriptures might provide norms or guidance.

---

[44]See Douglas H. Cook, "Negligence or Strict Liability? A Study in Biblical Tort Law," *Whittier Law Review* 13 (1992): 1-16.

The Exodus passages and principles regarding fault, personal responsibility, restitution, and reconciliation might prompt us to rethink our practices:

- There may be some cases that we won't handle as litigators if either the motivation for bringing the suit or the goals of litigation are contrary to what we discern as permissible in Scripture.
- We might advise our clients of moral obligations that they may have to others, regardless of legal consequences.
- There may be tactics that do not further what we discern to be legitimate goals of litigation. Will we engage in those? Will we inform our clients of our stance in this regard?
- We may change our practices regarding demands or defenses based on the principles of proportionality in restitution and retribution.
- Changing our orientation toward litigation, based on its proper ends, may reveal to us new avenues for ministry in our practice, showing us how we serve in very practical ways to foster justice.

One Colorado Springs lawyer orders his approach to criminal defense around reconciliation and restitution. He has his clients write letters of apology to victims and encourages his clients to raise money for restitution, even before sentencing.[45] His family law practice, too, bears witness to his passion for the human beings involved, as he encourages his clients to work with opposing parties for the good of the broken family and the children. It changes lives. A client sums it up: "He cares more about people than his pocketbook."[46]

Jurisdiction and the role of the civil ruler. The principles of jurisdiction, the role of the civil ruler, and the implications of Christ's atonement are important considerations for civil procedure. We should also consider the existence or procedural rules in the Old Testament laws, such as the two-witness requirement, judgment upon review of evidence, and the practice of calling witnesses as evidence of the necessity of moral procedure. The biblical foundations of the rule of law itself are likely also fertile ground for a normative perspective on procedure. Lawyers might also consider the *imago Dei* as a foundation central to the presumption of innocence, the prohibition against cruel and unusual punishment, and the right to confront one's accusers. Likewise, the doc-

---

[45]Dennis Huspeni, "Lawyer Practices His Faith," *Colorado Springs Gazette,* January 8, 2007, Metro, p. 3.

[46]Ibid.

trine of the Fall recommends procedural safeguards, appellate remedies, and limits on certain types of questionable evidence.

The applications of these central doctrines to law practice are virtually endless, but I'll suggest a few ideas for practical application in the law office or classroom. First, the various procedural requirements in the Old Testament can remind us of the importance of procedures in a moral system. Lawyers' general devotion to procedure as central to justice is not misplaced. For example, the requirement that "a single witness shall not suffice to convict a person of any crime or wrongdoing in connection with any offense that may be committed" (Deuteronomy 19:15) implies that even some obviously guilty people cannot be punished by human beings. If, for example, a reliable source with perfect eyesight were to witness a murder in broad daylight from a close distance, we would be quite sure that the murderer was indeed guilty. Yet, if the murder occurred under the jurisdiction of the Mosaic procedural law, there could be no punishment by the state. Why would God have instituted such a procedure?

Moral legal process is necessary to determine who can be held accountable in temporal legal systems. The "two witnesses" requirement, for example, ensured that the civil state did not execute judgment unless there was a significant degree of certainty that the party was, in fact, guilty. With this requirement, the state erred on the side of letting the guilty go unpunished, rather than overstepping its authority and punishing the innocent. As William Blackstone wrote in 1769, "It is better that ten guilty persons escape, than that one innocent suffer."[47] This is sound theology, since the state does not have the authority from God to punish all who are "guilty" of any sin or to cast so broad a net in pursuit of justice that it punishes the innocent as well as the guilty. This ought to remind us in daily practice that, as guardians of justice, lawyers guard procedure, respecting the technicalities that preserve jurisdictional boundaries.[48]

Second, Scripture reminds us that all human institutions derive their authority from God and are therefore limited in their *jurisdiction*. "Individuals, families, covenantal bodies, schools, all exist and have authority as prescribed

---

[47]William Blackstone, *Commentaries on the Laws of England* (Chicago: University of Chicago Press, 1979): 4:27.

[48]On this issue, see Michael P. Schutt, "What's a Nice Christian Like You Doing in a Profession Like This?" *Regent University Law Review* 11 (1998-1999): 137.

by God. A biblical doctrine of the state equally should affirm that the existence and authority of the state are prescribed by God."[49] This means that human governments lack the authority to punish every sin or wrong.

This ought to help to lawyers as legislators and judges, seeking to discern the limits and roles of the state, the church, the family, and the individual. It, too, should encourage us as practitioners to seek alternative means to resolve disputes and redress wrongs. In the same way that we have recognized the limits of political action, we should admit that the state is not supreme in all things and that there are limits to the civil law and legislation.

Furthermore, as Professor Stern has suggested (see the appendix), the doctrine of divine providence has vast implications for all types of procedural and substantive issues. In fact, without faith in God's sovereign justice, procedural limitations to effect human justice would be quite difficult to justify.

Why not, for example, permit perjured testimony to convict a child molester who would otherwise go free? Why forbid false evidence when it leads to the "right" result? J. Budziszewski explains:

> The motto "Do the right thing and let God take care of the consequences" makes sense only on the assurance that He will take care of the consequences. Without that assurance, doing the right things *means* taking care of the consequences—or trying to. And so unless there is providence, the urge to do good irresistibly consorts with evil. Unless God is just, *our* justice becomes unhinged.[50]

Summary of the advocate's role. Litigation can be a powerful means of justice. By way of summary, here are some guiding themes for the advocate's work.

Restoration and litigation. Litigation, despite the human cost, can restore victims and bring restoration. Yet attitudes and motivations are suspect. Are we willing to advise our clients of alternatives to litigation, to refuse to bring suits among believing individuals, or to seek reconciliation rather than generate further conflict?

The system. As advocates within an adversary system we must be willing to evaluate the content of the system itself to determine its creational structure and direction rather than hiding behind it. My own view is that the ad-

[49]Craig A. Stern, "Things Not Nice: An Essay on Civil Government," *Regent University Law Review* 8 (1998): 1.

[50]J. Budziszewski, *What We Can't Not Know: A Guide* (Dallas: Spence, 2003), pp. 69-70.

versary system itself is not structurally evil. The principle of advocacy is sound (since Christ himself is our advocate) and the system generally seeks to protect jurisdictional boundaries through procedural safeguards. But not everything permitted in the adversary system is permissible to the Christian lawyer. The fact that Christ is our advocate does not mean that we might advocate for evil, participate in the corruption of the system by permitting false testimony, or mislead the court, for example. Neither are all means of advocacy permissible. The Christian advocate must carefully evaluate the rules of the prevailing system in light of a biblical view of justice in order to determine the limits of his or her role within that system. Hiding behind the system is not an option.

As we evaluate our roles within the system, we'll have to take a position on a variety of practical issues. First, we'll need to decide if we can even work within the adversary system. I suggest that a lawyer may work within the adversary system, if he or she (1) recognizes the limitations of that system, (2) is committed to refraining from tactics—even ethically permissible tactics—that would undermine the integrity of the litigation or negotiation process, and (3) refuses to cooperate in evil that may be perpetuated by the system. The problem is figuring out what this means in the context of our daily practice. For example, a lawyer must decide how to distinguish between systemic practices that are morally justified as a result of being universally understood (such as "puffery" in negotiations and selective trial testimony) and practices often accepted by those in the system but not morally justified (such as abuse of opposing witnesses, offering evidence the lawyer believes to be false, and discovery tactics designed only to harass the opposing party). Is there really a valid distinguishing principle, and even if there is, are we able to make proper decisions in the heat of a trial, consultation, or negotiation?

Second, Christian lawyers will have to embrace a special responsibility to "push" the system in the direction of righteousness and goodness. When we see areas of oppression and loopholes for abuse, are we willing to take responsibility in this area?

Third, as part of an integrated approach to involvement in our system, I believe we ought to attempt to disabuse our clients of the notion that our primary job is to "work the system" to reach any desired result. We ought to be able to accomplish this through the process of moral conversation (see chap. 10). Are we ready for this sort of commitment with our clients?

Punishment. Sound views on the nature of punishment will help us evaluate and participate in the criminal justice system. Knowing that just desert, rather than rehabilitation or deterrence, is the primary end of punishment will determine our role and approach to both prosecution and defense work.[51] As we represent accused criminals, we will seek just sentences, require that the state prove its jurisdiction to punish, and honor moral procedural safeguards.

Candor with clients. Christian advocates, if they find themselves unable to work within certain aspects of the system, must advise their clients in advance of strategies or tactics that will be off limits. This requires wisdom and foresight. Imagine the difficulties, for example, that you might cause in assuring your client that you will never divulge communications between the two of you if, later, it turns out that the client lies on the stand and you are are morally obliged to inform the court.

Counselors. Attorneys whose role is to counsel encompass a broad range of expertise: in-house counsel, transactional lawyers, estate planners and financial advisers, negotiators, and corporate vice presidents. I'll list some historical-theological approaches to the specific areas encountered by these lawyers—corporations, contracts and property—but first, let's review some broad areas of concern for counselors.

Wisdom and advice. It is hard to imagine a more important way to love one's neighbor than by giving godly wisdom. Model Rule 2.1 tells us that in "rendering advice, a lawyer may refer not only to law but to other considerations such as moral, economic, social and political factors, that may be relevant to the client's situation."[52] In other words, we are "permitted" by the ethics rules to treat our clients as if they are fully human and not just legally challenged raw material to be solved by us.

Our clients are real people who often need more than mere technical advice when they need a lawyer, and most states' ethical rules recognize this. As we learn to communicate with our clients on the human level, we will find greater moral meaning in our practice and our service to the people we represent. If we fail to treat our clients as human beings that have social, familial, spiritual,

---

[51]This is not completely uncontroversial. See Professor Tuomala's argument for deterrence in the excerpts in the appendix, and see Jeffrey C. Tuomala, "The Value of Punishment: A Response to Judge Nygaard," *Regent University Law Review* 5 (1995): 13.
[52]*ABA Model Rules of Professional Conduct* R.2.1 (2002).

and economic obligations, we fail to serve them fully.

We do, of course, need to be aware of the reasons the client has come to us. Yet it seems wrong to ignore the plain needs of those seeking our counsel. A simple encouragement to seek moral, psychological, or spiritual advice is sometimes all that is necessary. Many lawyers are afraid to go even this far. But don't we a have a duty to go further? Whether particular religious, moral, or other nonlegal considerations—Scripture passages, specific prayer with the client, direct admonition—should be raised in a given situation requires wisdom and prayer.

If we claim that the pursuit of justice is a "worthwhile good," we must admit that ethical rules alone are insufficient to define our obligations to our communities, clients, and God. And if no such obligations exist, perhaps we are spinning our wheels in seeking to address matters of justice, right, and good at all in the practice of law.

Recently I was giving a continuing-legal-education ethics presentation using one of the early scenes from the movie *A Time to Kill* to generate discussion. In the scene, Carl Lee Hailey (Samuel L. Jackson) has come to see Jake Brigance (Mathew McConaughey), a young lawyer. Carl Lee's elementary-age daughter has been raped by two white men, and Carl Lee believes that they will be acquitted as a matter of course by an all-white jury in the rural south. He asks Jake, "What would you do?" and whether he would "help" him if he got into some trouble. Jake clearly believes (and he is right) that Carl Lee intends to shoot the accused men.[53] I show this clip to raise the issues of when the lawyer-client relationship begins and whether Jake may ethically divulge the conversation to his wife or the local sheriff. As I began to discuss these issues with the group, one lawyer interrupted. "I think we're missing an important point. This guy is about to ruin his life and the lives of his family. He is contemplating murder and risking everything he has for revenge. If I'm the lawyer, I tell him that. Then we get down to some serious prayer about the injustice he is facing and how best to handle it." In other words, forget the ethical quandaries for a minute; this man is a hurting human being in need of a wise counselor and the power of God to solve his real

[53]*A Time to Kill*, screenplay written by Akiva Goldsman, based on the novel by John Grisham, directed by Joel Schumacher (Regency Pictures, Warner Bros. 1996). University of Arkansas law professor Howard Brill directed me to this clip and others for use as ethics examples.

problems. That's what I call integrity in the law office.

We need to recall, too, Shaffer's advice regarding the ethics of care: our advice to the client is not the end-all. The moral conversation is the means to growth and a good first step toward justice.

Stewardship issues. Almost all counselors are in the business of loving their neighbors by helping their clients to be good stewards of what God has entrusted to them. This necessitates a proper view of mammon and a commitment to moral conversation about the ends to which money is a means. If our theology of wealth is properly developed, we will be able to better serve those who wish to faithfully use it to take dominion over creation (see Genesis 1:28), give to others in need (see, e.g., Proverbs 31:9) and leave an inheritance for their children (Proverbs 13:22).

Negotiations. When lawyers negotiate on behalf of clients, even outside the litigation arena, all sorts of predicaments may arise. While this is not as difficult an area *theologically*, negotiations do require clear moral thinking. In fact, the ethical rules regarding negotiations may permit more than a Christian lawyer will be willing to do. For example, Model Rule 4.1 arguably provides lawyers greater latitude in withholding facts than laymen, even under the same circumstances.[54] Lawyers may not knowingly "fail to disclose a material fact when disclosure is necessary to avoid assisting a criminal or fraudulent act by the client."[55] I can imagine examples in which a lawyer would feel honor bound to disclose material facts to third parties, even if the disclosure were not necessary to avoid assisting in criminal or fraudulent conduct.

Likewise, lawyers involved in negotiations will discover early in their careers how deep their commitment to truth really runs. Is "puffing"—making exaggerated (or false) statements that are not intended to be taken as true by parties on the other side of the table—permissible to the man or woman of integrity? Ethically, "both lawyers and their clients are free to indulge in the ritualistic and presumably harmless lying that is legally permissible under the concepts of puffing or chaffering."[56] A Christian lawyer will need a well-developed theology of misstatements to determine what's right in this regard. One way to approach it is to understand the conventions involved in

---

[54]ABA Model Rule 4.1(b). For possible alternative explanations and interpretations, see Charles W. Wolfram, *Modern Legal Ethics* (St. Paul, Minn.: West, 1986), pp. 722-27.

[55]Ibid.

[56]Wolfram, *Modern Legal Ethics*, p. 726.

negotiations and evaluate one's statements based on the effect they will have on one's neighbor. If the statement "My car is worth *way* more than that" isn't exactly true, but it isn't intended to be understood as a statement of value but as an invitation to offer more money, we might justify the statement as simply a negotiating convention. Another approach might be to change our conventions to be more precise, even if it requires evasion, in our negotiations. Our decision, once again, will rest on a theological decision: when, if ever, is lying permissible?[57]

I believe it possible to have significant nuance in answer to this question, and I agree with much in the analysis that says that a duty to tell the whole truth at all times does not exist in the abstract, and that our duty to speak is always based in the context of relationship and correlative duties. But I also know that a stance that lying in negotiations is always permissible, as long as we are wearing our lawyer's hat, seems, at this stage in our discussion, to be an act of complete disintegration.

Ken Sande, though writing for laymen more than for lawyers, suggests "cooperative" rather than "competitive" negotiation, pointing out that we have a duty to look to the interests of others and not only to our own interests (Philippians 2:4). While this is not literally the duty for lawyers when we are agents of others (our limited duty is to our clients over others), we represent clients who are or ought to be interested in both loving their neighbors and negotiating a deal that creates good will or benefits for others.

Sande's model requires significant effort; it is far more preparation intensive than a strategy that seeks to beat down the opponent as far as he or she will go. But Sande advocates cooperative negotiation because it creates *solutions to problems*. Granted, sometimes our clients cannot budge on a matter of principle or a financial limit. But most of the time, we are trying to help them solve problems. Cooperative negotiation, as most of us have probably seen, can do that more easily than competitive negotiation. In the process, we are often able to save money and relationships as well.[58] Our goal is not to cave in to others, but to understand their needs and how our clients might be able to meet those needs while also getting what the client needs. The key to cooperative negotiation is creative preparation; we need to take the time to understand what the

---

[57] An interesting and helpful historical-theological treatment is found in Paul J. Griffiths, *Lying: An Augustinian Theology of Duplicity* (Grand Rapids: Brazos, 2004).

[58] Sande, *Peacemaker,* p. 226.

opposing side really needs. Even in corporate struggles and stock battles, sometimes these needs are emotional or psychological (sometimes they even involve the lawyers!). Sande uses the acronym PAUSE to outline cooperative negotiation:[59]

Plan
Affirm relationships
Understand interests
Search for creative solutions
Evaluate options effectively and reasonably

Lawyers who take the time to really prepare for a negotiation by praying, understanding what the client really needs, learning what the other side is really after, studying Scripture related to the project, and developing creative strategies is serving the client beyond what a client will expect. But isn't our goal to be fully integrated servants? Don't we desire that our clients do more than just get what they want—we desire that they honor God and love their neighbors too. If we can help them do that in a way that meets their needs, so much the more pleasing we will be to them and to God. While we need to remain alert to varied tactics from others and be ready to stand firm on behalf of our clients, the time that it takes to prepare to negotiate cooperatively is certainly worth the effort. And our clients won't likely complain, because "social science research also indicates that [cooperative negotiation] is significantly more successful in advancing a client's interests."[60]

Contracts. In the words of Professor Pryor:

> The identification of normative standards relevant to [contracts] is not as bleak as might first appear. [One] could seek first to justify the use of contracts as a form of social activity by reference to the promise-keeping character of the God revealed in the Scriptures, and then move on to analyze the significance of humanity's creation in the image of God, the persistent use of the ancient Near Eastern practice of covenanting as the model of God's relationship with humanity, and the approbation of promise-keeping in the torah, poetry, and the Wisdom literature of the Hebrew Scriptures. [One] could then analyze the significance of those relatively rare occasions in which a biblical character receives tacit approval for breaching a promise and particularly those instances

---

[59]Ibid., pp. 227-28.
[60]Wofram, *Modern Legal Ethics*, p. 714.

when God does not carry out a threatened judgment due to an intervening contingency operating as an implicit condition.

The traditional or historical perspective on [contracts] could start with the Roman law and progress through the medieval and early modern period. Attention should be given to original archival research from a range of sources—theological, historical, and legal. This historical perusal must not be an end for itself. Instead, it should form part of the intellectual collage by which the faculty member can contribute to the goods of the common law tradition: criticism, analysis, and application.[61]

In the first paragraph of this excerpt, Professor Pryor lays out the basic theological justification of the calling of the lawyer who drafts, negotiates, and enforces contracts. There is still plenty of fertile ground to till, however, as we pursue our practice with Christian integrity. What obligations arise, for example, when I—or my clients—give our word on a matter? How might I advise a client who has made a promise yet has grounds for an "efficient" breach? How do I deal with these and other areas in which the law and my obligations to God may differ? How can I use and create agreements that will assist my clients in their stewardship and other duties? Does it matter whether I present these goals to them explicitly, or is it enough that I know how God is using me to love my neighbor and further his or her particular ministry in the community?

I have a friend who tells the story of learning the doctrine of "efficient breach" in law school. His professor had elaborated on the doctrine, opining that when economic benefits of breaching a contract outweigh the costs of breach, a lawyer should advise the client to breach the contract. My friend raised his hand. "What about a person's word? What about the moral commitment?" The professor was apparently amused. Years later, my friend had an opportunity of a lifetime come to him that would require him to go back on his word to another party, though there was no written contract. He remembered his law school experience, and God also reminded him of Psalm 15: "O LORD, . . . Who may dwell on your holy hill? / Those who walk blamelessly, and do what is right / . . . who stand by their oath to their hurt" (Psalm 15:1, 2, 4b). He kept is word, even though he was not legally bound. I'm not saying that my friend's position is the only possible theological approach to the doc-

[61]Pryor, "Mission Possible," p. 727.

trine of efficient breach. I am saying that behind virtually every legal stance we take there is a biblical-theological stance. If we don't decide in advance, based on our commitments to integrity, our decision on how to stand will make itself before we are prepared.

Professor Pryor also encourages us to mine all the resources available as we seek a faithful approach to serving our clients. Again, this is not something that we do alone; in fact, we see that scholars like Pryor and others have laid a good groundwork on which we can stand as practitioners. As we think and pray about our daily work, we can trust that God will show us how we need to study in order to be lawyers of integrity.

EXAM QUESTION

Proverbs 13:22: "The good leave an inheritance to their children's children."

Tom comes to your law office and would like you to draft his will. He wants to leave his entire estate to a nonprofit corporation and express in the instrument that his three children shall receive nothing.

Do you comment on his choice? Engage him in dialogue? Do as he wishes without comment or discussion? Other? Explain your answer. This is an open book test.

Private property. Michael Hernandez suggests the following building blocks for a normative perspective in his property class.[62]

- God created the Earth and everything in and on it (Genesis 1:1-27).
- God owns the Earth and everything in and on it (Leviticus 25:23; Deuteronomy 10:14; Job 41:11; Psalm 24:1).
- God's grant of dominion to humans (Genesis 1:26-31; Psalm 115:16).
- Humans have stewardship responsibility (Genesis 2:15; Matthew 25:14-30; Colossians 3:17, 23-24).
- Prohibitions/warnings against theft, covetousness and greed (Exodus 20:15, 17; Leviticus 19:9-11; Matthew 6:19-21; Luke 12:15-21; James 5:1-5).

These building blocks will be instructive for the practitioner seeking a normative grounding for his or her law practice as well. To understand the varied

[62]Michael V. Hernandez, Regent University School of Law syllabus of property class (on file with author).

duties that people owe God with regard to their property is probably essential to a law practice of integrity. Of course, working out these issues with clients is a matter for prayer, wisdom, and reflection.

An additional theological building block that any lawyer must grapple with in this type of law practice is a moral justification for private ownership of real and personal property. A lawyer who fails to come to grips with this fundamental question might have difficulty making tougher decisions down the road when it comes to assisting clients with stewardship, inheritance, or dominion issues.

We have some historical help on this issue, since Blackstone, James Kent, and John Locke all developed theories of private property ownership, and all based their analysis on Genesis 1 and 2:

> While both Blackstone and Kent agreed that the book of Genesis was the key to a correct understanding of the origin of private property, they did not have the same understanding. Blackstone believed that private property had been invented by men as the only solution to the problems of finiteness of resources and of the need for a stable civilization.
>
> Kent, however, claimed that private property was inherent in the nature of things.[63]

John Locke's theory, also based on Genesis, was that God had given property to all humankind in common, but when a human being "mixed his labor with it," it was removed from the common state.[64]

As lawyers build on these foundations, they must also revisit the fundamental distinctions in jurisdictions of church, state, and family. Is there a role for government protection of private property? Is there a duty to the state—or the church or family—regarding what we "own"? How do we balance the legal "ownership" of property against the truth that we are mere stewards of it, and how might we advise and assist our clients given these truths? There is plenty to consider when we practice in this area.

If our commitment to community means anything, we will also desire to think about how a client's place in various communities—cities, associations, family, parish—is relevant to the client's obligations and wishes regarding pri-

---

[63]Herbert W. Titus, *God, Man, and Law: The Biblical Principles* (Oakbrook, Ill.: Institute in Basic Life Principles, 1994), p. 237.

[64]Ibid., citing John Locke, *Second Treatise of Civil Government* (1690).

vate and real property. Again, we are not necessarily looking to substitute the lawyer's conscience for the client's, but we are looking for moral conversation on these issues—give and take—and if we haven't even thought about any of this, we will be poorer counselors for it.

Conclusion

Without expressly saying so, this chapter has suggested a further solution to our three stumbling blocks. We have discussed (1) theological thinking about law, (2) in light of a central commitment to vocation that (3) counters instrumental views of law and lawyering. Along with the lawyer's disciplines and an intentional pursuit of virtue in our client relationships, we have some building blocks for integrity in our practice and study. I'll conclude by briefly summarizing our pursuit of integrity in the law in chapter thirteen.

For Further Thought

1. Integrating faith and practice under the three-fold paradigm (revelation, community, self) is a lifelong project. Begin by making a list of passages, articles, and principles that already inform your approach to your practice or studies. How well are you doing at integrating your practice with your faith? Where do you think you are lacking?
2. Make a list of practices in your daily work (whether in law school, in law practice, or on the bench) that you believe you need to think more faithfully about. Set a time to sit down with another lawyer to discuss them.
3. What historical resources would you like to read in the next six months to help develop your thinking on law practice? How can you make that happen?
4. Consider whether a deeper, more biblically informed understanding of any of the following areas would help you in your daily practice:

- Compensation for injured parties
- The jurisdiction of the church, state, and family
- Procedural requirements necessary for justice
- Limits on the role of the state in punishing sin and crimes
- The purpose of punishment
- The ethical limits of living out the gospel with clients

- The adversary system and advocating for others
- The limits of negotiations
- The biblical justification for corporations, wills, private property, or contracts
- Other areas

Choose one topic and meet with another lawyer or your pastor to begin exploring the issue. Read the examples in the appendix to get started.

Conclusion

Dr. Benjamin Carson is the well-known director of the division of pediatric neurosurgery at Johns Hopkins and has performed many ground-breaking procedures and high-profile operations. He believes that God has called him to be a surgeon, and his life and testimony bear witness to that call. He has loved thousands of "neighbors" through his unique and special gifts.

In the mid-1980s, a young couple came to Dr. Carson and asked him to perform a dangerous type of surgery on the husband. They wanted him to operate on an area of the brain stem, on which no surgeon had ever operated, to remove a tumor. They were Christians, and Dr. Carson prayed with them about the surgery and advised against it. It would likely be fatal, and he told them he wouldn't do it. After much prayer, however, and further requests, he agreed. When the day of the surgery arrived, having prayed with them before the surgery, he said to them, "It's in God's hands."

"Yes it is," they replied, "but we believe that you let God use *your* hands."[1]

This is the great and mysterious call of God. That we are privileged to be his hands of healing, reconciliation, justice, peace, encouragement, hospitality, love, and all that he desires to do to restore our culture, our neighbors, and our world. He could do it alone, but he calls us as his colaborers, that we may experience relationship with him and with his creation. It is ultimately a mystery.

The heart of Christian lawyering is the abundant life lived before God at home, at church, and at the office. It is the life lived in the knowledge of a good and infinitely powerful Creator God who is active in his work among us

---

[1]Ben Carson, with Cecil Murphey, *Gifted Hands: The Ben Carson Story* (Grand Rapids: Zondervan, 1990), p. 183.

and who allows us the privilege of working with him to change the world through faithfulness in daily living.

Lawyers who see themselves in light of this deep mystery and as part of this great drama will never mistake a client for a mere mortal, will never call a case "ordinary business," and will never see the law as just a job.

> Like good stewards of the manifold grace of God, serve one another with whatever gift each of you has received. Whoever speaks must do so as one speaking the very words of God; whoever serves must do so in the strength that God supplies, so that God may be glorified in all things through Jesus Christ. To him belong the glory and the power forever and ever. Amen. (1 Peter 4:10-11)

Appendix

Examples of Integration Under the Paradigm

Let's consider three examples of the paradigm applied, to help us as we attempt to find an integrated perspective in our particular practice or scholarship. The clearest examples are those that are developed with an eye toward teaching others, so the examples I have chosen are all written evaluations of a biblical-theological-historical approach to a particular legal problem. Unfortunately, they were written by law professors rather than practitioners, so the results of the critique, analysis, and application tend to be more theoretical than immediately useful in daily law practice. On the other hand, I've chosen areas that are instructive not only as exemplary applications of the paradigm but also as introductions to transcendent norms, doctrines, and principles that practitioners and students will be able to build on when evaluating their own practices and studies under the paradigm.

We'll turn now to three examples: (1) the doctrine of the atonement as it relates to theories of punishment, (2) biblical perspectives on contract consideration in the common law, and (3) the Sermon on the Mount as it illuminates the criminal law doctrine of incomplete attempts.

Example 1. Christ's Atonement as the Model for Civil Justice

Professor Jeffrey Tuomala has demonstrated that "the doctrine of Christ's atonement is of singular importance for theories of punishment, as it is the judicial archetype of the way in which God deals with sin and crime."[1] He shows

[1]References in this section to Jeffrey C. Tuomala's theory are found in "Christ's Atonement as the Model for Civil Justice," *American Journal of Jurisprudence* 38 (1993).

the parallels between various views of what the atonement means and various resulting theories of civil justice. In so doing, he criticizes legal and theological doctrines with scriptural norms, analyzes historical facts and interpretations, and makes applications.

He begins his analysis by evaluating the relationship between theories of punishment and basic criminal-law doctrines, making the case that cases are always resolved on the basis of an underlying theory, which is not always justified. The justifications for these theories, he notes, are always based on one's worldview. He argues that the civil ruler, as "minister of God for justice" should deal with crime and sin according to the same principles that God does. Therefore, his starting place is the doctrine of the atonement.

Tuomala brings the normative perspective to bear on the theory of atonement on two levels. First, he lays out four views of the atonement (primarily developed through the historical perspective), evaluating each one scripturally (normatively). Second, he critiques the four views comparatively against each other and against Scripture. He calls on at least thirty or forty separate references to normative passages as he seeks to critique the views and establish the norm by which he may critique the legal doctrines of punishment. His point is that one's view of the atonement (worldview) will have consequences in one's theory of punishment: "The satisfaction, governmental, moral influence, and mystical theories of atonement correspond to retribution, deterrence, rehabilitation, and social justice."[2]

He brings the historical perspective to work in setting the normative passages in context and to explain the various views of the atonement, since they have developed historically. The historical development demonstrate norms as well, since the historical narrative informs us of the meaning of the doctrine itself.[3]

Tuomala sets out the satisfaction theory of atonement first, using Anselm's work *Why God Became Man* as the starting place. He describes Anselm's use of Roman law and the doctrine of penance to explain the satisfaction theory, developing it further through the historic perspective of the Reformation, citing John Calvin and engaging some contemporary legal historians as well.

---

[2]Tuomala, "Christ's Atonement," p. 223.

[3]Pryor notes that this is an important part of the historical perspective. See C. Scott Pryor, "Mission Possible: A Paradigm for Analysis of Contractual Impossibility at Regent University," *St. John's Law Review* 74 (2000).

Tuomala then critiques the theory with Scripture (again, the normative perspective) and then moves on to its implications for legal doctrine. He establishes the current status of the retributive theory of punishment, demonstrating the parallel between the satisfaction theory and retributive theory:

> The satisfaction theory teaches that justice is an immutable attribute of God's character demanding full payment of the law's penal and compensatory sanctions for human sin. It alone holds that Christ's vicarious death was necessary to satisfy justice as a condition of salvation, and that its primary effect was to change God's judicial disposition toward humanity. Likewise, only retribution requires punishment based on moral desert and does not focus on its prospective effect on the offender.[4]

Tuomala concludes that "Scripture characterizes Christ's death not only as a punishment but as a payment. Justice demands both. An offender deserves to be punished (retribution) and he owes payment (restitution) to the offended party." This view leads to the conclusion that criminals deserve punishment "proportionate to the moral blameworthiness of their offense." We cannot justify punishment by our own goals, whether to reduce crime or rehabilitate "bad" people. In order to reflect the atonement, punishment ought to include payment to the victim and payment to the offender (just desert).

Tuomala also adds that if the atonement is the model for civil justice, it also demonstrates another element always left unjustified by legal scholars—why the state has any right to punish at all:

> Most writers do not address the question of whether the state has a right to punish; however, it is answered in the course of showing why Christ's atonement is the model for civil justice. . . . Romans 13:1-7 says that God established the state with the magistrate as his servant, who is "an agent of wrath to bring punishment on the wrongdoer." As an agent exercising delegated authority, the magistrate must administer justice by the same principles that God dealt with all sin through Christ's atonement.[5]

Tuomala completes the same multiperspectival critique, analysis, and application for three other theories of the atonement, next discussing the moral theory of the atonement and its proponents, Abelard and Faustus Socinus. Grotius and the governmental theory of the atonement are next, followed by a

---

[4]Tuomala, "Christ's Atonement," pp. 223-24.
[5]Ibid., p. 232.

discussion of rehabilitation and deterrence, the theories of punishment that follow the moral and governmental theories of the atonement:

Both Grotius and Socinus believed that Christ's death was an unnecessary, but highly expedient, means to change man and preserve order. Utilitarian civil sanctions, like Christ's death, are selected for their expediency to a particular end. These utilitarian views of the atonement were quite compatible with, and perhaps smoothed the way for, an emerging view of the state which was becoming less concerned with exaction of perfect justice in individual cases, and more concerned with law as an instrument for advancing a particular vision of the common good.[6]

This brings together all three perspectives, since the suggested application to our current system is implied. Tuomala adds the jurisdictional kicker here as well: "Just as Arminian and Socinian theology confuse the work of Christ and the Holy Spirit, utilitarian views of civil justice confuse the roles of state and church."[7]

Finally, through scriptural norms and the historical perspective of Friedrich Schleiermacher, Tuomala describes, critiques, and analyzes the mystical theory of the atonement and its corresponding theory of punishment, social justice. The suggested application is already clear:

> In both the mystical and social justice views, issues of individual sin, and guilt as moral wrongs, are minimized or eliminated. The focus is on establishing a particular order, or effecting a change of relationship, without a satisfaction of justice. In effect, it is reconciliation without atonement and community without satisfaction of justice. The mystical view of atonement eliminated the duality between god and man, and in so doing, eliminated the separateness of individuals. Social justice, to overcome the problems of the welfare-corporate state, eliminates the separateness of individuals, and in so doing creates a new god.[8]

Tuomala concludes his analysis with application. "I have argued that only the satisfaction and retribution-restitution views are distinctly different and justifiable in terms of Christian theology and biblical worldview."[9]

---

[6]Ibid., pp. 243-44.
[7]Ibid., p. 244.
[8]Ibid., p. 254.
[9]Ibid., p. 255.

Example 2: A Biblical-Theological Critique of Contract Consideration

Professor Tuomala's project involved an important doctrine evaluated through a maze of historical variations. The perspectives, therefore, from which his criticism, analysis, and application flowed, were heavily historical and normative. Our second example, involving consideration in the common law of contracts, involves a complex evaluation of three doctrines applicable to contract law generally, evaluated under the three perspectives, in light of two important principles, liberty and jurisdiction. The benefits of this example for our purposes include, first, the inclusion of three important doctrinal issues that will help students and practitioners integrate biblical truth in many other areas of the law, and, second, the intentional and self-conscious use of the Pryor Paradigm, since Professor Pryor is the author of the example we will consider.[10]

Pryor begins "by describing three Christian doctrines that are particularly relevant to legal analysis. I will then follow with three perspectives that demonstrate how to apply the doctrines as tools for legal criticism. With these foundations, I will then move on to address consideration in two parts."[11] Due to the complexity of the analysis, our discussion here will focus on demonstrating the method itself and some of his broader conclusions, without an in-depth discussion of the bottom line on consideration.[12] As you might expect, however, it is the nuts-and-bolts discussion of consideration across the perspectives that takes up the bulk of the article. So you might say we're just hitting the introductory highlights in our treatment here.

The three doctrines. The three doctrines that frame the analysis are the Creator-creature distinction, the covenantal structure of understanding, and the law of God. In setting forth the first doctrine, Pryor emphasizes our dependence on God as part of his creation. "In other words, what we believe we know about justice in general and the law of contracts in particular is dependent on what God thinks about justice and contracts. Anything we say about these topics is subject to what God says about them." Doing all to the glory of

---

[10]References in this section are found in C. Scott Pryor, "Consideration in the Common Law of Contracts: A Biblical-Theological Critique," *Regent University Law Review* 18 (2005-2006): 1.

[11]Ibid., p. 2.

[12]If you are a contracts fanatic and simply need to know his evaluation of the doctrine of consideration, read the full treatment in ibid.

God, then, entails complete obedience to the One who created us in every single area of life, whether it be in the law of contracts or academic studies. "Our search for the correct rules and their accurate applications is not autonomous but rather is subject to the God whose will is revealed in Scripture."[13]

The second doctrine, the covenantal structure of understanding, tells us what form our dependant relationship with God takes. Covenant describes that relationship in a pervasive way, and leads to three conclusions:

- All humankind is covenantally related to God.
- There is no division between sacred and secular; all of life of every human being is embedded in covenantal relationship (including the law of contracts).
- Creation understood in terms of covenant entails that the cosmos is subject to God's kingship; therefore, neither law nor lawyering is a neutral, secular activity.

Our analysis of the law must reflect these truths:

> Human law is ultimately grounded in the divine character; the law of contracts is dependent. Human law is administered on earth; the law of contracts flourishes in God's Kingdom. Human beings dispense human law; the law of contracts is subject to God's kingship. In short, all human knowledge, including knowledge of the law of contracts, is servant knowledge, and the Christian's concern should be to discover what the LORD thinks about this law, to agree with that judgment, and to carry it out in loving obedience.[14]

The third doctrine, the law of God, tells us that law may be discovered from "the full range of God's revelation including the world around us, our consciences, and human experience as well as the Bible."[15] We often have too narrow a conception of what it means to seek application of God's will to the law. Scripture is the "best evidence" of God's will on any topic and provides "the standard against which all other truth claims must be evaluated." It also "justifies other means by which God's will about the law of contracts may be discovered."[16]

The three perspectives. The three perspectives (normative, situational, and

---

[13]Ibid., pp. 5-6.
[14]Ibid., p. 9.
[15]Ibid.
[16]Ibid., p. 10.

existential) help relate the various aspects of a system to each other and ultimately relate them to the whole (described in the three doctrines). "Each element of the system of the law of contracts is perspectivally related to another and to the whole. . . . These three perspectives can be summarized . . . as the normative, the situational, and the existential."[17] Professor Pryor describes his task in applying the perspectives:

First, all human activity is "normed" by the law of God, but the law is not simply "out there," it is part of the covenantal constitution between the personal independent God and personal dependent human beings. Second, every human application of the law of God must take place in a particular setting; situations differ and provide differing fora or spheres in which to apply the correct norm. Last, the law is applied in a particular situation by and to human beings.[18]

In applying these perspectives Pryor first sets out the basic conclusions as to the perspectives in light of the doctrines to contract law generally. First, he applies the normative perspective across the doctrines, discussing our mandate to rule the earth (the "dominion mandate"), the authority of human beings that flows from that "dominion mandate," the effect of the Fall and the mandate to continue nonetheless in God's work as cocreators. The normative perspective leads to the conclusion that "contracts are a means by which human beings exercise dominion." He warns that dominion can be distorted and become oppressive if not understood in light of the situational and existential perspectives.[19]

The situational perspective, which leads to a discussion of both office and spheres of dominion, "suggests two useful insights on the law of contracts." First, the dominion mandate and the covenantal relationship from which it flows, suggests "universal opportunity to contract." Second, *office* defines who may enforce contracts and in what sense *justice* might require enforcement.[20]

Finally, the existential perspective links contractual ability with the imago Dei: human beings are capable of making promises and keeping their word. Tying the three perspectives together across the doctrines, Pryor concludes: "God created human beings in His image and with liberty to exercise domin-

---

[17]Ibid., p. 11
[18]Ibid.
[19]Ibid., pp. 12-15.
[20]Ibid., p. 18.

ion by making certain promises enforceable at law when they communicate decisions to act or refrain from acting in some definite way in the future, subject to other stipulations of His covenant(s)."[21]

He spends most of his pages in detailed analysis of the liberty principle and a second principle, jurisdiction, which is also discerned from the criticism, analysis, and application of the three doctrines across the perspectives.

By framing the discourse in this way, Pryor has given us both building blocks for our own future integrative tasks and ideas about how to approach contracts faithfully.

Example 3: Crime, Moral Luck, and the Sermon on the Mount

"Moral luck" is the strange label applied to the problem represented in the following hypotheticals:

> Alexander, intending to kill Carl, takes careful aim, fires, and inflicts a wound that proves instantly fatal. Alexandra, intending to kill Carol, takes careful aim, fires, and inflicts the merest dent in Carol's bicycle. Alexander and Alexandra share equal intention, skill, and equipment. But the wind unexpectedly blows askant Alexandra's bullet, saving Carol's life. If both shooters suffer arrest and conviction for their shots, Alexander likely will face the death penalty or a long prison term, while Alexandra will receive a relatively short prison term. A difference in wind has rendered Alexander guilty of murder, Alexandra of attempted murder.
>
> Whatever the theory of criminal law and punishment, these results appear anomalous, if not unjust. Both shooters harbored the same intent, both indulged in the same conduct and both imposed the same risks. . . . The conduct to be deterred is identical for both actors. Both manifest equal need for reform or incapacitation. Both seem to deserve equal punishment for the wickedness of their intent and conduct. Can the wind really matter so much? The criminal law of perhaps every jurisdiction in the United States would treat Alexander and Alexandra very differently.[22]

This issue is known as the problem of moral luck: "How can the moral quality of an act or an actor hinge upon luck?"[23] Professor Craig Stern applies a

---

[21]Ibid., p. 19.

[22]Craig A. Stern, "Crime, Moral Luck, and the Sermon on the Mount," *Catholic University Law Review* 48, no. 3 (spring 1999): 801, 802-3.

[23]Ibid., p. 804.

biblical-theological-historical lens to the problem in our final example of the Pryor Paradigm.

Whereas Pryor began by explicating three doctrines and Tuomala discussed the historical varieties and consequent of one doctrine, Stern concludes that two doctrines shed light on the current legal rule. Unlike our first two examples, however, he does not set out the doctrines until the middle of the discussion. He begins with the situational (historical) perspective, discussing the rules relating to the law of incomplete attempts and evaluating what philosophers, legal theorists, and theologians have had to say in study of this issue. Finding these wanting, he brings in the normative perspective, primarily from the Sermon on the Mount. "Two fundamental Christian doctrines support the view that simultaneously finds Alexandra as morally guilty as Alexander and yet not deserving of equal criminal punishment. Both doctrines are central to the faith that largely shaped the laws and morals of America. Both find expression in the Sermon on the Mount."[24]

Stern spends considerable time in exegesis and evaluation of Christ's words, demonstrating the thread of two doctrines in the Sermon: (1) "the unique stringency of God's standard of 'perfect humanness;' " and (2) the "beneficent omnipotence of God's Divine Providence." God's standard of "perfect humanness" is set out in the context of comparing the law ("an eye for an eye") with perfection ("turn the other cheek"). Jesus does not criticize the law, but his lengthy discourses on these matters "demonstrate the gap between the civil law and the moral law for humankind."[25]

> What is especially striking in the passage, however, is the repeated and insistent call not to find moral justification in adherence to a civil law standard of behavior. One may not be committing murder, and yet hate; one may not be committing the act of adultery, and yet commit adultery in one's heart. Again, it is not that the civil law itself is defective—God himself ordained the civil law in this case. Rather, Jesus warns of the confusion of the types of law and of the appropriate forum—the judgment of goodness before humans and the judgment of goodness before God. Even God's rules for social governance do not establish perfect rules for human behavior, though, of course, they do plainly suggest them.[26]

---

[24]Ibid., p. 812.
[25]Ibid., p. 815.
[26]Ibid.

The first fundamental Christian doctrine involved, then, is a *jurisdictional* principle regarding the limits of civil law.

The second doctrine, divine providence, is taught by Christ in the beatitudes, the teaching on alms, the teaching on fasting, and the familiar passage on the lilies of the field and the birds of the air. Stern connects the two doctrines and the cases of murder and bicycle-denting:

> First, the most just and perfect law for social use—for example, civil or church law—does not prescribe the total justice and perfection of ideal human behavior. Recognition of this principle does not necessarily entail the notion of inner-morality versus outer-legality, or the idea that law for society is instrumental and consequentialist while private morality is deontological, or some other such dichotomy. Rather, the principle may entail the Christian view that all authority comes from God, and that human authorities have various roles or ministries in recognizing, adopting, and applying law. The nature and purpose of law may not change from forum to forum, but the authority of a forum does. Justice remains a universal standard of law, no matter the forum, but no sublunary forum has commission to do total, absolute justice. That power is God's alone.
>
> So the moral luck that seems to damn Alexander's act more than Alexandra's because the wind shapes the trajectory of bullets is not really moral luck at all. If, before God, their hearts, acts or characters are equally guilty, he will judge. But our human response, including the response of our laws, may with justice treat them as guilty of different offenses to be punished differently. Leaving absolute justice to God, a Christian approach understands that the human role in responding to these acts is limited. The luck is not moral but "jurisdictional."[27]

The doctrine of divine providence completes the discussion, since it tells us that wind itself depends on God's will. It is God who "assigns cases to various fora, where God's justice may be administered in part according to jurisdictional rules that are themselves expressions of God's justice." Stern concludes:

> This view explains how we see Alexander and Alexandra as perhaps equally guilty in one sense, and yet not equally guilty in another, without compromising on standards of justice in either estimation. Before God and His absolute and complete standards of human moral perfection, Alexandra may be as guilty as Alexander. Before fellow humans in state, church, and other social contexts, and

[27]Ibid., pp. 817-18.

> the limited authority they possess to accomplish limited justice as cases providentially come before them, Alexander may be guiltier than Alexandra.[28]

The discussion does not end there, as Stern develops a further application of the jurisdictional principle through the normative and existential perspectives. First, the role of the civil ruler is to punish wicked acts, not to punish faulty character. Second, not all sinful acts may be punished by the civil ruler. In short, the "law of human behavior is stricter and more complete" than the law of civil government. The civil law "need not reflect absolute desert," but its morality and jurisdictional principles must be just:

> The Sermon on the Mount emphasizes the difference between God's absolute justice and the more limited justice to be administered by human beings, including ministers in civil government. . . . Both realms of justice are truly just and express the same nature of justice. Civil rulers are ministers of the wrath of God Himself and their judgment must reflect His. It is the scope of the justice, not its essence, that separates God's own from that share to be administered by civil government.[29]

Summary

The three examples we've just seen have provided a taste of thoroughgoing integration that honors our commitments to unity, community, and truth. In addition to seeing that it is possible to evaluate legal doctrines or conventions in light of history, revelation, and our role, we should also be encouraged that there is work out there for us to build and rely on. We need not reinvent the wheel or spend hours with the concordance as the first step to figuring out if God has any purpose in human law.

---

[28]Ibid., p. 818.

[29]Ibid., pp. 831-32. Within this paragraph was a footnote referring to John E. Witte and Thomas C. Arthur, "The Three Uses of the Law: A Protestant Source of the Purposes of Criminal Punishment?" *Journal of Law and Religion* 10 (1994): 451. The authors assert the following: "Like the theologians, early modern jurists accepted a general moral theory of government and criminal law. God has created a moral or natural law. . . . State magistrates are God's vice-regents in the world. They must represent and reflect God's authority and majesty on earth. The laws which they promulgate must encapsulate and elaborate the principles of God's moral law, particularly as it is set out in the Ten Commandments. The provisions of the criminal law, therefore, must perforce parallel the provisions of the moral law. The purposes of criminal punishment must perforce parallel the purposes of divine punishment. As William Blackstone put it, 'the state's criminal law plays the same role in man's social life that God's moral law plays in man's spiritual life.' "

The atonement, covenantal structures, the law of God, jurisdiction, providence, and the dominion mandate are central doctrines in the faith. This discussion has demonstrated, albeit in a whirlwind of ideas, how fundamentals of the faith make a difference in how we see the law. Again, these examples were developed by scholars who have dedicated large chunks of their lives to considering these things. Yet that is our call as practitioners and law students as well. It is not necessary to write a hundred-page treatise, but we ought to be continually thinking about how to take every thought—even thoughts about contracts, litigation, and corporations—captive in service to Christ. Again, "Neither the law nor lawyering is a neutral, secular activity."[30]

[30]Pryor, "Consideration in the Common Law," pp. 1, 9.

Author and Subject Index

Page numbers followed by "sb" indicate information found in a sidebar.

Scripture Index

Page numbers followed by "sb" indicate information found in a sidebar.

The Institute for Christian Legal Studies is a cooperative ministry of the Christian Legal Society and Regent University School of Law.

With more than 200 chapters and 2900 members in more than 1500 cities, the Christian Legal Society (CLS) is the largest national not for profit association of lawyers, law students, and law professors bound together by a common confession of Christian faith in the world. Founded in 1961, inspired by Jesus' admonition to the lawyers and judges to *"do justice with the love of God, never forgetting the weightier matters of the law: justice, mercy, and faithfulness"* (Luke 11:42, Matt.23:23), the Christian Legal Society exists to inspire, encourage, and equip lawyers, jurists, law professors, law students, and associated friends of the society to follow Jesus in life and the study and practice of law, thereby transforming our profession, laws, and society for the common good, one heart and mind at a time. CLS conducts its operations through its five ministries: Law Student Ministries (campus ministry); the Center for Law and Religious Freedom (legal defense of the inalienable right to life and religious liberty for all people from Congress to the courts); Legal Aid Ministries (legal aid for the poor and needy, Biblical reconciliation, and legal referral); Attorney Ministries (pastoral care and support for attorneys through various publications, member benefits, mentoring, and other voluntary service opportunities); and Conferences (national and regional meetings of attorneys, law students, law professors, and jurists).

For more information on CLS contact:
8001 Braddock Rd., Suite 300
Springfield, VA
703-642-1070
www.clsnet.org

The mission of Regent University School of Law is distinctive among accredited law schools. That mission is to bring to bear the will of our Creator, Almighty God, upon legal education and the legal profession. Regent understands that law is more than a profession; it's a calling. To help future leaders fulfill this calling, Regent is committed to equipping them to display both excellence and integrity. Regent offers superb training in the skills of legal writing, negotiation, trial advocacy, and appellate advocacy. Regent students regularly win competitions testing these skills at both the regional and national levels. But Regent recognizes that training in legal skills alone is not enough. What makes Regent unique is that it thoroughly integrates a Christian perspective into the classroom. Regent is committed to the proposition that there is truth—eternal principles of justice—about the way men and women should practice law and about the law itself.

For more information about Regent University School of Law, contact:
Regent University School of Law
1000 Regent University Dr.
Virginia Beach, VA 23464
757-226-4040
www.regent.edu/law